CHRISTIAN
DISCIPLESHIP

Fulfilling the Great Commission in the 21st Century

Self care very important.

Steven Collins, PhD

May 22nd 2022
joined Metropolitan.
18 days after my
birthday

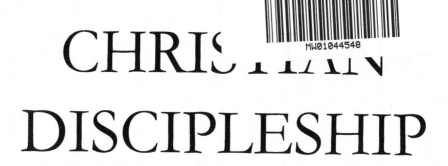

Trinity Southwest University Press
Albuquerque, New Mexico

Trinity Southwest University Press
5600 Eubank NE Suite 130
Albuquerque, New Mexico 87111

CHRISTIAN DISCIPLESHIP: Fulfilling the Great Commission in the 21st Century
By Steven Collins, PhD
Copyright ©2013 Steven Collins

Library of Congress Number: 2013948771
ISBN-13: 978-0615874487
ISBN-10: 0615874487

All rights reserved. Published in the United States of America by Trinity Southwest University Press. No part of this work may be reproduced, stored in a retrieval system, or transmitted, in any form or by any means, electronic, digital, mechanical, photocopying, recording or otherwise, without the written consent of the publisher.

All scripture quotations, unless otherwise indicated, are taken from the Holy Bible, New International Version®, NIV®. Copyright ©1973, 1978, 1984, 2011 by Biblica, Inc. ™ Used by permission of Zondervan. All rights reserved worldwide. www.zondervan.com The "NIV" and "New International Version" are trademarks registered in the United States Patent and Trademark Office by Biblica, Inc. ™

Scripture references marked KJV, are from the King James Version of the Bible. Public Domain.

Scripture references marked NASB are from the New American Standard Bible. Scripture quotations taken from the New American Standard Bible®, Copyright © 1960, 1962, 1963, 1968, 1971, 1972, 1973, 1975, 1977, 1995 by The Lockman Foundation. Used by permission." (www.Lockman.org).

Cover photo courtesy of NASA (www.NASA.gov).

DEDICATION

CHRISTIAN DISCIPLESHIP is dedicated to Dr. Irwin "Rocky" Freeman,
whose devotion to Christ and commitment to the Bible
have greatly influenced my life.

About Photocopying This Book

Some people who would never walk into a store and shoplift a book may think nothing of photocopying the same book. The results are the same. Both acts are wrong. Many people have the mistaken understanding that making copies of copyrighted material is legal if it is for their own personal use and not for resale. Making unauthorized copies of any copyrighted material is against Federal law for any purpose and may result in imprisonment and fines up to $50,000.

I Timothy 5:17, 18 instructs us to give the laborer his wages, specifically those who labor in the Word and doctrine. As the publisher we have a moral as well as a legal responsibility to see that our authors receive fair compensation for their efforts. Many of them depend on the income from the sale of these books as their sole livelihood. So, for that matter do the artists, printers, and the numerous other people who work to make these books available to you.

Please help us abide by the laws of both man and God by discouraging those who would copy this material in lieu of purchase. Since this book is protected by USA copyright laws and treaties, we would appreciate being notified of any violations.

Publisher's Note

It is our hope that you will write liberally in this book as you work your way through it. To assist you with using this book in a group setting, a downloadable PDF file is available on the TSU Press web site (www.TSUPress.com) containing all of the forms from within this book that you may freely print.

John 10:10b   Matt 6:33

TABLE OF CONTENTS

INTRODUCTION

"Go, make disciples…." These powerful words of Jesus in Matthew 28:19 are meant for every believer. The purpose of *CHRISTIAN DISCIPLESHIP* is to help you, a follower of Christ, to fulfill this Great Commission in your personal life. Of course, making disciples means more than just teaching through this manual. It involves pouring your life into another (as Paul did with Timothy).

CHRISTIAN DISCIPLESHIP will guide you through the disciplemaking process, step-by-step, and help you to make the most of your time and effort in discipling new believers and others who need this vital training. Whether you are a youth minister, pastor, young person or adult, this manual will get you involved in teaching others for Christ and then training them to make disciples.

Part One

BASICS OF
ABUNDANT LIVING

6306/52

CHAPTER 1

FOLLOWING CHRIST

Matthew 16:24, 25

> "If anyone wishes to come after Me, let him deny himself, and take up his cross, and follow Me. For whoever wishes to save his life shall lose it; but whoever loses his life for My sake shall find it."

When you made a decision to follow Jesus Christ, you made the most important, crucial decision of your life. But Jesus didn't offer eternal life to you based in "saying the right words," "having a warm religious feeling," an emotional moment when you felt you ought to do something, and "walking an aisle seemed like the appropriate thing to do," or "a need for assurance that you wouldn't have to go to hell." There is one, and only one, way to receive eternal life (be "saved") and it isn't how a great many people think it is.

In the verses above (Matthew 16:24, 25) Jesus made it very clear how a person becomes a true follower of His. When you look at these verses carefully it isn't difficult to understand what He was talking about. What did Jesus mean by these phrases?

"come after Me"

To follow him, walk with him, be with him, Jesus life as the ultimate example

"deny himself"

deny your flesh, don't do things your own way

"take up his cross"

take responsibility for your own walk and life.

"follow me"

Follow Christ's example.

Look carefully in your Bible at verse 25. What does Jesus mean by this? How do you **"lose your life in order to find it"**? *Lose your life that ends in death and find life eternal by following God.*
These are serious words describing a life-changing
relationship to Jesus Christ. Actually, what we have
in **Matthew 16:24, 25** is Jesus' own definition of
faith. Many have tried to water down the real New
Testament meaning of faith by saying things like,
"Faith is taking God at His word, or "Faith is trusting
God to do what He says He will do," or "Faith is
believing what you can't see." These are very nice,
but they don't communicate the reality of the king
of **living faith** demanded by the Lord Jesus Christ.

Before we talk about the details of becoming a believer in Christ, a follower of His,
it will be helpful to examine what the Bible itself has to say about faith. **Just how
does God's Word define faith?**

Hebrews 11:1
> "Now faith is the reality of things hoped for, the proof of things not seen."
> (author's rendering of the Greek text)

According to the Word,

FAITH IS: REALITY AND PROOF.

The Greek word translated "reality" (often translated "substance" or "assurance")
was used in the first century to designate real estate and other accumulated
personal property. It is a very tangible term.

The word translated "proof" (sometimes translated "evidence" or "conviction")
was a legal term used to describe the evidence which gave strength to a legal case,

allowing it to be brought into a higher court. On the basis of this weighty evidence, a legal position could be demonstrated to be true or false.

The phrases "of things hoped for" and "of things not seen" refer to that which God has supplied for us on the basis of Jesus' **death** and **resurrection**. They are reference to the eternal, abundant life of those who are in Christ. The life that we have through Christ Jesus has benefits which stretch far beyond this life into the aeons of infinity. The things which we hope for and have not yet seen are the sure realities of all that awaits the followers of Christ. They are as real and as certain as He is. And included in this "unseen" reality is the very presence of Jesus in the person of the Holy Spirit who indwells every one of His followers.

1Corinthians 2:9

"... 'Things which eye has not seen and ear has not heard, And which have not entered the heart of man, All that God has prepared for those who love Him.'"

Hebrews 11:1 tells us that faith is much more than mental assent. It involves the utmost reality and proof. What kind of reality and proof? The kind Jesus described in **Matthew 16:24, 25**...

"Come ... deny yourself ... take up your cross ... follow me."

This is the reality and proof of a **personal relationship** with Christ. The reality of the relationship is demonstrated by the proof of a transformed life. Merely to say that you are "accepting " Christ or "trusting" Him is not to have the faith that brings personal salvation. As **Hebrews 11:1** says, faith is having a life-response which not only claims a title-deed to eternal life in His Kingdom, but also demonstrated (proves, gives evidence) that you have truly turned from self to follow Christ.

Faith isn't a fleeting emotional desire, nor is it blind acceptance. Faith is not merely accepting a set of facts. Faith is not believing in the teaching of Jesus. **Faith is the reality of following Christ which, by its nature, give evidence of a transformed life.**

As James put it, the "faith" that fails to produce a changed life is not the kind of faith which brings one to salvation.

James 1:21, 22; 2:14, 18, 19, 26

"Therefore putting aside all filthiness and all that remains of wickedness, in humility receive the word (the Gospel) implanted which is able to save your souls. But prove yourselves doers of the word, and not merely hearers who delude themselves... What use is it, my brethren, if a man says he has faith, but he has no works? Can that faith save him? But someone may well say, 'You have faith, and I have works'; show me your faith without works, and I will show you my faith by my works. You believe that God is one, you do well; the demons also believe, and shudder … For just as the body without the spirit is dead, so also faith without works is dead."

As we have seen, faith is one's **life-response** to Christ. To be sure, one is not saved by works – this is heresy! But the quality of genuine faith is shown in Scripture to be that which is living and productive.

Faith is sharing a common "real estate" with Jesus Christ ("come after me," "follow me") by denying one's self and talking up one's cross. The cross is an instrument of death. It is symbolic of your total commitment to Christ – total abandonment to His desire. The cross of self-death, which must be taken up in order to follow Him, produces evidence of one's relationship to Christ because one is then walking (following) in

A NEW DIRECTION.

As you can see, faith is a difficult concept to understand! From this point on, whenever we speak of faith, be sure that you understand it to mean the life-changing kind of faith taught in the Bible.

The verb for of the noun "faith" found in the New Testament is translated "believe." It means "to have faith" or, literally, "to faith." We don't have such a verb as "to faith" in English, so we use "believe." Whenever you see the words "faith" (noun) and "believe" (verb) in the New Testament, remember that they are speaking of the same thing – one emphasizes that fact of it, the other the action of it – faith!

Jesus said if you would place your faith in (believe in) Him that He would grant to you eternal, abundant life. He didn't say just to believe "about" Him, but to make a life-response to Him – to give up yourself to His lordship.

John 3:16
> "For God so loved the world, that He gave His only begotten Son, that whoever believes in Him should not perish, but have eternal life."

John 1:12
> "But as many as received Him, to them He gave the right to become children of God, even to those who believe in His name."

1 John 5:10-13

> "The one who believes in the Son of God has the witness in himself; the one who does not believe God has made Him a liar, because he has not believed in the witness that God has borne concerning His Son. And the witness is this, that God has given us eternal life, and this life is in His Son. He who has the Son has the life; he who does not have the Son of God does not have the life. These things I have written to you who believe in the name of the Son of God, in order that you may know that you have eternal life."

John 11:25, 26

> "I am the resurrection and the life; he who believes in Me shall live even if he dies, and everyone who lives and believes in Me shall never die."

John 3:36

> "He who believes in the Son has eternal life; but the who does not obey the Son shall not see life, but the wrath of God abides on him."

John 10:10

> "I came that they might have life, and might have it abundantly."

At a time in the past, whether a few days or years ago, you responded to Jesus' personal call to you that you turn from your self-life to follow Him – no reservation, nothing held back. When you placed your faith in Him (your life-response) you became a new member of God's family. That's very exciting!

YOU ARE A CHILD OF GOD!

But the purpose of this lesson is to examine your salvation **experience** in the light of God's Word. So, having come to an understanding of what faith is, let's look at the salvation which God has supplied to you in Jesus Christ...

Why does a person need Christ, anyway? Let's look at what the Bible says...

Romans 3:23

> "...for all have sinned and fall short of the glory of God."

Sin is self-willed rebellion against God. Because we have all sinned, we are hopelessly separated from God.

Romans 6:23

> "...for the wages of sin is death."

This death refers to **spiritual separation** from God because of sin. The separation exists because sinful man cannot meet the standards of a perfect and holy God. No matter how hard you might try, you could never be good enough to bridge the gap between you and God. All the clean living, religion and education in the world isn't sufficient to reach God. The chasm that separates God and man is just too great.

You had to realize that there was nothing you could do to make yourself right before God.

Romans 5:8

> "God demonstrates His own love toward us, in that while we were yet sinners, Christ died for us."

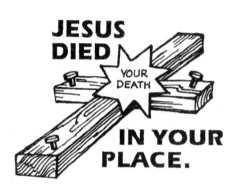

After you realized that you were a sinner and that it was hopeless to try to reach God on your own, God showed you the way out! Jesus Christ died in your place. The death that you deserved because of your sin, He took on Himself.

John 14:6

> "I am the way, and the truth, and the life; no one comes to the Father but through Me."

JESUS IS THE ONLY WAY TO COME TO GOD, NOTHING ELSE WORKS.

John 1:12

> "As many as received Him, to them He gave the right to become children of God, even to those who believe in His name."

You realized that you must receive Jesus Christ personally. No one could do it for you. He had to become your personal Savior. And you discovered that there was only one way to receive Him into your life – faith.

Ephesians 2:8, 9

"For by grace you have been saved through faith; and that not or yourselves, it is the gift of God: not as a result of works, that no one should boast."

It wasn't enough just to believe that He exists. It wasn't enough to know everything about Jesus. The key to receiving Jesus Christ is faith.

Faith – your life-response to the living Christ – became a reality when you turned from your old life and began following Him as your Lord. That's the meaning of repentance – turning from self to follow Christ. Through faith you gave your life to the Lord Jesus Christ.

Let's look at it this way:

Revelation 3:20

"Behold, I stand at the door and knock; if anyone hears My voice and opens the door, I will come in to him..."

Jesus knocked on the door of your life wanting to enter into a close personal relationship with you. You could have turned Him away, but you have opened up your life to Him and He has come in to stay. Not only do you have this new relationship with Him, but also

YOU HAVE BEEN BORN AGAIN.

John 3:7

"You must be born again."

The analogy of birth is quite appropriate to describe your salvation experience. The new birth is an irreversible event through which you are born into God's family.

When a baby is born, can he be un-born? _____

When a person is born spiritually, can that person be un-born spiritually? _____

You have been born again and you now have a new life! You have been granted this new life based on your life-response to Christ (your faith) and you will be a new person for the rest of your life on earth and throughout eternity. You'll never be the same as you were before because

YOU HAVE A NEW NATURE.

If this new nature cannot be detected in your life, you must take a close look at your claim to be a follower of Christ and make an honest evaluation of your relationship to Him. Don't be so proud that you can't humbly admit that you've never made a true life-response of faith to Jesus Christ. A failure to make this test could leave you in the position of the people in **Matthew 7:21-23**. Read these verses now.

Check your life against God's Word. The following verses tell us what we can do to check this all-important area of our lives:

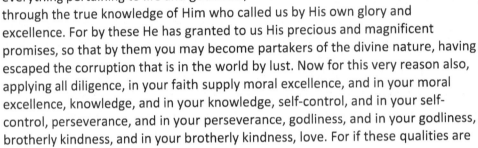

II Peter 1:3-11

"...His divine power has granted to us everything pertaining to life and godliness, through the true knowledge of Him who called us by His own glory and excellence. For by these He has granted to us His precious and magnificent promises, so that by them you may become partakers of the divine nature, having escaped the corruption that is in the world by lust. Now for this very reason also, applying all diligence, in your faith supply moral excellence, and in your moral excellence, knowledge, and in your knowledge, self-control, and in your self-control, perseverance, and in your perseverance, godliness, and in your godliness, brotherly kindness, and in your brotherly kindness, love. For if these qualities are yours and are increasing, they render you neither useless nor unfruitful in the true knowledge of our Lord Jesus Christ. For he who lacks these qualities is blind or short-sighted, having forgotten his purification from his former sins. Therefore, brethren, be all the more diligent to make certain about His calling and choosing you; for as long as you practice these things, you will never stumble; for in this way the entrance into the eternal kingdom of our Lord and Savior Jesus Christ will be abundantly supplied to you."

II Corinthians 13:5

"Test yourselves to see if you are in the faith; examine yourselves! Or do you not recognize this about yourselves, that Jesus Christ is in you—unless indeed you fail the test?"

Do you pass the test? Do you have the confidence that Christ truly lives within your life? If this is so, praise God! You have been made new.

YOU ARE A
NEW CREATURE.

II Corinthians 5:17

> "Therefore if anyone is in Christ, he is a new creature; the old things passed away; behold, new things have come."

In Christ you are a brand new person. You have new life. This life is described by God's word as **abundant** and **eternal**. Study these verses closely:

John 10:10

> "I came that they might have life, and might have it abundantly."

John 3:16

> "For God so loved the world that He gave His only begotten Son, that whoever believes in Him should not perish, but have everlasting life."

John 10:27, 28

> "My sheep hear My voice, and I know them, and they follow Me; and I give eternal life to them, and they will never perish; and no one will snatch them out of My hand."

1 John 5:11-13

> "God has given us eternal life, and this life is in His Son. He who has the Son has the life; he who does not have the Son of God does not have the life. These things I have written to you who believe in the name of the Son of God, so that you may know that you have eternal life."

As a believer, you have begun the exiting journey of life in Christ.

THE ABUNDANT LIFE IS YOURS.
ETERNAL LIFE IS YOURS.

How do you know these things are true? Because the Bible, God's Word, is true.

Because Jesus Christ lives in you, there is something very important that you should know; You are not saved by how you feel. **You are saved by what God has done.**

Look at it like this:

The Bible is the Word of God. It is the truth on which we base our trust. The truth is that Jesus Christ is who He said He is, and that He has done for you everything He said He would do.

By placing your trust in Jesus Christ (He is the truth) you experience the forgiveness of sin and new life that's abundant and eternal. Your trust has been placed completely in Him as your personal Savior.

Emotions are an important part of your life, to be sure. But you should be careful to realize that feelings are often fickle. They can even be affected by what you ate for lunch! You may have moments when you think. "Well, I don't feel saved."

When your feelings cause you to doubt that you really belong to Jesus Christ, go back to the truth of God's Word and remember, it's not how you feel, but what God has done. That's what counts.

Study the following verses: **1 John 5:11-13; John 10:27-29**.

Once you are a child of God you cannot cease to be His. When you were born physically, you became the child of your parents in an irreversible way. No matter what, you will always be their child. That's the way it is with God. He is our Heavenly Father. He will never leave you. You are eternally His. Every moment of every day.

YOU ARE ALWAYS
HIS CHILD.

APPLICATIONS...

1. Use the space provided here to write your personal salvation testimony using the outline of Jesus' statement in Matthew 16:24, 25 as a guide. Specifically,

    a. How have you denied yourself?

    _____

    _____

    _____

    b. How have you taken up your cross in self-death?

    _____

    _____

    _____

    c. What evidence is there that you are truly following Christ?

    _____

    _____

    _____

d. How have you lost your life for Jesus' sake?

_____

_____

_____

2. On what basis has God granted eternal, abundant life to you?

_____

_____

_____

3. Define the kind of faith that brings one to salvation?

_____

_____

_____

4. Give three good examples of the fact that you are a new creature.

_____

_____

_____

5. Is there any doubt whatsoever in your mind that if your life were terminated this very moment that you would be with Jesus Christ eternally? Why?

_____

_____

_____

6. Have you begun to share your life in Christ with your friends?

_____ (Look for these important opportunities to share Jesus with others.)

7. As soon as the opportunity arises, share your testimony with other believers. Get involved in a local church body that believes and teaches God's Word.

CHAPTER 2
THE LORDSHIP OF CHRIST

You have often heard it said. "Make Jesus the Lord of your life." This sounds good, but it's not accurate. Why? Because He is Lord.

Philippians 2:9-11

> God highly exalted Him, and bestowed on Him the name which is above every name, so that at the name of Jesus EVERY KNEE WILL BOW, of those who are in heaven and on earth and under the earth, and that every tongue will confess that Jesus Christ is Lord, to the glory of God the Father.

Revelation 19:16

> And on His robe and on His thigh He has a name written, **"KING OF KINGS, AND LORD OF LORDS."**

There's no doubt about it. There's no debate. Jesus Christ is Lord whether you recognize it or not.

Jesus' lordship – His absolute rule and authority over all things – isn't diminished one little bit by your failure to realize it. His lordship isn't increase by your submission to it. In all situations, from eternity past to eternity future.

JESUS CHRIST IS LORD.

When you became a Christian, a follower of the living Christ, you bowed before his authority and obeyed His command to place your life in Him by **faith**. You became obedient to His lordship.

But those who fail to acknowledge the lordship of Christ are under it whether they like it or not. Those who do not humble themselves before Jesus Christ and become obedient to Him are condemned.

REBELLION PRIDE APATHY IGNORANCE

John 3:18

"Whoever believes in Him [Jesus] is not condemned; but whoever does not believe stands condemned already, because he has not believed in the name of the only begotten Son of God."

All people, believers and unbelievers, are under Jesus' lordship. Those who reject it stand condemned. Those who receive it stand in Christ. A refusal to bow to His lordship results in judgment. A life lived in recognition of Jesus' lordship brings about His blessing.

As a Christian, **everything in your life is subject to Jesus' lordship.** Nothing in your life is so insignificant that it goes unnoticed by God. God cares about everything in your life, no matter how small or unimportant you may think it is.

BUT GOD DOESN'T CARE ABOUT MY ... FRIENDS OR HOBBIES, JOB, THOUGHTS HABITS, DESIRES ... DOES HE?

Matthew 10:29-13

"Are not two sparrows sold for a cent? And yet not one of them will fall to the ground apart from your Father. But the very hairs of your head are all numbered. So do not fear; you are more valuable than many sparrows."

The fact is that **Jesus cares about you infinitely more than you care about yourself!** And not one single thing about your life in unimportant to Him. Everything you think, say or do is subject to His approval. Jesus Christ is Lord over every aspect of your life.

As a Christian, you have died with Christ and your life belongs to Him, not to you.

1 Corinthians 6:19, 20

"Do you not know that your body is a temple of the Holy Spirit who is in you, whom you have from God, and that you are not your own? For you have been bought with a price: therefore glorify God in your body."

Romans 6:11

"Even so consider yourselves to be dead to sin, but alive to God in Jesus Christ."

Galatians 2:20

"I have been crucified with Christ; and it is no longer I who live, but Christ lives in me; and the life which I now live in the flesh I live by faith in the Son of God, who loved, me, and delivered Himself up for me."

Colossians 3:17

"Whatever you do in word or deed, do all in the name of the Lord Jesus..."

Of course, that which is done in His **name** is that which meets Jesus' divine **approval**. Jesus' name represents His personal character and honor. That which is done in His name upholds His honor and reveals his character. Anything less than this is not pleasing to the Lord.

As a believer, you should possess the desire to please Christ in every area of your life. But how can you know what is pleasing to Him and what is not? The Bible promises that those who truly seek to please God will get the direction they need from Him. God will show you what He desire for your life. That's a promise from God Himself.

Proverbs 3:5, 6

"Trust in the LORD with all your heart, and do not lean on your own understanding. In all your ways acknowledge Him, and He will make your paths straight."

Matthew 7:7, 8

"Ask, and it will be given to you; seek, and you will find; knock, and it will be opened to you. For everyone who asks receives, and he who seeks finds, and to him who knocks it will be opened."

BUT WHAT ABOUT... DRINKING, LUST, BAD MOODS, CHEATING, DRUGS, PRIDE, ANGER, SMOKING, GOSSIP, DIRTY MIND, LYING, TEMPER?

Because of Jesus' lordship, you should desire to please Him in everything. He died in your place. He has given you eternal life. Your gratitude and love for Him will make you want to please Him.

Colossians 1:10

"...walk in a manner worthy of the Lord, to please Him in all respects..."

So how will you know what is pleasing to Him? Jesus will provide definite answers to every question in your life if you are serious about pleasing Him.

1 John 3:22

"...whatever we ask we receive from Him, because we keep His commandments and do the things that are pleasing in His sight."

Knowing God's desire for your life in any situation is possible when three important conditions are met. These important ingredients come from truly seeking His mind in any matter.

These three conditions can be seen by asking three important questions.

1. DO I REALLY WANT AN ANSWER FROM GOD?

Some people go around asking questions not because they want an answer, but because they want someone to agree with their preconceived ideas. When they find someone "important" who supports their opinion, they stop asking their questions.

But looking for an opinion is **not** looking for an answer. God has an answer for every one of the questions about anything and everything in your life. But, you must want an answer.

If the desire of your life is to please the Lord Jesus Christ, you must ask with a desire to know His answer.

2. AM I COMPLETELY WILLING TO ABIDE BY GOD'S ANSWER?

God won't provide an answer to your question just because you're curious to know what He thinks. You must be willing to obey God's answer when it comes. It may not be the answer you expected or wanted. But if you aren't ready to be obedient to His answer, He won't give you one. It's as simple as that.

If you are truly seeking God's will in a matter, you must be ready to follow His leadership, **instantly** and **joyfully**.

When you truly desire God's answer and are willing to abide by it, one crucial step remains...

3. AM I READY TO RECEIVE AN ANSWER FROM GOD?

At this point many Christians back off. They fear God's mind in the matter. They're afraid because they know that if the first two conditions are true, God will answer. But for them, no answer comes. They want to hang on to what the flesh wants. They just can't seem to take that final step of obedience, to do what God says. This kind of hesitance to follow God's answers results in what the Bible calls **carnality**. Carnal Christians don't have a joyful obedience to the lordship of Christ.

The spiritual believer, however, realizes that God loves and cares for those who belong to Him and that God's answer is the ultimate best.

GOD KNOWS WHAT'S
BEST FOR YOUR LIFE.

He sees things from His divine perspective. He wants His best for you as His child. So when you...

1. **really want God's answer, and**

2. **are willing to abide by His answer, and**

3. **desire to receive His answer,**

get ready! God is going to provide an answer to your question! You must trust God to provide His answer.

The lordship of Jesus Christ can be experienced in your everyday life by obedience.

List some areas of obedience which are obvious for every Christian:

_____

_____

_____

_____

_____

To many people there seem to be areas in life that are somewhat ambiguous in reference to God's desires. But let's face it, God is neither ambiguous nor silent on any issue if we will only let His Word speak to us by being honest and open to His leadership.

True, there are some things that God doesn't spell out exactly in modern terms. But His Word is very revealing in all aspects of living. And, too, some things are just downright obvious for the thinking person. For example, God made our bodies to glorify Him (**1 Corinthians 6:18-20**). Therefore, one could by sheer common sense conclude that God would not be glorified if you (1) beat your forehead with a hammer until you bleed, (2) eat broken glass, (3) suck smoke into your lungs, (4) burn holes in your skin with hot coals, (5) drink substances that make you stumble or fall down or have head-on collisions or beat your wife and kids, or (6) lay down in front of a speeding semi-truck.

Some things just aren't good for you. Some things by their very nature cannot glorify God. The same reasons that parents give to their children for not doing certain things apply to the parents as well! God doesn't label some things "for adult use only." Most of the time adults do that in order to rationalize their disobedience to God.

The fact is that you will never fully experience the lordship of Christ in your practical experience until you take care of the **obvious**. When you are obedient in these areas, God will begin to show you other areas where you need to experience Christ's lordship.

THE POWER TO OBEY GOD COMES FROM THE SPIRIT OF CHRIST, THE HOLY SPIRIT, WHO INDWELLS EVERY BELIEVER.

Philippians 2:13
> "...for it is God who is at work in you, both to will and to work for His good pleasure."

GOD'S ANSWERS COME IN SEVERAL WAYS ...

1. THROUGH SCRIPTURE

II Timothy 3:16, 17
> "All scripture is inspired by God and profitable for teaching, for reproof, for correction, for training in righteousness; that the man of God may be adequate, equipped for every good work."

God's Word, the Bible, tells us what He wants us to know about how we should live our lives. Spending time in His Word is the best way to build a Christ-like character. As the Word reveals God's will to you, submit to it gladly. The Holy spirit will give you the strength for obedience as the Word works to transform your life.

2. THROUGH COUNSEL

Proverbs 12:15
> "...a wise man is he who listens to counsel."

Another way that God provides answers for our lives is through the spiritual counsel of godly Christians. The Lord is able to use mature, spiritual believers to help guide us because they are strong in His Word. Listening to the counsel of fellow believers will allow you to draw upon the wisdom that God's Word has built into the lives of others.

3. THROUGH PARENTS

Colossians 3:20
> "Children be obedient to your parents in all things, for this is well-pleasing to the Lord."

For young people, parents are a source of direction, guidance and protection. God blesses young people who honor their parents with an obedient heart. Christian parents have an awesome responsibility to make sure that their own lives are pleasing to Christ so that they can be used by God to mold and shape the lives of their children in a godly fashion.

4. THROUGH SPIRITUAL INTUITION

1 Corinthians 2:16
> "... we have the mind of Christ."

1 John 2:27
> "... His anointing teaches you about all things."

1 Corinthians 2:15
> "He who is spiritual appraises all things."

The Holy Spirit indwells every believer in Jesus Christ. He is actively involved in the transformation of our lives from the inside out. As we read and study God's Word, pray, experience the dynamic of fellowship with other believers, and continue in our daily walk with Christ, we are guided by the Holy Spirit from within. As you live the Christian life, you will often sense the **prompting** of the Holy Spirit leading you in your service to Christ. Or course, the guidance of the Holy spirit will always be consistent with God's Word.

So, God wants to answer every question about everything in your life with reference to the lordship of Christ. **But what happens when you ignore God's answers and refuse to recognize Jesus' lordship by obedience? He disciplines you.**

Hebrews 12:5-11
> "My son, do not regard lightly the discipline of the Lord, nor faint when you are reproved by him; for those whom the Lord loves he disciplines, and He scourges every son whom he receives. It is for discipline that you endure; God deals with you as with sons; for what son is there whom his father does not discipline? But if

you are without discipline, of which all have become partakers, then you are illegitimate children and not sons. Furthermore, we had earthly fathers to discipline us, and we respected them; shall we not much rather be subject to the Father of spirits, and live? For they disciplined us for a short time as seemed best to them, but He disciplines us for our good, so that we may share His holiness. All discipline for the moment seems not to be joyful, but sorrowful; yet to those who have been trained by it, afterwards it yields the peaceful fruit of righteousness."

WHEN YOU ARE OBEDIENT, JESUS' LORDSHIP RESPONDS IN BLESSING.

WHEN YOU ARE DISOBEDIENT, HIS DIVINE AUTHORITY RESPONDS IN DISCIPLINARY ACTION.

There are two ways to learn a lesson…

1. Obey God's answer for your life as they are given.

2. Experience God's disciplining action.

Remember, God loves you and wants His best for you. Don't get caught trying to second-guess God's motives behind wanting you to live a life that's pure and clean and pleasing to Him. From His infinite, divine and sovereign perspective, God knows what's best for you.

Don't settle for the "leftovers" by rejecting God's best. But don't be fooled by thinking that God's best is what appears best from the human point of view. God's best for you just might be to make less money than you're making now, or have fewer clothes, or drive a lesser automobile, or give up all material possessions to serve Christ in a poverty-stricken country. The mentality that "God made Cadillacs for Christians" is straight from Satan himself. Don't let the world dictate your standards as a believer. Get into God's Word and let His divine standard prevail. We are here, as Christ was, not to be served, but to serve (**Luke 22:27**).

APPLICATIONS …

1. Describe the lordship of Christ.

_____

_____

_____

2. How have you submitted to His lordship?

_____

_____

_____

3. List three specific things that have changed in your life as a direct result of your obedience to answers from God.

_____

_____

_____

4. How will God deal with you when you refuse to heed His answers?

_____

_____

5. You have areas in your life badly in need of transformation. Make it a point to share these with fellow believers so that they can pray for you.

6. Take some time right now to express to the Lord, in prayer, your true desire to be obedient to Him.

7. Together with your discipler (and group, if applicable) study **Romans 12:1, 2** and discuss its implications in the light of this lesson.

_____

_____

_____

_____

_____

_____

CHAPTER 3
FELLOWSHIP IN CHRIST

This is one of the weakest points in the lives of many believers. But the importance of fellowship isn't just overlooked. Many people ignore it altogether. It's appalling how many Christians don't know the first thing about it, much less how to do it. Should you learn this lesson well, you will begin to experience one of the basic elements of the abundant life.

When you became a follower of Christ, something exciting happened! **You became part of a family.** This family includes all those who have received Jesus Christ. God calls this group of believers the Body of Christ, the Church.

1 Corinthians 12:18, 20

> "But now God has placed the members [believers in Jesus Christ], each one of them, in the body, just as He desired...now there are many members, but one body."

YOU'RE NOT ALONE.

When you accepted Christ, God didn't stick you off somewhere by yourself in isolation.

The fact that you are in Christ **automatically** makes you a part of the family. Every member of the body has an exact and specific function. In order for the members of the body of Christ to exercise their individual functions, the local church is a necessity. Local churches provide a context in which the members of Christ's body can minister to one another, building up each other in the faith.

As a Christian, God's plan for your life includes a definite and dynamic relationship to a

LOCAL CHURCH.

That's why it's so important to spend time getting to know other Christians. Get to know the members of your family.

I Corinthians 12:25

> "...there should be no division in the body, but that the members should have the same care for one another."

What kind of relationship must we have with other believers? Let's look deeper ...

The Bible points out many ways that Christian should, and must, relate to each other. The relationship of one believer to another is called

FELLOWSHIP.

By accepting Christ you became a member of God's family. Being born again is being born into the family. Fellowship is the practical application of your family membership. At this point it's important to remember two things:

1. Membership in the family is automatic.

2. Fellowship must be developed and practiced.

The dynamics of fellowship don't happen automatically. There are certain conditions to be met for fellowship to be successful. For one thing fellowship cannot exist unless Christians are walking with Jesus in their daily lives.

1 John 1:7

> "...if we walk in the light as He himself is in the light, we have fellowship with one another..."

As a local group of believers matures together, fellowship becomes a meaningful experience. Here are some basic facets of fellowship that are crucial to the life of every Christian...

1. SPIRITUAL MOTIVATON

Hebrews 3:13

> "..encourage one another day after day..."

Hebrews 10:24, 25

> "...let us consider how to stimulate one another to love and good deeds; not forsaking our own assembling together, as is the habit of some, but encouraging one another..."

One of the things fellowship does is to encourage believers to live for Christ. As Christians have opportunities to share together, God provides a dynamic spiritual motivation that can't take place under any other circumstances. Jesus promises His special presence when believers gather together...

Matthew 18:20

> "For where two or three have gathered together in My name, there I am in their midst."

2. SPIRITUAL SUPPORT

II Corinthians 1:3, 4

> "…God…comforts us in all our troubles, so that we can comfort those in any trouble with the comfort we ourselves have received from God."

I Thessalonians 5:11

> "…build up one another…"

When believers learn the principle of fellowship, they experience comfort and support from one another. Basically, fellowship means burden-sharing. No one in the church body should have to shoulder the weight of the Christian life alone. True fellowship is caring and supportive.

3. LOVE

John 13:34, 35

> "a new commandment I give to you, that we also ought to love one another, even as I have loved you, that you also love one another. By this all men will know that you are My disciples, if you have love for one another."

I John 4:11; 5:1

> Beloved, if God so loved us, we also ought to love one another…Whoever believes that Jesus is the Christ is born of God; and whoever loves the Father loves the child born of Him."

WITHOUT LOVE
FELLOWSHIP CAN'T EXIST.

Everything that takes place in true fellowship is brought about by love. Love is certainly the most vital factor in the fellowship of a local church body.

I Corinthians 13:4-8 describes the properties of love. (The word translated "love" in these verses is the Greek word "agape." The quality of agape love is summed up by the word selfless. Agape is the attitude of self-sacrifice displayed by the Lord Jesus Christ.)

Study **I Corinthians 13:4-8** and write down these important aspects of love and what each means.

_____

_____

_____

_____

WHY IS FELLOWSHIP SO IMPORTANT?

The Bible shows us that the world is filled with all kinds of things that are contrary to God's will. Paul describes the condition of the world as spiritual blindness.

II Corinthians 4:4

> "...the god of this world (Satan) has blinded the minds of the unbelieving, that they might not see the light of the gospel of the glory of Christ."

Because of this blindness, an unbeliever has no spiritual kinship with you. As a believer, the foundation and central theme of your life is Jesus Christ. Because of this there is no common spiritual ground for fellowship between you and an unsaved person....

II Corinthians 6:14-16

> "Do not be bound together with unbelievers; for what partnership have righteousness and lawlessness, or what fellowship has light with darkness? Or what harmony has Christ with Belial (Satan), or what has a believer in common with an unbeliever? Or what agreement has the temple of God with idols? For we are the temple of the Living God..."

The **principle of fellowship**, which is the basis for friendship, does not exist between believers and unbelievers.

GOD WANTS YOU TO BUILD FRIENDSHIPS ON THE BASIS OF THE PRINCIPLE OF FELLOWSHIP.

Whenever this principle is violated, your ability to grow spiritually is severely hindered. Any close friendship between you and an unbeliever is **defective**.

Of course, we are to treat unbelievers graciously and with compassion for the specific purpose of **leading them to Jesus Christ**.

This is a very difficult thing for many Christians to accept. But the fact remains that when God's desire in this matter is ignored, spiritual development is hindered. The people you hang around with the most are those who influence you the most. God wants you to make sure that you're drawing your closest and most meaningful friendships from those who have **a heart for God**.

I Corinthians 15:33

"Do not be deceived: 'Bad company corrupts good morals.'"

Psalms 1:1, 2

"How blessed is the man who does not walk in the counsel of the wicked, nor stand in the path of sinners, nor sit in the seat of scoffers! But his delight is in the law of the Lord, and in His law he meditates day and night."

According to **Psalm 1:1, 2** God says you will be blessed if you avoid what three things?

_____

_____

_____

What does "counsel" mean?

_____

_____

_____

What does "stand in the path of sinners" mean?

_____

_____

_____

What does "sit in the seat of scoffers" mean?

_____

_____

_____

How does fellowship with other believers help strengthen our love for Christ and our ability to serve Him?

Fellowship with other Christians provides a positive environment for spiritual growth. Remember this...

THERE'S NO SUCH THING
AS A FREELANCE CHRISTIAN!

The principle of fellowship is something that must be put into practice. Many groups of believers have difficulty maintaining a healthy environment of fellowship. Individually, a desire to experience fellowship with Christian brothers and sisters must be developed if proper spiritual growth is to take place.

It is important that the group of believers to which you belong (this includes your church, a specific group within the church, or other groups of believers with whom you meet on a regular basis) learns the principle of fellowship. If this principle is not operating, each person needs to examine the reasons why.

When you meet together, take this test:

Be honest. Answer "yes" or "no."

1. Do I have a genuine desire to meet together with other believers? _____

2. Is meeting with this group of believers a priority in my life? _____

3. Do I easily let other activities take up the time when I could meet with this group? _____

4. Are my closest friends involved in this group? (Or would they be if they had the opportunity?) _____

5. Is there someone here that I don't like? _____

6. Am I willing to spend enough time with this person to get to know and understand him or her? _____

7. Am I willing to go to this person (or persons) and ask his (their) forgiveness for my failure to fulfill my spiritual responsibility to love and support them? _____

8. Do I sincerely desire to do my part to help this group grow spiritually and become what God wants it to be? _____

9. Can I honestly stand before God and say that I have been the kind of person who provides help and encouragement to others in their spiritual growth? _____

10. Do I desire to be that kind of person? _____

11. Am I willing to do whatever God wants me to do in order to make my group the best it can be? _____

12. Will I make it a point of prayer to ask God to make me a part of the answer and not a part of the problem? _____

When you have finished this brief test, take all the time necessary to do what's asked in questions 7 and 12. The proper responses to the above questions are obvious. Your responses will give you an indication of what you need to improve regarding this important principle of fellowship.

Let's review the principles of fellowship...

1. When I became a believer in Jesus Christ, I was made a part of a

   _____.

2. My family includes _____ and is called

   _____.

3. Another name for my family is the _____.

4. As a member of the body of Christ, I have a specific _____.

5. The relationship of one believer to another is called

   _____.

6. Fellowship is the _____ of my membership in

   _____.

7. Fellowship must be _____ and

    _____.

8. I am capable of having fellowship when I _____.

9. Three of the things fellowship provides are: _____

    _____

    _____

10. Of these three things, _____ is the most vital element.

11. The world is corrupted by sin and _____ blindness is
    everywhere.

12. Because of spiritual blindness, a believer has no _____

    _____ for fellowship with an unbeliever.

13. The scriptural command concerning this fact is _____.

14. The principle of fellowship is the basis for _____.

15. My relationship to the unbelievers is that of _____.

16. When I ignore this important principle, my spiritual development is

    _____.

17. My friends should have a _____.

18. Fellowship with other believers provides a positive _____

for _____.

CHAPTER 4
POSITION IN CHRIST

What an exciting thing it is to know that you have eternal life! You belong to Jesus Christ and absolutely nothing can remove you from Him (**1 John 5:12, 13; John 10:27, 18**).

Now let's look at something so important that you can't experience abundant Christian life without it. Sad to say, many believers never learn it. Because they haven't learned it they are still spiritual infants.

How about you? Have you been a Christian for several years, but still crawl around in spiritual diapers? It's common for people to be Christians for years and years, yet never grow to spiritual maturity.

I Corinthians 3:1, 2

> "I could not speak to you as to spiritual men, but as to men of flesh, as to babes in Christ. I gave you mild to drink, not solid food; for you were not yet able to receive it."

Hebrew 5:13

> "Every one who partakes only of [spiritual] milk is not accustomed to the word of righteousness for he is a babe."

Spiritual maturity does not automatically accompany the natural physical/mental maturing process. And unless one very important factor is integrated into the Christian life, spiritual maturity is virtually impossible. What is this thing that's so vital to spiritual maturity? What is this most basic key that unlocks the door to the abundant Christian life?

THE PRINCIPLE OF POSITION

The principle of position can best be explained by introducing two import facts:

1. POSITION IN CHRIST

2. PRACTICAL EXPERIENCE

The Bible makes it crystal clear that **sin was removed by Jesus' death on the cross**...

Romans 8:2
> "For the law of the spirit of life in Jesus Christ has set you free from the law of sin and death."

II Corinthians 5:21
> "He made Him who knew no sin to be sin on our behalf, that we might become the righteousness of God in Him."

Hebrew 9:26
> "Now once, at the consummation of the ages, He has been manifested to put away sin by the sacrifice of Himself."

Now, you must ask yourself a crucial question:

If Jesus has truly cancelled sin and its power by His death and resurrection...

WHY DO I STILL STRUGGLE WITH SIN?

The answer to this question is found in what seems to be a contradiction. Actually, the seeming contradiction exists only because of our limited human point of view.

Let's remember our two basic facts:

POSITION in Christ and practical **EXPERIENCE**.

Both are true. But one is **eternal** (unchanging forever) and one is **temporal** (subject to change in time and space). One is **permanent** while the other is **temporary**.

First, let's look at your

POSITION IN CHRIST.

Because you responded in faith to Christ as Lord., God has done something that's so fantastic it's almost hard to believe; but you must.

God has placed you IN CHRIST.

Ephesians 1:3
> "Blessed be the God and Father of our Lord Jesus Christ who has blessed us with every spiritual blessing in the heavenly places in Christ."

Ephesians 2:4-7
> "God, being rich in mercy , because of His great love with which He loved us, even when we were dead in our transgression, made us alive together with Christ (by grace you have been saved), and raised us up with Him, and seated us with Him in the heavenly places, in Christ Jesus, in order that in the ages to come He might show us the riches of his grace in kindness toward us in Christ Jesus."

Romans 8:1
> "There is therefore now no condemnation for those who are in Christ Jesus."

What does it mean to be IN CHRIST? It means that **everything Jesus is, you are, because He has credited all of Jesus' righteousness to your account (Romans 4).** When god looks at you He sees the sinless perfection of Christ.

YOUR SIN IS COVERED BY JESUS' BLOOD ...

Psalm 32:1 (see also **Romans 4:7, 8**)
> "How blessed is he whose transgression is forgiven, whose sin is covered!"

1 John 1:7
> "The blood of Jesus...cleanses us from all sin."

When God looks at you in Christ He sees you as **pure and clean**.

GOD SEES YOU AS A PERFECTLY FINISHED PRODUCT!

This is God's **eternal** point of view. From His vantage point (the finished work of Christ in His death and resurrection), you are already complete and therefore totally acceptable to God. Your position in Christ is **God's perspective** and

1. **God's perspective is that of eternity;**

2. **You are eternally placed in Christ;**

3. **God sees you as a finished product.**

Your position in Christ is one of **ACCOMPLISHED FACT**.

Some of the accomplished facts of being in Christ are (fill in your name)...

_____ died with Christ on the cross (**Galatians 2:20; Romans 6:6**).

_____ is dead to sin (**Romans 6:7, 11**).

_____ is risen with Christ from the dead and now has eternal life (**Romans 6:5, 8, 11; John 3:16; I John 5:12, 13**).

_____ is completely and eternally forgiven of all sin (**Psalm 103:11, 12; Hebrews 10:17; Romans 8:1**).

_____ has already been blessed with every available spiritual blessing (**Ephesians 1:3**).

_____ is seated with Christ in the heavenly places (the presence of God) (**Ephesians 2:6**).

_____ is a fellow-heir with Jesus Christ (**Romans 8:17**).

WOW! You say, "You mean, all these things are true of me?"

Yes!

This position doesn't change. It's not affected by personal performance. It's not altered by how you feel. Position in Christ is a spiritual absolute. Because it is God's perspective, your position in Christ is as unchanging as God Himself.

Colossians 3:1-4

> "Since you have been raised up with Christ, keep seeing the things above, where Christ is, seated at the right hand of God. Set your mind on the things above, not on the things that are on earth. For you have died and your life is hidden with Christ in God. When Christ, who is our life, is revealed, then you also will be revealed with Him in glory."

Next, we need to take a close look at your

PRACTICAL EXPERIENCE.

Let's ask that tough question again:

"If I am in Christ and all the things concerning my position in Him are true, WHY DO I STILL STRUGGLE WITH SIN IN MY LIFE?"

Remember, the first basic fact, **position in Christ, is true**.

The second basic fact, **personal experience, is also true.**

Your position as a believer is guaranteed because it is God's perspective. But your practical experience is **your** perspective.

If you compare the two you can see the important differences:

YOUR VIEW

1. **TIME AND SPACE (HISTORY)**

2. **YOUR LIFE ON EARTH**

3. **LOTS OF ROOM TO GROW SPIRITUALLY**

But God's point of view is very different from ours:

GOD'S VIEW

1. **ETERNITY**

2. **YOUR LIFE IN CHRIST**

3. **A PERFECTLY FINISHED PRODUCT**

Look at it this way...

You experience history only in the present. You look back on the past and forward to the future. But God, because He is not bound by space or rime (He created it!), is able to view history as a completed act. Past, present and future are all within God's "eternal present" viewpoint (**Revelation 1:8; John 8:58**).

You must live in a world corrupted by sin. You retain the old nature and must deal with it on a daily basis (**Romans 7:25; John 17:11, 14-18**). But God sees that you have been crucified with Christ, raised up with Him and that you possess His life. In His eyes, you are sinless because of Jesus' substitutionary death (**Hebrews 10:1-7, 11, 12, 14**).

You are experiencing a maturing process according to your obedience (**I Peter 2:1-3; II Peter 3:18**). But God knows you as the finished product of His grace, complete in Jesus Christ (**Colossians 2:10**).

When you receive Jesus Christ, you immediately gained your position in Christ. What a privilege! Even now, while you 're still a sinner, you have been given the right to be a child of God.

John 1:12

> "But as many as received Him, to them He gave the right to become children of God..."

But remember...

SALAVATION DOES NOT EXEMPT YOU FROM LIFE!

You are here for a reason. **God has allowed you the privilege of remaining on earth as His personal representative!**

II Corinthians 5:17-20

> "Therefore, if any man is in Christ, he is a new creature; old things passed away; behold, new things have come. Now all these things are from God, who reconciled us to Himself through Christ, and gave us the ministry of reconciliation, namely that God was in Christ reconciling the world to Himself, not counting their trespasses against them, and He has committed to us the word of reconciliation. Therefore, we are ambassadors for Christ..."

While living day to day, you are a walking, breathing, public example of the grace of God. Someday, you'll be just like Christ. When He returns, you'll be transformed into everything that God has made you by your position in Christ.

1 John 3:2

> "Beloved, now we are the children of God, and it has not appeared as yet what we shall be. We know that, when He appears, we shall be like Him, because we shall see Him just as He is."

Your complete redemption, from your perspective, is coming! When Jesus comes back, your perspective of practical experience will miraculously merge with God's perspective of position in Christ.

I Corinthians 15:51-53

> "Behold, I tell you a mystery; we shall not all sleep, but we shall all be changed, in a moment, in the twinkling of an eye, at the last trumpet; for the trumpet shall sound, and the dead will be raised imperishable, and this mortal must put on immortality."

Your position in Christ will become your practical experience when you see the Lord Jesus face to face at His return. But in the meantime, you are to **deal with the old self, the sin nature, by living according to God's perspective**. The old self rules in your life when you live according to your own desires. The new self is evident when you live according to your position in Christ through obedience to His desires. **God wants you to live as He sees you in Christ.**

THE PROCESS OF SPIRITUAL MATURITY OCCURS AS YOU REALIZE YOUR POSITION IN CHRIST AND PUT IT TO WORK IN YOUR PRACTICAL EXPERIENCE.

II Corinthians 5:7

> "For we walk by faith, not by sight."

From what you have learned so far, how can this verse be restated?

_____

_____

If you get caught up in your daily experience and ignore your position in Christ, you are sure to be defeated.

KEEP YOUR EYES ON CHRIST.

Read **Matthew 14:22-23**.

What happened when Jesus said to Peter, "Come!"?

_____

_____

Why did Peter become afraid?

_____

_____

What happened when Peter took his eyes off Jesus and looked at the rough water?

_____

_____

What did Peter do then?

_____

_____

What was Jesus' response to Peter's cry?

_____

_____

THE CHRISTIAN LIFE IS AN ADVENTURE IN TRUSTING GOD.

It's amazing what God has done for us in Christ. In Christ we have an unchangeable, immovable position. When God looks at us through Christ, He sees people who are fully restored to a personal relationship with Him, just as if they had never sinned at all. Oh sure, we still commit sins; our old nature is still hanging around and we have to deal with it on a daily basis. But our eternal position in Christ guarantees us that, whatever happens, we will always be **IN CHRIST**. That's an absolute from God Himself. **As believers we must learn to look at ourselves as God sees us.** This is accomplished by faith. We must, no matter how rough the water gets, keep our eyes on Christ and what He has done for us.

Let's review for a moment...

1. As a Christian, what is my position?

   _____

2. Can that position ever change or be altered in any way?

   _____

3. Whose point of view places me in this position?

   _____

4. From God's perspective, is my salvation complete? Why?

   _____

   _____

5. When will it be complete from the standpoint of my practical experience?

   _____

6. Until that time, how can I live an effective Christian life and mature spiritually?

   _____

   _____

7. I experience the process of spiritual maturity when my

_____ is applied by

_____ to my

_____.

Life, with all its ups and downs, is an experience of becoming like Jesus. Even the problems are used to make us more like Him.

Romans 8:28

> "We know that God causes all things to work together for good to those who love God, to those who are called according to His purpose."

As we have seen, your position in Christ gives you the exciting prospect of becoming more like Jesus every day, until He returns, at which time you'll become what you already are in Christ.

But here's what's happening to you NOW…

II Corinthians 3:18

"But we all…are being transformed into the same image from glory to glory…"

Romans 8:29

"For whom He foreknew, He also predestined to become conformed to the image of His Son…"

Ephesians 4:12, 13

"…building up the body of Christ; until we attain to the unity of the faith, and to the knowledge of the Son of God, to a mature man, to the measure of the stature which belongs to the fullness of Christ."

THE PRINCIPLE OF POSITION IS THE KEY TO SPIRITUAL GROWTH.

Because of your position in Christ, you possess the ability to effectively deal with sin in your life, and live a victorious spiritual life.

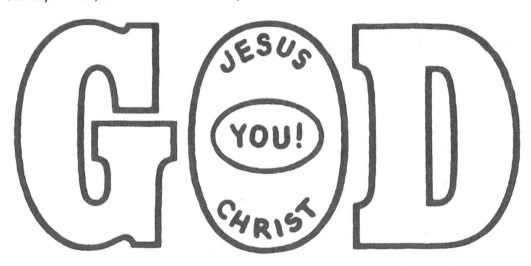

CHAPTER 5

FORGIVENESS THROUGH CHRIST

Although many people have accepted God's love and forgiveness by receiving Christ, they often find it hard to experience that love and forgiveness in their daily lives. The reason this happens is that they have taken their eyes off their unchangeable position in Christ.

Let's trace the problem from the start...

Sometimes your old nature (the flesh) gets the upper hand in your life and you disobey God. Immediately you sense that something is wrong. Up to this point everything has been going great; but now, suddenly, you realize that the presence and power of Jesus Christ in your life don't seem as strong as before.

You have sinned against God and you know it. **What do you do now?**

Before we answer this question there is something important to consider. Pay very close attention...

There are two kinds of Christians in the world,

SPIRITUAL and CARNAL

Spiritual believers live according to the POSITION.

Carnal believers live according to their EXPERIENCE.

The experience of the spiritual believer is most often controlled by **position in Christ**. On the other hand, the experience of the carnal believer is most often controlled by the **environment of experience**. (In the second section of this manual we will examine the subject of spirituality in detail.) Being spiritual (or spirituality) is a **condition**. It's not exactly the same thing as spiritual maturity, but they are related.

True **spirituality** exists when you act according to the **new self**, Jesus Christ being in control. When you are spiritual – when the new creature created in Christ Jesus dominates your experience – you are able to mature spiritually. **The process of spiritual growth is active when you are spiritual.**

Carnality exists when the **old sin nature**, (the self, the flesh) is in control. Carnality, too, is a condition. When this condition prevails in your life, spiritual growth is hindered and your relationship with Christ isn't vital and active.

Look at some of the differences between a spiritual believer and a carnal believer:

A spiritual believer relies on **God's power**. A carnal believer relies on his **own strength**.

A spiritual believer is **spiritually sensitive**. A carnal believer is **spiritually dull**.

A spiritual believer has a **fruitful life**. A carnal believer **rarely produces fruit** in the Christian life.

A spiritual believer **realizes his unworthiness**, but trusts his position in Christ. A carnal believer often **doesn't realize that he's carnal**.

A spiritual believer has **victory over sin**. A carnal believer lives in **slavery to sin**.

The Bible has much to say about these two kinds of Christians.

I Corinthians 3:1
> "I [Paul], brethren, could not speak to you as to spiritual men, but as to men of flesh…"

Romans 8:5-11
> "For those who are according to the flesh set their minds on the things of flesh, but those who are according to the Spirit, the things of the Spirit."

At this point carefully study **Romans 8:5-11**.

The spiritual believer is controlled and empowered by the Holy Spirit (the indwelling Christ) and sees life from God's perspective.

The carnal believer lives by his own power and sees life from his own perspective.

WHICH KIND OF CHRISTIAN ARE YOU?

Both spiritual and carnal believers have God's love and forgiveness. They both share the same position in Christ. Both are equally saved from God's point of view. So what's the difference?

One has learned to apply the principle of position to daily experience, while the other has not.

Now, let's see how each kind of Christian handles the sin in his life…

THE CARNAL BELIEVER

Has just disobeyed God. He has sin in his life. And then it beings to set in...

GUILT

Because he doesn't understand his position in Christ and the love and forgiveness that are already his, he tries to relieve himself of the guilt by one or more of several methods:

1. **IGNORING IT** ("What sin?")
2. **MAKING EXCUSES** ("Everybody's doing it!")
3. **RATIONALIZING** ("It's the way I was raised.")
4. **COMPENSATING** ("I'll just attend church more often.")
5. **SELF PUNISHMENT** (I'm such a terrible person!")
6. **TRYING HARDER** ("I know I can do better.")

7. **MAKING PROMISES** (I promise I won't do it again!")
8. **SHIFTING THE BLAME** ("It really was her fault.")
9. **FALSE DEPRESSION** ("I just want some sympathy!")
10. **GIVING UP** ("I just can't live the Christian life.")

The carnal believer tries one, then another. Then in combinations. But the guilt just won't go away.

But in a few days it doesn't seem so bad. He starts feeling better – and then it happens again! Up one day and down the next – the carnal believer seems to be riding a spiritual roller-coaster. How in the world can he ever get off?

If this is you, you know the frustration. Every Christian struggles with this. You come to the point in your life where you say, "OK, Lord! If you think this is so easy, then **you** try it!"

Guess what. **He did.** He knows all about it.

Hebrews 4:15
"For we do not have a high priest who cannot sympathize with our weaknesses, but one who has been tempted in all things as we are, yet without sin.

Hebrews 2:18
'"For since He Himself was tempted in that which He has suffered, He is able to come to the aid of those who are tempted."

Hebrews 4:16
"Let us therefore draw near with confidence to the throne of grace, that we may receive mercy and may find grace to help in time of need."

JESUS UNDERSTANDS.

Although it hurts Him deeply when you sin, God still loves you because you are His child – this is your position. **Remember your position.**

Romans 8:38, 39
"For I am convinced that neither death, nor life, nor angels, nor principalities, nor things present, nor things to come, nor powers, nor height, nor depth, nor any other created thing, shall be able to separate us from the love of God, which is in Christ Jesus our Lord."

Carnal Christian, it's time to get off the GUILT TRIP!

Because of your position in Christ Jesus, **you have the answer to the question of sin** in your daily life. It's no secret. (By the way some Christians live, you might think it's a secret!)

Learn the solution that the spiritual believer knows, and you can overcome being carnal. **Here's the way out...**

PUT YOUR SPIRITUAL POSITION TO WORK!

When you sin realize two things:

1. GOD LOVES YOU.

2. YOU ARE ETERNALLY FORGIVEN.

This is your position. These things are eternally true. Now, apply your position to your sin problem by practicing

SPRITUAL GROOMING

First you must bathe spiritually by **confessing your sins**. Confession means "to agree with God concerning your sing." Confess your sins according to this promise:

1 John 1:9

> "If we confess our sins, He is faithful and righteous to forgive us our sins and to cleanse us from all unrighteousness."

Confession involves three things...

1. **Acknowledge** that your sins are wrong in God's sight.

2. **Recognize your position in Christ** and realize that God has forgiven your sins— past, present and future – on the basis of Jesus' death on the cross.

3. **Repent**: that is, turn from your sin. The power to do this is provided by the Holy spirit who indwells you.

Why do you need to confess sins?

CONFESSION IS THE PRACTIAL APPLICATION OF POSITION IN CHRIST.

CONFESSION DOES NOT RESULT IN MORE FORGIVENESS.

CONFESSION IS NOT THE REASON FOR FORGIVENESS.

Forgiveness of sin is granted to you on the basis of Jesus' sacrifice for sin, once and for all (**Hebrews 10**).

FORGIVENESS IS POSITION.

CONFESSION IS EXPERIENCE.

Confession allows you to experience in your daily life that which is already true by your position in Christ. When you confess your sins, God makes real in your experience what He has already done for you in Christ.

When you refuse to confess your sins, even though your position in Christ doesn't change, you hinder your ability to experience God's presence and power in your life, and you will become a carnal Christian.

Here's an exercise in **spiritual bathing** that will help you apply your position in Christ:

1. Pray and ask God to reveal to you the unconfessed sin in your life.

2. Make a list of each one as the Holy Spirit brings them to your attention.

3. Confess these to God.

4. In bold letters across your list write "1 John 1:9" and stand on that promise.

5. Tear up your list! Thank God for His forgiveness.

6. If you have wronged someone, make it right with them at the first opportunity.

When you have confessed your sins, you are as pure and clean in your practical experience as you are in God's sight because of your position in Christ! Not only that, but also

GUILT IS REALLY GONE.

Any feeling of guilt which remains is Satan's lie. Reject it!

God truly loves you and has a marvelous plan for your life; however, He will not bless you and use you until you deal with the problem of sin in your daily walk with Him.

YOU CAN EXPEIENCE GOD'S CLEANSING
NOW OR ANYTIME. DO IT!

Now that you know how to **bathe spiritually**, you need to learn how to be **spiritually clothed**...

Romans 13:14
> "...put on the Lord Jesus Christ..."

This is the subject of the next lesson.

Let's review...

1. Spiritual believers live life according to their _____.

2. Carnal believers live according to their _____.

3. List some differences between spiritual and carnal believers.

   _____

   _____

   _____

   _____

4. What kinds of things do we often do in order to rid ourselves of guilt?

   _____

   _____

   _____

5. Describe the process of spiritual bathing.

   _____

   _____

   _____

   _____

   _____

   _____

   _____

   _____

CHAPTER 6
THE WORK OF THE HOLY SPIRIT

The practice of spiritual grooming not only involves being bathed (cleansed), but also being clothed.

Being clothed spiritually means to put on Christ (**Romans 13:14**). Putting on Christ in your daily experience means to be directed and empowered by the spirit of Christ, the Holy Spirit. This is what it means to be

FILLED WITH THE HOLY SPIRIT.

Before we look at the filling with the Holy Spirit in detail, it will be helpful to examine the relationship of the Holy Spirit to everyone who is in Christ.

WHO IS THE HOLY SPIRIT?
HE IS GOD.

No one can adequately explain the fact that God is **ONE**, and reveals Himself in **THREE PERSONS** – the Father, the Son and the Holy Spirit.

The Bible teaches us that when God, who is infinite, reveals Himself in the three-dimensional, temporal universe he appears as **TRINITY**. God the Holy Spirit is the third person in the Triune Godhead. (Although the term "Trinity" does not appear in the Bible, Scripture plainly reveals that God is Trinity by His very nature).

The **Old Testament** speaks frequently about God the Spirit. Study these passage of Scripture:

Genesis 1:2; 6:3; II Chronicles 15:1; Isaiah 11:2; 61:1.

The **New Testament** tells us that the Holy Spirit is one with both the Father and the Son:

Matthew 10:20; Acts 16:7; Romans 8:9; Galatians 4:6.

THE HOLY SPIRIT DOES SEVERAL INSTANTENEOUS, SIMULTANEOUS THINGS IN THE LIFE OF EVERY PERSON WHO RECEIVES CHRIST...

1. The Holy Spirit REGENERATES.

The Holy Spirit has always been active in regeneration. Regeneration (being saved, justified, born again, made righteous, redeemed, renewed through faith in Christ) is performed by the Holy Spirit in the life of every person who receives Christ.

Romans 4:3 (see Genesis 15:16)
"For what does the Scripture say 'And Abraham believed God, and it was reckoned (credited) to him as righteousness.'"

Titus 3:5-7
"He saved us, not on the basis of deeds which we have done in righteousness, but according to His mercy, by the washing of regeneration and renewing by the Holy Spirit, whom He poured out upon us richly through Jesus Christ our Savior, that being justified by His grace we might be made heirs according to the hope of eternal life."

Every person who receives Jesus Christ as Savior is immediately regenerated by the Holy Spirit. The Spirit of God, when you place your faith in Christ, instantaneously brings your spirit to life.

John 6:63
"It is the Spirit who give life…"

I Peter 3:18
"…made alive in the spirit…"

Regeneration, then, is that point in time when the Holy Spirit joins Himself to your spirit, restoring communication and fellowship with God as His child.

Romans 8:16
"The Spirit Himself bears witness with our spirit that we are children of God."

Not only does the Holy Spirit bring about regeneration, He also guarantees your position in Christ.

2. The Holy Spirit SEALS.

Ephesians 1:13, 14
"In Him you also, after listening to the message of truth, the gospel of your salvation – having also believed, you were sealed in Him with the Holy Spirit of promise, who is given as a pledge of our inheritance…"

Your position in Christ is sealed by the Holy Spirit. This seal is God's mark of ownership upon you. You belong to Him.

3. The Holy Spirit BAPTIZES you into the body of Christ.

1 Corinthians 12:13
"For by one Spirit we were all baptized (placed) into one body, whether Jews or Greeks, whether slaves or free, and we were all made to drink of one Spirit."

Here the Holy Spirit is the baptizer, not the element of baptism as in **Matthew 3:11** and **Acts 1:5-8**. Sometime this is a little confusing, but just remember that the word translated "baptize" simply means "to place within," "to immerse in,' or even "to be under the influence of."

The Holy Spirit places each believer into the body of Christ, the Church. It is the Spirit who unites believers together in spiritual union.

4. The Holy Spirit permanently INDWELLS.

John 14:17

> "...the Spirit of truth...will be in you."

Romans 8:9-11

> "You are not in the flesh but in the Spirit, if indeed the Spirit of God dwells in you. But if anyone does not have the Spirit of Christ, he does not belong to Him. And if Christ is in you, though the body is dead because of sin, yet the spirit is alive because of righteousness. But if the Spirit of Him who raised Jesus from the dead dwells in you, He who raised Christ Jesus from the dead will also give life to your mortal bodies through His Spirit who indwells you."

The indwelling Holy Spirit is the key to our life in Christ, both now and in eternity.

5. The Holy Spirit ANOINTS.

1 John 2:20, 27

> "But you have an anointing from the Holy One. And as for you, the anointing which you received from Him abides in you, and you have no need for anyone to teach you; but His anointing teaches you about all things, and is true and is not a lie, and just as it has taught you, you abide in Him."

Every believer is anointed by the Spirit for the purpose of assimilating the truth of God's Word. Human teachers are important to the Church (they are given to the church by God), but we are actually taught by the Holy spirit through the inner man. It is the Holy Spirit who takes the teaching of the word and infuses it into our lives.

These FIVE acts (or works) of the Holy Spirit take place the very moment a person trusts Christ as Savior, and

THEY ARE POSITIONAL IN NATURE.

Together these five acts of the Holy Spirit comprise what Jesus spoke of as being **"baptized with the Holy Spirit."**

Acts 1:5

> "John baptized with water, but you shall be baptized with the Holy Spirit not many days from now."

The baptism with the Holy Spirit means that every believer has been placed within the sphere of God's Spirit. This baptism is unique to the Church, the body of Christ. Many are confused in their understanding of these facts, so pay close attention.

When Jesus said "You shall be baptized with the Holy Spirit not many days from now, He was being very specific. He was speaking to the body of gathered disciples. He addressed them as a group. They were the **Church** of that day. They represented the entire church-to-be, which would become a reality on the Day of Pentecost (a Jewish holy day) when the baptism with the Holy Spirit occurred.

Acts 1:8

> "You shall receive power when the Holy Spirit has come upon you (plural); and you shall be My witnesses both in Jerusalem, and in all Judea and Samaria, and even to the remotest part of the earth."

It's obvious that none of those who heard Jesus' words that day ever personally reached "the remotest part of the earth" with the Gospel. So the "you" must certainly include more that those physically present. The coming baptism with the Holy Spirit would result in the spread of the Gospel to all the earth. Yet is it spoken of as a **single** event, a **once-occurring phenomenon**. Jesus didn't present the baptism with the Spirit as having several or continuing occurrences. **Jesus made it clear that his baptism ultimately included the Church throughout all ages – every believer without exception.**

When the Day of Pentecost came (**Acts 2**), **the entire body of Christ, the Church, was baptized with (placed under the influence of, or within the sphere of) the Holy Spirit.** All of those present were the Church of that day. No more. No less.

After that day, the baptism of the Holy spirit is never mentioned as something to be anticipated or that would occur again. Why?

BECAUSE THE BAPTISM WITH THE HOLY SPIRIT WAS A ONCE-AND-FOR-ALL COLLECTIVE BAPTISM WHICH CREATED THE CHURCH.

The baptism with the Holy Spirit occurs only once – the Day of Pentecost. As you study God's Word, note carefully that **before the Day of Pentecost this baptism is spoken of as a future event.** It is predicted by John the Baptist and Jesus. **After the events of Acts 2, the baptism with the Holy Spirit is always referred to as a past event in which all believers are included.**

The baptism with the Holy Spirit is a singular historical event. It is not repeated. From that point on, others were **brought under the sphere of that baptism** as they received Christ. When you received Christ you were **instantaneously** placed within the sphere of the Holy Spirit, the baptism with the Holy Spirit, making you a part of the spirit-baptized body of Christ, His Church.

As people respond to the Gospel and receive Christ, they are included in the baptism which occurred in **Acts 2**. The Holy Spirit does not "come again" every time someone is saved. He came – His vertical arrival – on the Day of Pentecost to stay! He has been here ever since. He abides as the bond of the Church.

The following diagram will help you understand this baptism...

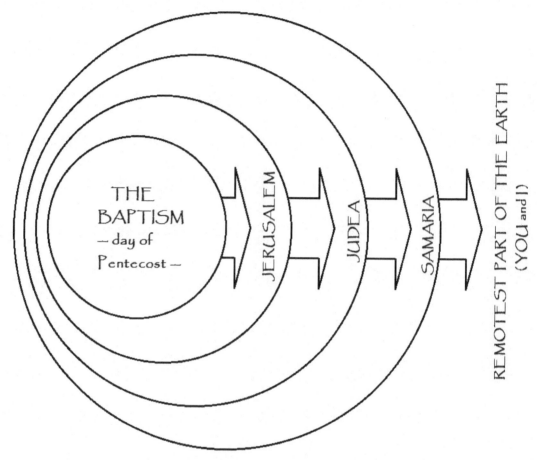

The event of the baptism with the Holy Spirit was once-and-for-all.

The sphere of this baptism increases numerically as more people receive Christ and are included in the Church.

Note the **all-inclusive, past-tense** nature of the following verses that speak of the baptism with the Holy Spirit:

I Corinthians 12:13

> "For by one Spirit we were all baptized into one body, whether Jews or Greeks, whether slaves or fee, and we were all made to drink of one Spirit.

Romans 6:3, 4

"...do you not know that all of us who have been baptized into Christ Jesus have been baptized into His death? Therefore, we have been buried with Him through baptism into death, in order that as Christ was raised from the dead through the glory of the Father, so we too might walk in newness of life."

Ephesians 4:4-6

"There is one body and one Spirit, just as also you were called in one hope of your calling; one Lord, one faith, one baptism, one God and Father of all who is over all and through all and in all."

Colossians 2:12

"...having been buried with Him in baptism, in which you were also raised up with Him through faith in the working of God, who raised Him from the dead."

Galatians 3:26-28

"For you are all sons of God through faith in Christ Jesus. For all of you who were baptized into Christ have clothed yourselves with Christ. There is neither Jew nor Greek, there is neither slave nor free man, there is neither male nor female; for you are all one in Christ Jesus.

All of the Scripture passages above refer to the universal baptism with the Holy Spirit, and all speak of this once-and-for-all positional event as a **completed act for all believers**. The Bible in no way teaches or implies that there is, for any believer, a "second act of grace" subsequent to the experience of salvation.

Salvation in the New Testament sense, under the New Covenant, is the five-act baptism with the Holy Spirit. This baptism is what makes every believer what he or she is in Christ. The baptism with the Holy Spirit is **positional**. It's not an experience in and of itself, but it is the dynamic of the new birth, our spiritual birth, and it equivalent to our position in Christ.

Shortly, we will examine the experiential aspect of the Holy Spirit's work.

Ephesians 1:3-14

"Blessed be the God and Father of our Lord Jesus Christ, who has blessed us with every spiritual blessing in the heavenly places in Christ, just as He chose us in Him before the foundation of the world, that we would be holy and blameless before Him. In love He predestined us to adoption as sons through Jesus Christ to Himself... to the kind intention of His will, to the praise of the glory of His grace, which He freely bestowed on us in the Beloved. In Him we have redemption through His blood, the forgiveness of our trespasses, according to the riches of His grace...He made known to us the mystery of His will...In Him also we have obtained an inheritance...to the end that we who were the first to hope in Christ would be to the praise of His glory. In Him, you also, after listening to the message of truth, the gospel of your salvation—having also believed, you were sealed in Him with the Holy Spirit of promise, who is given as a pledge of our inheritance, with a view to the redemption of God's own possession, to the praise of His glory."

When you received Christ you were immediately included in the baptism with the Holy Spirit. This is position in Christ. The instant you received Christ, you became a part of that Holy Spirit-baptized Church which has as its responsibility the spreading of the Gospel to the "remotest part of the earth."

Your position in the sphere of the Holy Spirit (the baptism) became a reality the moment you responded to Christ through your life-response of faith. This baptism included all five acts of the Holy Spirit:

1. **REGENERATION**

2. **SEALING**

3. **BAPTISM** (into the body, the Church)

4. **IDWELLING**

5. **ANOINTING**

(Note again the difference between the baptism with the Holy Spirit which was the arrival of the Holy Spirit and the baptism which is an act of the Holy Spirit. The common word "baptize" is simply used to describe different but related things.)

So the baptism with the Holy Spirit is not repeatable. It is not an experience. **It is your position in Christ as it relates to His Church universal and eternal.** It's important to comprehend this fact because many believers are still seeking for something to "zap" their lives and make them into spiritual giants. The fact is that the power to live the abundant life is **already** present in every believer! All that remains is for the believer to experience this power by **OBEDIENCE.**

As we have seen, the five acts of the Holy Spirit already mentioned are positional.

DOES THE HOLY SPIRIT ALSO OPERATE IN YOUR PRACTICAL EXPERIENCE? YES.

The working of God's Sprit in your daily walk is called being

FILLED WITH THE HOLY SPIRIT.

We are not commanded to be baptized with the Holy Spirit – we don't have anything to do with that beyond receiving Christ as Savior and Lord. **But we are commanded to be filled with the Holy Spirit:**

Ephesians 5:18

> "And do not get drunk with wine, for that is dissipation, but be filled with the Spirit."

The verb "be filled" is an imperative. It's a command.

This filling is our **personal experience of the Holy Spirit**. It's based on the fact of the positional baptism with the Holy Spirit – specifically that we have already been placed in the Holy Spirit who has regenerated, sealed, baptized, indwelled, and anointed us. He awaits our **obedience** to His Word so that he may fill us to overflowing. Again, as is always true, our experience is based on what God has already done. In the Christian life, experience is forever based on position.

The experience of the presence and power of Christ in your life is a result of being filled with the Holy Spirit. This is what it means to **"clothe yourselves with Christ."** The work "fill" (Greek, "plerao") suggest the process of bringing something to its intended level. When you allow the Holy Spirit to direct and empower your life, you are clothing yourself with Christ, that is, you are allowing Him to fill you to the point where He overflows into your visible, public, daily life.

Romans 13:14

> "...clothe yourselves with the Lord Jesus Christ, and do not think about how to gratify the desires of your sinful nature."

TO BE FILLED WITH THE HOLY SPIRIT IS TO BE FILLED TO OVERFLOWING WITH CHRIST AND TO BE ABIDING IN HIM (JOHN 15:1-8).

Being filled with the Holy Spirit has a two-fold significance:

1. GOD'S WORD WILL BECOME MEANINGFUL TO YOU.

The Word is basic for spiritual growth (**Colossians 3:16**). The Holy Spirit will bring the Scripture alive in your life (**1 Corinthians 2:6-16**).

2. YOU WILL BEAR SPIRITUAL FRUIT.

The power of the Holy Spirit working in your life will cause you to bear at least five kinds of spiritual fruit:

1. the fruit of souls won to Christ (**John 15:16; Matthew 4:19**)

2. the fruit of the Spirit (**Galatians 5:22, 23**)

3. the fruit of righteousness (**Philippians 1:11; James 3:18**)

4. the fruit of service (**Romans 1:13; 15:27, 28**)

5. the fruit of praise (**Hebrews 13:15**)

MANY CHRISTIAN ARE NOT FILLED WITH THE HOLY SPIRIT BECAUSE THEY HAVE NOT LEARNED TO APPLY THEIR POSITION TO THEIR EXPERIENCE.

How can you clothe yourself with Christ and be filled with the Holy Spirit? You became a Christian through faith. You must also walk in the Spirit **by faith**.

Colossians 2:6

"As you therefore have receive Christ Jesus the Lord, so walk in Him."

Galatians 5:16

"Walk by the Spirit, and you will not carry out the desire of the flesh."

II Corinthians 5:7

"For we walk by faith, not by sight."

Remember, you are commanded to be filled with the Spirit (**Ephesians 5:18**). This is an act of your will, an act of **OBEDIENCE**.

You have confessed your sins (spiritual bathing) and have claimed by faith the forgiveness that is already yours by your position in Christ. Now, you must claim the power of the Holy Spirit by faith, realizing that by your position you are already regenerated, sealed, baptized, indwelled, and anointed by the Holy Spirit.

Being filled with the Spirit is repeatable and should be a daily experience. Just as you physically dress every day, so also you must clothe yourself with Christ, allowing His Spirit access to your daily life.

YOU CANNOT LIVE THE CHRSITAN LIFE ON YOUR OWN POWER.

Galatians 3:3

"Are you so foolish? Having begun by the Spirit, are you now being perfected (matured) by the flesh?"

You must realize your inability to live on your own strength and ask God to fill you with His Spirit. His power is already yours by position in Christ. Let Him direct and empower your daily life by asking Him to fill you, knowing by faith that He will!

Just for review…

1. The baptism with the Holy Spirit occurred on the Day of Pentecost and the

   _____ was formed.

2. Jesus baptized the _____ with the Holy Spirit.

3. Therefore, when a person receives Christ, he is _____ in the
   baptism with the Holy Spirit and becomes a part of the Church.

4. The five acts of the Holy Spirit are:

   _____

   _____

   _____

5. Baptism with the Holy Spirit, along with its five acts, is identical to your

   _____ in _____.

6. The filling with the Holy Spirit is based on your position, but is to be repeated

   often in your _____.

7. The filing is experience by _____.

8. Before you dress spiritually (the filling with the Holy Spirit), spiritual bathing

   must be done by _____ your

   _____.

9. Being filled means to be _____ and

   _____ by God's Spirit.

In **II Corinthians 1:21, 22**, Paul gives us a fantastic statement which includes all five
of the positional acts of the Holy spirit. Fill in the five blanks with the correct acts
of the Holy Spirit:

"Now He who establishes us (_____) with you

(_____) in Christ and anointed us

(_____) is God, who also sealed us

(_____) in our hearts

(_____) as a pledge."

To be filled with the Holy Spirit on a daily basis means that He is making of your life an open letter to those who don't know Christ.

II Corinthians 3:3

"You are a letter of Christ...written not with ink, but with the Spirit of the living God, not on tablets of stone, but on tablets of human hearts."

CHAPTER 7

FEEDING ON GOD'S WORD

The Bible is the most important book ever written.

The history contained within it pages has been confirmed time and time again my modern historical investigation and archaeology, yet the Bible isn't just a history book. From a literary standpoint the Bible is a masterpiece, but it isn't simply a collection of literature. Although civilization's greatest ethical systems have been patterned after its concepts, it isn't merely a book of ethics and morals.

THE BIBLE IS THE WORD OF GOD.

Although the authors were human beings, God directed the production of His Book in such a way that it is totally free from error. That's the meaning of the term **"inspired."**

The Bible is the record of God's dealing with mankind. The theme is **salvation**. The central character is **Jesus Christ**. The Bible traces how God has revealed Himself down through history. His final and complete revelation being Jesus Christ, the God-man.

The **Old Testament** shows us the sinfulness of mankind and the need for a Savior. It predicts the coming of the Messiah, the Redeemer.

The **New Testament** tells of the entrance of God into the world in the person of Jesus Christ (Messiah). It tells how Jesus provided salvation for you and me by His substitutionary death on the cross and His resurrection from the dead. It predicts His second coming and gives us a picture of eternity.

THE BIBLE TELLS US EVERYTHING GOD WANTS US TO KNOW ABOUT OUR RELATIONSHIP TO HIM.

It says exactly what God wants to say to everyone, no more, no less. Now think about that for a minute. Everything God has to say to you is in His Book! **The** person who doesn't read and study the Bible can't know what God has to say about anything at all!

The Christian who overlooks God's Word will never discover God's plan and direction for his or her life.

MOST SPIRITUAL PROBLEMS ARE A DIRECT RESULT OF FAILURE TO STUDY AND APPLY GOD'S WORD.

Most believers spend embarrassingly little time probing, searching, and studying God's word, and some Christians never even bother to read it at all.

IMAGINE HAVING THE VERY WORD OF GOD WITHIN YOUR GRASP AND NEVER INVESTIGATING IT!

Christian, it's time for you to stop fooling around and get serious about Bible study because

GOD HAS SOMETHING TO SAY TO YOU

and you'll never know what it is until you begin to

SEARCH THE SCRIPTURE

Just how important is Bible study to you as a believer in Jesus Christ? Let's allow the Bible itself to answer that question.

Matthew 4:4
> "It is written, 'Man shall not live by bread alone, but on every word that proceeds out of the mouth of God.'"

You must feed on the Word.

Physically, you must eat to survive.

Spiritually, you must feed on God's Word in order to experience the abundant life.

IF YOUR PHYSICAL EATING HABITS WERE THE SAME AS YOUR SPIRITUAL ONES, WHAT KIND OF SHAPE WOULD YOU BE IN?

The Bible is an essential part of your Christian life.

Colossians 3:16
> "Let the word of Christ richly dwell within you."

James 1:21

> "...in humility receive the word implanted, which is able to save your souls."

1 Peter 1:23-2:2

> "For you have been born again not of seed which is perishable but imperishable, that is, through the living and abiding word of God...'The word of the Lord abides forever'...like newborn babes, long for the pure milk of the word, that by it you may grow in respect to salvation."

Without Bible study you soon become spiritually anemic.

Spiritually anemic Christians live in constant defeat because they refuse to feed on the essential spiritual nutrients contained in Scripture.

The problem isn't hard to diagnose. Try this test...

SELF-TEST FOR SPIRITUAL ANEMIA
DUE TO DEFICIENT SCRIPTURE DIET:

Rate yourself on a scale of 0-to-10 in response to each of the following statements. Maximum agreement with a statement is 10. Write the degree of your response (0, 1, 2, 3, 4, 5, 6, 7, 8, 9, 10) in the blank following each statement.

1. _____ I feel a definite need in my life to study God's Word.

2. _____ I have a specific time set aside each day for Bible study.

3. _____ I am currently following a set plan to read through the Bible.

4. _____ I have invested (or plan to) some of my own money in Bible study aids

   (such as a concordance, Bible dictionary, word-study books, etc.)

5. _____ I make notes of my study.

6. _____ I can cite specific changes in my life as a result of studying God's Word

   and applying it to my life.

7. _____ When I confront problems or questions, one of the first things I do is

consult the Word.

8. _____ I internalize key Scripture verses through meditation, memorization, or

application.

9. _____ My prayer life is centered around God's Word, realizing that through it

God speaks personally to me.

10. _____ Bible study is a constant source of strength and joy in my life.

MY TOTAL SCORE IS: _____

Interpret your score as follows:

90-100

Consistently experience the abundant life; genuine concern for lost friends; share Christ freely with others; consistent prayer life; joyful attitude; able to overcome problems, depression, temptation; helpful to others; thoughtful; teachable attitude; worship freely; involved in local church ministry.

80-89

Fluctuating spiritual experience; genuine concern for lost friends; fear or embarrassment in witnessing; spasmodic prayer life; sometimes moody; difficulty with certain problems, temptations, and occasional depression; usually helpful to others; usually thoughtful; some difficulty in learning spiritual truths; easily distracted in worship; fair degree of local church involvement.

70-79

Spasmodic spiritual experience (seek spiritual highs, but lack any consistency); some concern for lost friends; rarely share Christ, if at all; pray when desperate; moody; difficulty in handling problems; often overcome by temptation; easily depressed; generally self-centered; mind easily wanders when confronted with spiritual truth; rarely experience true worship; inconsistent involvement in local church.

69 and Below

General spiritual disinterest; no concern for the lost; never share Christ; rarely pray; predictable moods because easily swayed or influenced; generally poor attitude; try to cover up or escape problems; unable to overcome most temptations; frequent depression; self-centered; unable to comprehend spiritual truths; unable to experience true worship; inability to function in a fellowship context.

This test serves to emphasize the various problems that can result from an inadequate relationship to the Word of God. It's amazing how accurate this test has proven to be with the thousands who have taken it. All of each set of basic tendencies may not be true of your life, even if you scored in the range. But many of them are true, and others will become true depending on your obedience to the Lord concerning His Word.

This is very serious business. So many believers suffer needless problems and difficulties simply because they have not learned to

FEED ON THE WORD.

You must realize that you can't be an effective disciple apart from God's word.

John 8:31, 32
> "If you abide in My Word, then you are truly disciples of mine; and you shall know the truth, and the truth shall make you free."

You cannot gain spiritual truth outside the Bible. "Spiritual" investigation which goes beyond the boundaries of God's Word and the sound doctrine it contains in mere human speculation and is cultic or occultic in nature. The Bible is the only guide for the life of a Christian.

IN ORDER TO BE A TRUE DISCIPLE, YOU MUST ABIDE IN THE TRUTH WHICH IS THE WORD OF GOD.

When Jesus prayed for His followers (present and future) He requested specifically for God to reveal truth to them.

John 17:17
> "Sanctify them in the truth; Thy word is truth."

Not only is the Bible the exclusive source of spiritual truth, but also it is the only reliable guide for your daily life and spiritual growth.

II Timothy 3:16, 17
> "All Scripture is inspired by God and profitable for teaching, for reproof, for correction, for

training in righteousness; that the man of God may be adequate, equipped for every good work."

Verses 16 and 17 outline four basic functions for the Word of God as it applies to your daily walk with Christ.

They are:

1. _____

2. _____

3. _____

4. _____

What do they mean?

TEACHING is the systematic declaration of truths from God's Word.

REPROOF is the recognition (conviction) of sin, error, and spiritual deficiency;

CORRECTION is the improvement of spiritually deficient life-patterns with ultimate restoration to scriptural norms.

TRAINING IN RIGHTEOUSNESS is the development of scriptural life-patterns through discipline.

It is important to notice that verses 16 and 17 of **II Timothy 3** go together. This is crucial! It's crystal clear that the believer can't be adequately equipped to experience the abundant life unless God's word is allowed to perform **all four** of these essential functions.

When you make a serious commitment to read and study it, God's Word will begin to render dynamic changes in your thoughts and attitudes.

Hebrews 4:12
"...the word of God is living and active. Sharper than any double-edged sword, it penetrates even to dividing soul and spirit, joints and marrow; it judges the thoughts and attitudes of the heart."

The Christian life is radically contrary to the world, and Jesus' call to discipleship demands a radical transformation of your entire life. God's word plays an important part in this exciting transformation.

Now, there's one very important thing you need to realize:

YOU MUST SCHEDULE A TIME IN YOUR DAILY ROUTINE FOR BIBLE STUDY.

The fact is that **if you don't set aside a time to study the Bible, you won't ever do it!** The first step (after you have realized the need in your life to feed on God's Word) is to set a specific time to do it.

Make no mistake, there is time for you to study the Bible. You may have stolen that time for other uses, but it's there.

Stop and think for a moment. Did you know that by reading the Bible only five or ten minutes a day, you could finish it in less than a year? That's right. Reading at average speed, you can read through the Bible in less than 72 hours. By reading ten chapters a day, you could finish it in just eighteen weeks.

READ GOD'S BOOK!

Why not ask God how much time He wants you to devote to His word each day? Then, make a commitment to read for a certain amount of time every day, or to read a set number of chapters per day.

If you happen to miss a day, confess your negligence, ask God's forgiveness, and start again, Ask God to help you keep your commitment to His word. He will.

Don't forget, Satan will try his best to keep you from reading and studying the Bible. He knows that if he can keep you out of God's Word, he can stunt your spiritual growth.

Here are some helpful hints that will help you in your Bible study:

1. USE A GOOD TRANSLATION.

There are so many versions of the Bible on the market that people often get confused about which one to use. Well, which one is best, anyway? The three most popular versions are the King James Version (or Authorized Version), the New American Standard Version, and the New International Version. These three are certainly the best of the best in the English language. Each has its good and not-so-good points.

YOU CAN READ YOUR BIBLE LATER... GO ON OUTSIDE AND RELAX WITH YOUR FRIENDS... YOU NEED A BREAK! WHY DON'T YOU...

The KJV uses language and style that is often archaic to modern readers (the new King James corrects some of this). But if you like the lofty style of the KJV, use it.

The NASB is a very literal translation (as it the KJV), and is the English version of choice for many who know the original languages, Hebrew and

Greek. Because the NASB is so literal, it's often awkward in style. But all things considered, the NASB is an excellent translation for the contemporary reader who takes notice of technical details (often reflected in the literal word order and structure) which reflect the original languages.

The NIV is probably the best all-around version in the English language. Structural literalness has been sacrificed for a smooth, readable style. Grammatically, it has the best English of all versions. The NIV makes for enjoyable reading. It is also an excellent translation from a technical point of view.

The fact is that there isn't one version that does everything perfectly. Go with the one you like the best. Of course, if you want to bypass translations altogether, you can study Hebrew and Greek until you're proficient enough to study God's Word in the original languages. That's the best way to go, but not always the most practical! If you can't make up your mind, get a parallel Bible that contains several versions side by side.

The main thing is to have a Bible that's useable. Don't get one with tiny print that strains your eyes. Select a type-style that's easy to read. Wide margins are nice for making notations. Each of the "big three" version introduced above is available in several different study Bible formats. If you get one that will last, you'll pay a good bit for it. So take your time and get one that will give you good service for many years to come.

2. ALWAYS READ AND STUDY FROM CONTEXT.

When verses are isolated from their contexts, they sometimes lose the force of their true meaning. Don't make verses say what they don't mean. Always seek to discover what the original author meant to say.

3. REMEMBER THAT THE BIBLE MEANS WHAT IT SAYS.

Just make sure you know what it is saying. Take any passage literally unless the context suggest otherwise. It will usually be obvious whether a passage is literal of symbolic. As you study, ask questions like, "Who is speaking?" "Who is being spoken to?" "What is the historical setting?" "What cultural elements are important?"

4. DON'T WORRY ABOUT WHAT YOU DON'T UNDERSTAND.

There will be passages that are puzzling to you. As you continue to read and study deeper into God's Word, the difficult passages will come into focus and the pieces will begin to fit together. Interpret difficult passages in the light of clear, understandable passages that deal with the same subject matter. Concentrate on what you can understand and trust that God will provide understanding of the hard passages as you gain knowledge and spiritual insight from His Word.

5. LEARN TO USE BIBLE STUDY HELPS

A good concordance (a kind of bible index) is very helpful. Keep a dictionary of the English language handy. Bible dictionaries, Bible encyclopedias, commentaries and word-study books are valuable aids to Bible study.

6. KEEP A NOTEBOOK

This can be a rewarding practice. Write down key thoughts. Jot down questions. Take notes. A notebook helps you keep up with your own thinking and progress.

You know how important Bible study is to your life as a follower of Jesus Christ. **Do it!**

Let's take a brief look at what you've learned...

1. The Bible is the _____

2. The theme of the Bible is _____

3. _____ is the central character of the Bible.

4. Most spiritual problems are a direct result of failure to _____

   and _____ God's Word.

5. Without Bible study, you become spiritually _____

6. Can you be an effective disciple apart from God's word? _____

7. The Bible is the only _____ on Christian living.

8. What are the four basic functions of the Word of God as it applies to your life?

   _____

   _____

9. Define the following:

a. Teaching _____

_____

b. Reproof_____

_____

c. Correction _____

_____

d. Training in Righteousness _____

_____

10. Without these four things, you are not properly _____ to serve Christ.

11. God's word will cause dynamic changes in your _____ and

_____.

12. You need a daily _____ for Bible study.

CHAPTER 8
LEARNING TO PRAY

One of the most important aspects of the Christian life is prayer. It's also one of the most difficult things to learn and experience.

Jesus' first disciples realized the importance of prayer...

Luke 11:1

> "While He was praying in a certain place, after He had finished, one of His disciples said to Him, 'Lord, teach us to pray.'"

Why do you think prayer is so essential?

_____

_____

Why do you think so many Christians (even you) have such a hard time establishing a consistent prayer life?

_____

_____

Why do you think the early disciples asked Jesus to teach them how to pray?

_____

_____

Let's begin probing deeper in the subject of prayer by asking

WHAT IS PRAYER?

Prayer involves several things...

1. THE CONSCIOUS EXPERIENCE OF GOD'S PRESENCE

Hebrews 4:16

> "Let us therefore draw near with confidence to the throne of grace, that we may receive mercy and may find grace to help in time of need."

What is the "throne of grace"?

_____

What should our attitude be when we approach God?

_____

The privilege to come before God is guaranteed by your position in Christ. When we come to God, He responds in GRACE.

What is grace?

_____

Because of what Christ has done (our position in Him) we have the privilege of experiencing the very presence of God in prayer. As a result of our personal communion with God in prayer, He supplies us with His grace in order to meet our needs, whatever they are.

2. COMMUNICATING YOUR THOUGHTS AND DESIRES TO GOD

Philippians 4:6, 7

> "Be anxious for nothing, but in everything by prayer and supplication with thanksgiving let your requests be made known to God. And the peace of God, which surpasses all comprehension, shall guard your hearts and your minds in Christ Jesus."

WORRIES CARES FRETS ANXIETIES TROUBLES

What kinds of things does God want me to communicate to Him?

_____

_____

_____

Psalm 37:4

> "Delight yourself in the Lord, and He will give you the desires of your heart."

What does it mean to "delight yourself in the Lord"?

_____

_____

God wants you to communicate with Him—your thoughts, hurts, desires, joys, sorrows. God is interested in what you have to say!

3. ALLOWING GOD TO COMMUNICATE HIS WILL TO YOU

God answers many prayers specifically from His Word.

Matthew 7:7-11

> "Ask and it shall be given to you; seek and you shall find; knock, and it shall be opened to you. For everyone who asks receives, and he who seeks finds, and to him who knocks it shall be opened. Or what man it there among you, when his son shall ask him for a loaf, will he give him a stone? Or if he shall ask for a fish, he will not give him a snake, will he? If you then, being evil, know how to give good gifts to your children, how much more shall your Father who is in heaven give what is good to those who ask Him!"

True prayer is always answered.

So the, prayer can be defined as **COMMUNICATING WITH GOD IN HIS PRESENCE.**

HOW SHOULD YOU PRAY?

Jesus give us a **MODEL**:

Matthew 6:91-13

> "Our Father in heaven, hallowed be your name; your kingdom come, your will be done on earth as it is in heaven. Give us today our daily bread. Forgive us our debts as we also have forgiven our debtors. And lead us not into temptation, but deliver us from the evil one."

Examine each point in this prayer closely. What does each point suggest? Explain what you think Jesus means by each statement:

1. "our Father in heaven"

_____

2. "hallowed be your name"

_____

_____

3. "your kingdom come"

_____

_____

4. "your will be done on earth as it is in heaven"

_____

_____

5. "give us today our daily bread"

_____

_____

6. "forgive us our debts as we also have forgiven our debtors"

_____

_____

7. "lead us not into temptation, but deliver us from the evil one"

_____

_____

Each of these seven elements in the model prayer gives us some idea of the kinds of things we should include in our communication with God.

WHEN AND WHERE SHOULD YOU PRAY?

Jesus made it clear that sometimes it's best to pray alone.

Matthew 6:6
> "When you pray, go into your inner room, and when you have shut the door, pray to the Father who is in secret, and your Father who sees in secret will repay you."

Jesus Himself often went alone into the mountains or other private places to pray (**Matthew 14:23; Mark 1:35, 6:46; Luke 5:16; 9:18; 9:28; 11:1**).

SPEND TIME ALONE WITH GOD

Sometimes it's important to come together and pray with a group of believers. The book of Acts is full of examples of believers praying together…

Acts 1:14

"These all (the disciples) with one mind were continually devoting themselves to prayer..."

PRAY WITH OTHERS, TOO.

So, you need time both to pray alone and to pray with other believers.

It's obvious that we should pray, and pray often. In light of these there's an important question that we've saved until now...

WHY PRAY?

Doesn't God know what my needs are even before I pray?

Doesn't He know what I'm going to ask even before I ask it?

The answer to both of these questions is **"YES."**

THEN WHY PRAY?

God wants you to experience His plan for your life and to participate together with Him in a

PERSONAL RELATIONSHIP.

God has granted to you freedom of choice. You're not a robot. He wants you to exercise your own unique individual personality in your relationship to Him.

GOD IS A PERSON, and He created you as a person. Prayer is an important part of your dynamic friendship with God through Jesus Christ. Just as you respond to God in a personal way, **GOD RESPONDS TO YOU IN A PERSONAL WAY.**

1 Corinthians 8:3

"...if anyone loves God, he is known by Him."

The person who loves God (the Christian) is known by God. As a believer

GOD KNOWS YOU.

This means that He has an intimate, personal friendship with you.

PRAYER IS AN INTIMATE, PERSONAL CONVERSATION BETWEEN YOU AND GOD.

You don't need any special vocabulary in order to pray. God wants you to be you. Talk to God in your own personal manner.

We have seen that prayer involves many things – like praise, adoration, requesting, and confessing. At this point, let's focus on one of these aspects of prayer...

ASKING.

The Bible has a lot to say about asking. Jesus, especially, spoke often about it.

Matthew 7:7, 8
> "Ask, and it shall be given to you...everyone who asks receives..."

Matthew 18:19
> "Again I say to you, that if two of you agree on earth about anything that they may ask, it shall be done for them by My Father who is in heaven."

Matthew 21:22
> "And all things you ask in prayer, believing, you shall receive."

Asking must be done in God's will. We must learn to ask truly desiring the Lord's will to be done – **NOT OUR WILL, BUT HIS!** This is what Jesus meant when He talked about praying in His name.

John 14:13, 14
> "And whatever you ask in My name, that will I do, that the Father may be glorified in the Son. If you ask Me anything in My name, I will do it."

When we ask out of our own selfishness, we cannot expect an answer.

God wants you to ask, but your asking must be properly motivated by **LOVE**.

1 John 3:21-23
> "Dear friends, if our hearts do not condemn us, we have confidence before God and receive from Him anything we ask, because we obey His commands and do

what pleases Him. And this is His command: to believe in the name of His son, Jesus Christ, and to love one another as he commanded us." (NIV)

Proverbs 28:9

"He who turns away his ear from listening to the law, even his prayer is an abomination."

Remember, God hears and answers every true prayer.

Here are several things about **TRUE PRAYER** that are very important.

1. SEEK GODS WILL, NOT YOUR OWN.

1 John 5:14, 15

"And this is the confidence which we have before Him, that, if we ask anything according to His will, He hears us. And if we know that He hears us in whatever we ask, we know that we have the requests which we have asked from Him."

2. LIVE A LIFE THAT'S PLEASING TO GOD.

1 John 3:21, 22

"...do the things that are pleasing in His sight."

3. DON'T HAVE UNCONFESSED SIN IN YOUR LIFE.

Psalm 66:18

"If I regard wickedness in my heart, the Lord will not hear."

HOW DOES GOD ANSWER PRAYER?

Basically, God answers prayer in three ways:

"YES"   "NO"   "WAIT"

Whatever the answer is, receive it joyfully, knowing that God has His best in mind for your life.

What are some ways God might answer **"YES"**?

_____

_____

What are some ways God might answer "NO"?

_____

_____

What are some ways God might answer "WAIT"?

_____

_____

_____

Prayer is an extremely vital part of your walk with Christ. Make it a part of your daily life by having a specific time to pray each day. Besides your set prayer times, pray throughout the day. Talk to the Lord. He is right there with you every second of every day. The apostle Paul reminds us in I Thessalonians 5:17 that we should

PRAY WITHOUT CEASING.

Let's think through what we've talked about...

1. Prayer is experience the _____ of God.

2. Prayer is _____ with God.

3. _____ is always answered.

4. When should I pray? _____

5. Where should I pray? _____

6. God responds to us in a _____ way.

7. We must always ask according to God's _____

8. Asking must be properly _____

9. True prayer can take place when se seek God's _____

   instead of our own, live a life that's _____

   to God, and keep our _____ confessed.

10. God answers in three ways: _____,

    _____ , and _____.

CHAPTER 9
FRUIT IN THE CHRISTIAN LIFE

As a Christian, your relationship with Jesus Christ is living and vital. When Jesus spoke of this relationship, He compared it to a growing, thriving vine.

John 15:1, 5

> "I am the vine, and My Father is the vinedresser...I am the vine, you are the branches; he who abides in Me, and I in him, he bears much fruit; for apart from Me you can do nothing."

In this beautiful analogy, Jesus spells out the intimate nature of the believer's relationship to Himself. The life-giving "sap" which flows from the main vine into each individual branch is the divine power of the Lord Jesus Christ which sustains growth.

It's important to recognize that this passage (**John 15:1-8, 16**) isn't dealing with the issue of salvation. Jesus uses the vine analogy to express the critical nature of an abiding personal relationship to Him in order to produce fruit in the Christian life. The issue is the PRODUCTIVITY of the believer's life, not eternal salvation. (Keep this in mind, especially as you approach the end of this lesson.)

So, as a believer in Jesus Christ and as His disciple, you have the responsibility to **produce fruit**. When fruit comes forth in your life, God is glorified.

John 15:8

> "By this is My Father glorified, that you bear much fruit, and so prove to be My disciples."

Romans 7:4

> "Therefore, my brethren, you also were made to die to the law through the body of Christ, that you might be joined to another, to Him who was raised from the dead, that we might bear fruit for God."

THERE ARE SEVERAL KINDS OF FRUIT.

As a believer in Christ, there are many varieties of fruit to be produced in your life.

1. THE FRUIT OF THE SPIRIT

Galatians 5:22, 23

> "But the fruit of the Spirit is love, joy, peace, patience, kindness, goodness, faithfulness, gentleness, self-control..."

The fruit of the Spirit consists of various **CHARACTER QUALITIES** and attitudes which are a result of being filled (directed and empowered) by the Holy Spirit.

Galatians 5:25

> "If we live by the Spirit, let us also walk by the Spirit."

What does it mean to "live by the Spirit"?

_____

What does it mean to "walk by the Spirit"?

_____

As you experience the ministry of the Holy Spirit, the fruit of the Spirit will begin to mature in your life.

2. THE FRUIT OF RIGHTEOUSNESS

Philippians 1:11

> "...having been filled with the fruit of righteousness which comes through Jesus Christ, to the glory and praise of God."

James 3:18

> "And the seed whose fruit is righteousness is sown in peace by those who make peace."

The fruit of righteousness is the **CONDUCT** of the believer. As you abide in Jesus, the True Vine, righteous living is the sure result. When your conduct as a Christian does not please the Lord, you'll be disciplined by Him."

Hebrews 12:11

> "All discipline for the moment seems not to be joyful, but sorrowful; yet to those who are trained by it, afterwards it yields the peaceful fruit of righteousness."

Conduct is an important part of discipleship.

3. THE FRUIT OF THE GOSPEL

Colossians 1:5, 6

> "...the gospel, which has come to you, just as in all the world also, it is constantly bearing fruit and increasing...."

The fruit of the Gospel is produced by **WITNESSING**. It is your job as a believer to proclaim the Gospel to others.

John 4:35, 36

"Behold, I say to you, lift up your eyes and look on the fields, that they are white for harvest. Already he who reaps is receiving wages, and is gathering fruit for eternal life; that he who sows and he who reaps may rejoice together."

Acts 1:8

"...you shall be My witnesses both in Jerusalem, and in all Judea and Samaria, and even to the remotest part of the earth."

4. THE FRUIT OF SERVICE

Romans 1:13

"And I do not want you to be unaware, brethren, that often I have planned to come to you.. .in order that I might obtain some fruit among you also, even as among the rest of the Gentiles."

In this passage Paul tells the believers in Rome that he wants to come and minister to them as he has done among other groups of Gentiles (non-Jews). The fruit that he refers to is the fruit of service rendered in the name of Jesus Christ.

You are to serve others in Jesus' name. Every believer has a **MINISTRY** to perform.

When Paul spoke concerning the Macedonian and Achaian believers and their willingness to serve by sending a financial contribution to help the poor saints at Jerusalem, he said...

Romans 15:27, 28

"For if the Gentiles have shared in their spiritual things, they are indebted to minister to them also in material things. Therefore, when I have finished this, and have put my seal on this fruit of theirs, I will go on by way of you to Spain."

Paul recognized the fruit of their service to the Jerusalem believers. Serving others is a joyful and rewarding fruit of the Christian life.

5. THE FRUIT OF PRAISE

Hebrews 13:15

"Through Him then, let us continually offer up a sacrifice of praise to God, that is, the fruit of lips that give thanks to His name."

Praise is an important part of the Christian life. Praise is our recognition of God's greatness and the expression of our absolute dependence upon Him as the source of all things.

Psalm 22:3

"Thou art holy, O Thou who art enthroned upon the praises of Israel."

Now, let's look at the importance of

ABIDING IN CHRIST.

Remember, your position in Christ cannot change. Once you have received Christ, you are positioned in Him eternally. Jesus often speaks of abiding in Him with reference to bearing fruit in your life.

Being in Christ is POSITION.

ABIDING IN CHRIST IS EXPERIENCE.

To abide in Jesus is to maintain a close, personal daily walk with Him. Without this intimate personal relationship you will not produce fruit.

Let's look at **John 15:1-8** very carefully...

John 15:1

"I am the vine, and My Father is the vinedresser."

Jesus is the vine, the source of nourishment for the branches and the fruit. The Father is the gardener who takes care of the vine, making sure that it grows properly.

John 15:2

"Every branch in Me that does not bear fruit, He takes away; and every branch that bears fruit, He prunes it, that it may bear more fruit."

The phrase "He takes away" may refer to the removal, by death, of the fruitless believer. It may also be rendered "picks up," suggesting that the fruitless branch is provided extra support by the vinedresser, encouraging it to produce fruit. The branches which bear fruit are trimmed (pruned) to insure maximum production. This pruning is often in the form of discipline. (Hebrews 12:3-11).

John 15:3

"You are already clean (same root as "pruned") because of the word which I have spoken to you."

The Word of God is the pruning instrument (**Hebrews 4:12**).

John 15:4

"Abide in Me, and I in you. As the branch cannot bear fruit of itself, unless it abides in the vine, so neither can you, unless you abide in Me."

"Abide" means to continually experience the personal presence and power of Christ, living a life that's pleasing to Him.

John 15:5

> "I am the vine, you are the branches; he who abides in Me, and I in him, he bears much fruit; for apart from Me you can do nothing."

As a branch, the believer must abide continually in Christ, the vine, in order to produce fruit. When you do not abide continually, you rely on your own strength and accomplish nothing.

John 15:6

> "If anyone does not abide in Me he is thrown away as a branch, and dries up; and they gather them, and cast them into the fire, and they are burned."

Remember, Jesus is not discussing salvation. He is talking about producing fruit. (Fruitless Christians are not lost, they are disobedient and, therefore, under God's disciplinary action.) The analogy of burning in this verse describes the testing of the believer's works by fire. All fruitless activities in your life will be burned up. Only what is done through your faith-relationship with Jesus Christ will stand the test (**Romans 14:23; I Corinthians 3:10-15**).

John 15:7

> "If you abide in Me, and My words abide in you, ask whatever you wish, and it shall be done for you."

Jesus specifically points out that the Word in your life is the basic ingredient in an effective prayer life. The Word teaches us to ask according to God's will.

John 15:8

> "By this is My Father glorified, that you bear much fruit, and so prove to be My disciples."

You aren't proving your discipleship to the Lord, but to the world. Fruitless believers don't make an impression on unbelievers. A transformed, fruitful life **witnesses to the life-changing power of the cross.**

BE A FRUIT-BEARING CHRISTIAN.

Now, it's time for a little **FRUIT INSPECTION**.

You aren't authorized to inspect other's fruit, just your own!

Rate yourself on a 1-5 scale. One is lowest, five is highest. Circle your answer.

1. Genuine love for others	1	2	3	4	5
2. Deep abiding joy	1	2	3	4	5
3. Peace in life	1	2	3	4	5
4. Patient temperament	1	2	3	4	5
5. Kindness toward others	1	2	3	4	5

6. Goodness in character	1	2	3	4	5
7. Faithfulness to Christ and others	1	2	3	4	5
8. Attitude of gentleness	1	2	3	4	5
9. Quality of self-control	1	2	3	4	5
10. Christ-like conduct	1	2	3	4	5
11. Share the gospel freely	1	2	3	4	5
12. Actively minister to others	1	2	3	4	5
13. Heart full of praise to God	1	2	3	4	5
14. Desire to be a fruitful Christian	1	2	3	4	5

TAKE THIS TEST OFTEN.

Let's review…

1. In **John 15:1-8** Jesus compares Himself to a _____.

2. The Father is the _____.

3. You are a _____.

4. You have the responsibility to produce _____ in your Christian life.

5. What are the five kinds of fruit?

    _____

    _____

    _____

6. The fruit of the Spirit is character _____

    and _____.

7. The fruit of righteousness is your _____ as a believer.

8. _____ is the fruit of the gospel.

9. The fruit of service means that I have a _____ to perform in the lives of other people.

10. The fruit of praise can be described as _____.

11. Abiding in Christ is _____.

12. To abide in Christ is to maintain a close personal daily _____

_____.

13. Jesus is the source of _____ power for your life.

14. Pruning means to be _____

by the _____.

15. Not abiding means that you must rely on your own

_____ which results in a

_____ of your fruitless activities.

16. Much fruit is produced in your life by _____,

_____, and true _____.

17. A fruitful Christian life is a _____ to the

life-changing power of the cross _____.

CHAPTER 10
DEVELOPING A CHRIST-LIKE ATTITUDE

As a believer in Christ, as His disciple, your attitude is very important.

Attitude is the state of mind which causes you to **act** or **react** in a certain way. Attitude is the manner of responding (whether properly or improperly) to any life situation.

As a Christian,

PROPER ATTITUDE MEANS A CHRIST-LIKE RESPONSE TO GOD, PEOPLE, AND SITUATIONS.

The fruit of the Spirit relates to our attitude as followers of Jesus (previous chapter).

The primary characteristic of a Christ-like attitude is

SELF-SACRIFICE.

Jesus lived His life in complete selflessness.

Philippians 2:5-9
> "Your attitude should be the same as that of Christ Jesus: Who, being in very nature God, did not consider equality with God something to be grasped, but made Himself nothing, taking the very nature of a servant, being made in human likeness. And being found in appearance as a man, He humbled Himself, and became obedient to death-even death on a cross!" (NIV)

This is a graphic description of Jesus' attitude. These verses reveal to us that He didn't exploit His divine nature to the exclusion of others. As Creator (**Genesis 1; John 1:1-18**), when sin entered the world, Jesus, the Second Person of the Trinity, could have spoken the whole universe out of existence. But because His attitude was permeated by self-giving love, He came to die in our place. He died the death we deserved in order that we might live.

Your attitude should be like that of your Lord. Anything less than a Christ-like attitude is self-centeredness.

SELF-CENTERED ATTITUDE = IMPROPER RESPONSES

CHRIST-CENTERED ATTITUDE = PROPER RESPONSES

Your actions and reactions are determined by your attitude.

Let's consider three categories of response which are directly affected by your attitude...

1. RESPONDING TO GOD

Hebrews 4:12,13

> "The word of God is living and active. Sharper than any double-edged sword, it penetrates even to dividing soul and spirit, joints and marrow; it judges the thoughts and attitudes of the heart. Nothing in all creation is hidden from God's sight. Everything is uncovered and laid bare before the eyes of Him to whom we must give account." (N IV)

God knows the motive behind everything you do. In order to properly respond to His plan and purpose for your life, you must respond to Him through an attitude of **truthfulness**.

John 4:24

> "God is spirit, and those who worship Him must worship in spirit and truth."

and humility...

Matthew 18:4

> "Whoever then humbles himself as this child, he is the greatest in the kingdom of heaven."

Micah 6:8

> "He has told you, O man, what is good; and what does the Lord require of you but to do justice, to love kindness, and to walk humbly with your God."

James 4:6,10

> "But He gives a greater grace. Therefore, it says, 'God is opposed to the proud, but gives grace to the humble'... Humble yourselves in the presence of the Lord, and He will exalt you."

The attitude of the old self (the carnal nature) is ego-centered and can't respond to God's leadership. The attitude of the new self (the Spirit-controlled nature) is tempered with humility and truth.

Ephesians 4:22-24

"You were taught, with regard to your former way of life, to put off your old self...to be made new in the attitude of your minds; and put on the new self, created to be like God in true righteousness and holiness." (NIV)

A CHRIST-LIKE ATTITUDE IS SENSITIVE TO THE HOLY SPIRIT.

When we maintain an ego-centered attitude we become hardened to the movement of God's Spirit in our lives.

Hebrews 3:13

"Encourage one another day after day...lest any one of you be hardened by the deceitfulness of sin."

When a Christ-like attitude is present, we are ready to respond to the Holy Spirit.

I Corinthians 2:12

"Now we have received, not the spirit of the world, but the Spirit who is from God, that we might know the things freely given to us by God."

When you are directed and empowered by the Holy Spirit, you are a spiritual Christian and possess a Christ-like frame of mind.

I Corinthians 2:16

"But we have the mind of Christ."

Romans 8:5, 6

"Those who live according to their sinful nature have their minds set on what that nature desires; but those who live in accordance with the Spirit have their minds set on what the Spirit desires." (NIV)

2. RESPONDING TO PEOPLE

Philippians 2:3-5

"Do nothing out of selfish ambition or vain conceit, but in humility consider others better than yourselves. Each of you should look not only to your own interests, but also to the interests of others. Your attitude should be the same as that of Christ Jesus...." (NIV)

Romans 12:16

"Be of the same mind [attitude] toward one another; do not be haughty in mind [attitude], but associate with the lowly. Do not be wise in your own estimation."

1 Peter 5:5, 6

"Clothe yourselves with humility toward one another, because, 'God opposes the proud but gives grace to the humble.' Humble yourselves, therefore, under God's mighty hand, that He may lift you up in due time."

THINK OF OTHERS FIRST.

When you develop a Christ-like attitude, you begin to respond to others according to their needs instead of reacting only to their surface actions. Jesus always responded to others according to their true needs. He didn't treat symptoms, but causes. He always responded to the root of the problem.

Study the following passages:

John 3:1-1 5—NICODEMUS

What was Nicodemus' surface (symptomatic) approach to Jesus?

_____

_____

What was Nicodemus' real need (the root problem)?

_____

_____

How did Jesus respond to this need?

_____

_____

John 4:3-26—THE WOMAN OF SAMARIA

What were some of the woman's symptoms?

_____

_____

What might some people say (many already had, no doubt) to the woman if their attitudes allowed them to see only her surface symptoms?

_____

_____

What was her real problem?

_____

_____

How did Jesus respond to her need?

But how do we usually respond to the surface actions of others?

If your attitude is self-centered, you'll always be reacting to other people's symptoms. When a family member yells at you, you'll scream back. When a friend says something you don't appreciate, you'll stop talking to him for a week. When someone calls you a #*#!!*!#!, your first reaction will be to retaliate. When someone cheats you, slanders you, or makes fun of you, your desire will be to get even. **GET THE PICTURE?**

Jesus expressed His attitude of selflessness when He said:

Luke 6:27-31

> "I say to you who hear, love your enemies, do good to those who hate you, bless those who curse you, pray for those who mistreat you. Whoever hits you on the cheek, offer him the other also; and whoever takes away your coat, do not withhold your shirt from him either. Give to everyone who asks of you, and whoever takes away what is yours, do not demand it back. And just as you want people to treat you, treat them in the same way."

A SELF-CENTERED ATTITUDE REACTS TO SYMPTOMS.

A CHRIST-CENTERED ATTITUDE RESPONDS TO THE REAL NEED.

Surface symptoms are the result of root problems. When people act in a certain way, it's basically a reflection of their spiritual condition. Ungodly behavior stems from a spiritual deficiency in a person's life. When you react to other people's symptoms, you become a part of their problem and throw away the blessing of being used by God to minister to their spiritual needs.

God wants to transform your attitude so that you'll be able to meet the spiritual needs of others.

Remember, when someone says, "I hate you!" deep down inside he's really crying out, "I have a spiritual need in my life—please help me!"

I Peter 4:1, 2
> "Therefore, since Christ suffered in His body, arm yourselves with the same attitude, because he who has suffered in his body is done with sin. As a result, he does not live the rest of his earthly life for evil human desires, but rather for the will of God." (NIV)

3. RESPONDING TO SITUATIONS

A Christ-like attitude will cause you to respond to situations in a manner pleasing to God.

One of the sure signs of carnality in the Christian life is the inability to give a definite answer of "yes" or "no." Many believers have a hard time trying to make up their minds as to what they want to or should do.

Matthew 5:37
> "Simply let your 'Yes' be 'Yes,' and your 'No,' 'No'; anything beyond this comes from the evil one." (NIV)

Jesus says here that you should have an unequivocal answer for every question in your life. As Christians, what we say we will do, we should do. And our word about any matter should be specific and sure. Whatever the situation might be, you must be able to respond in a responsible way, ready to be used by God to affect the situation with a **positive Christian influence.**

MAKE EVERY SITUATION
COUNT FOR CHRIST!

Ephesians 5:1 5,1 6
> "Therefore, be careful how you walk, not as unwise men, but as wise, making the most of your time, because the days are evil."

II Timothy 4:2
> "...be ready in season and out of season..."

When you respond to situations in a manner pleasing to Christ, the definite "yes" or "no" of your responses will cause others to question you further about your personal devotion to Him. Why do you choose to serve Christ and not the world or fleshly desires? And when they begin to question you concerning the reason for the way you are and what you do, or don't do, you have ready-made opportunities to witness to the transforming power of Jesus Christ in your life.

I Peter 3:13-17

"And who is there to harm you if you prove zealous for what is good? But even if you should suffer for the sake of righteousness, you are blessed. 'And do not fear their intimidation, and do not be troubled,' but sanctify Christ as Lord in your hearts, always being ready to make a defense [give evidence] to everyone who asks you to give an account for the hope that is in you, yet with gentleness and reverence; and keep a good conscience so that in the thing in which you are slandered, those who revile your good behavior in Christ may be put to shame. For it is better, if God should will it so, that you suffer for doing what is right rather than for doing what is wrong."

This is the kind of attitude that makes a difference. And there will be times when your commitment to Jesus Christ will cause people to slander you or poke fun at you. But stand firm, always being ready to testify to the gospel of Christ.

Pray that God will cause your attitude to be transformed into a Christ-like attitude.

Let's review what you've learned...

1. Attitude is the state of _____ which causes you

   to _____ or _____ in a certain way.

2. A proper attitude means a _____ response to every situation and every person.

3. The primary characteristic of a Christ-like attitude is

   _____

4. Without a Christ-like attitude, you are _____.

5. A proper attitude is sensitive to the _____.

6. An ego-centered attitude disrupts the _____ of God's Spirit in your life.

7. You must learn to respond to the true _____ of others

   and not to their surface _____.

8. Ungodly behavior is caused by a spiritual _____.

9. God wants to transform your attitude so that you'll be able to meet the

_____needs of others.

10. Every situation is an opportunity to _____

_____

CHAPTER 11
SPIRITUAL WARFARE

Of all of the subjects addressed by God's Word, that of spiritual warfare is one of the most avoided, even ignored. There are a number of reasons for this. One is that we live in a scientific/technological age, and it's difficult for "modern" people to accept the reality of the existence of Satan, the devil, and his evil helpers, the demons. Another reason is that humanistic psychology is most often approached from a purely materialistic standpoint and, therefore, denies the reality of the spiritual realm and its influence, good or evil. Still another is that many believers who have taught on the subject have not done so scripturally and have gone to extremes which distort the true Biblical perspective. One final reason (certainly there are more) is that most Christians are frightened about the whole idea and avoid it as much as possible.

But the fact is, the Bible teaches the undeniable reality of the devil and his dark forces. To believe and accept God's Word is to believe in the existence of Satan and demons. To deny their existence is to put the entire Bible in doubt. For the believer who holds to the historicity and credibility of Scripture, there is the necessity of becoming acquainted with what God has to say about Satan and demons and their activities, for the purpose of dealing with their attacks in daily living. That is the purpose of this chapter.

We will discuss the subject in four parts: (1) Satan, (2) demons, (3) their methods of operation, and (4) the Christian's warfare. (Please read and study all Scripture references given, looking up those not quoted.)

First, let's look at the **reality** and **personality** of

SATAN.

Satan is called by many names and titles; among them are: the devil (**I Peter 5:8**), the dragon (**Revelation 12:9**), the evil one (**Matthew 13:19**), the serpent (**Revelation 20:2**), Abaddon (**Revelation 9:11**), Belial (**II Corinthians 6:15**), the god of this world (**II Corinthians 4:4**), the ruler of this world (**John 12:31**), the prince of the power of the air (**Ephesians 2:2**), the angel of the abyss (**Revelation 9:11**), Apollyon (**Revelation 9:11**), and Beelzebul (**Matthew 12:24**).

But just what or who is Satan? Satan is a person, a **created being**. He isn't omnipresent as God is. God is infinite—Satan is finite. Certainly, Satan is far more powerful than any human, but still he is only a meager, confined being, totally under the sovereignty of God, along with all creation.

Satan was created an angelic being, one of the highest and most beautiful of all God's creatures. He was a great and magnificent angelic leader. Satan, having free choice, became proud concerning his exalted position in the angelic realm. The Bible says Satan sought to diminish the worship and glory that were due only to the eternal God, his Creator, and to receive that worship and glory for himself. Certainly Satan could never usurp God's position as Infinite Sovereign, but evidently he deceived himself enough to believe it possible.

When Satan rebelled against God, great numbers of the angelic host followed him in rebellion. Thus, Satan and his followers were cast out of the heavenly realm. Satan, formerly Lucifer the high angel, became the adversary ("Satan" means adversary) of God's purpose in the universe. His followers, formerly angels, took on the role of demons, subservient pawns in their leader's evil pursuits. (See the following passages of Scripture which deal with the origin, fall and judgment of Satan: **Ezekiel 28:11-19; Isaiah 14:12-20; Genesis 3:14,15; John 12:31; Revelation12:13; 20:2,10**.)

Satan was defeated at the cross and through the resurrection of the Lord Jesus Christ. Jesus rose victorious over all sin and death. Satan's judgment at the hand of the Messiah is sure and absolute. The devil is only allowed to operate under the permission of God until the time when the Lord terminates, with eternal finality, his freedom to work.

The following verses will give you an idea of what Satan is like: His **character** and **personality** are seen in **Ezekiel 28:14; Ephesians 6:11; 12, John 8:44; I John 3:8; Revelation 12: 10; I Peter 5:8**. Satan's **work** is described in **Genesis 3:15, Matthew 2:16; 4:1-11; 13:38, 39; 16:23; John 8:44; 13:27; II Corinthians 4:4; Luke 8:12; I Corinthians 7:5; Acts 5:3; I Thessalonians 2:18; Revelation 2:13; 12:10**.

Satan is a **deceiver**. He puts on a beautiful facade in order to delude people.

II Corinthians 11 :14
> "...Satan disguises himself as an angel of light."

We'll learn more about Satan's activities later, but if you'll study the Scripture passages given above, you'll get a good idea of what he's like.

Next let's examine what the Bible has to say about

DEMONS.

Demons are spiritual beings—angels, who participated in Satan's rebellion and were cast down from their heavenly position (**Revelation 12:7, 9**). They ceased to be ministers of God and became ministers of the devil (**Luke 4:35; 9:1, 42; John 10:21**). Demons are under the direction of Satan and are organized to war against the purposes of God in the world (**Matthew 9:34; 12:24; Mark 3:2; Luke 11:15; Ephesians 6:10-12**). They, too, are finite. Because neither Satan nor his demon agents can be in more than one place at a time, they are highly regimented and organized in order to accomplish their work.

Scripture seems to indicate that neither Satan the prince of demons (the highest demon), nor other demons underwent a transformation in "appearance" as a result of their fall; in fact, they seem to have retained their original composition and, therefore, are quite capable of presenting themselves as angels of light (**II Corinthians 11:14, 15**). Only their activities have changed from good to evil. Presently some demons are free to operate in Satan's organization, while others are imprisoned until the end time or judgment and eternal destruction with Satan (**II Peter 2:4; Jude 6**).

[You might be wondering when the fall of Satan and demons took place. The Bible doesn't specifically state when this occurred, but it does indicate that, because Satan had already fallen by the time Adam and Eve were created, he fell before the creation of man. Whether or not Satan's rebellion occurred before the creation of the world is not entirely clear in Scripture.]

Now let's look at the workings of

SATAN'S DEMONIC SYSTEM.

Satan and his demons are spiritual beings. The term "spiritual" simply indicates that, as created beings, they have the ability to operate in more dimensions than the three in which we are presently confined. Still, whether they are able to operate in four or 40 dimensions, they are still confined to their created realm. God, on the other hand, is omnidimensional. He possesses the ability to operate in an infinite number of dimensions, all of His own creative design. God is not bound by any dimensional restrictions—not time, not space, nor anything beyond.

This is important to understand because many people have the erroneous idea that Satan is somehow God's arch rival, an alternate spiritual force of evil that is equal or nearly equal to God in power. This is not taught in the Bible. As we have seen, Scripture teaches that Satan is one of God's created beings. He is only allowed to do his work because he has a purpose to fulfill in God's plan for the ages. When God's purpose for Satan and demons is complete, they will be eternally deposited in hell, the lake of fire (**Revelation 20:10**).

Still, you and I must not underestimate the power and craftiness of Satan and his dark forces as they operate in this world. The Bible tells us very plainly that, as believers, our struggle is not with other human beings, but with the organized operation of evil carried on by demons and led by their prince, Satan.

Ephesians 6:10-12
> "Finally, be strong in the Lord, and in the strength of His might. Put on the full armor of God, that you may be able to stand firm against the schemes of the devil. For our struggle is not against flesh and blood, but against the rulers, against the powers, against the world forces of this darkness, against the spiritual forces of wickedness in the heavenly places."

Certainly, as Christians we possess all of the resources necessary to be victorious in this daily struggle against the forces of the devil. But what kinds of things is Satan doing today as he orchestrates his demonic followers in a rampage of evil? (By the way, if you don't believe that this rampage is real, get a newspaper and read it!)

The **satanic organization** sets itself to accomplish the following:

1. TEMPTATION (James 1:13-16; I Corinthians 7:5; Galatians 6:1; I Thessalonians 3:5)

"Tempt" means to try, to test, to prove. Satan, through his demonic agents, tries to get us to disobey Christ. He is out to make us fail in proving our love for Jesus and to make us gratify the flesh instead of pleasing the Lord. Temptation is through the mind; it is not sin. Sin occurs when temptation is followed and Satan's suggestions are obeyed.

2. DECEPTION (II Timothy 3:13; Revelation 12:9; II Corinthians 11:14, 15)

Deception occurs when we see things in a manner different from what they are in reality. Partial truths, half-truths, distortions of the truth, infusions of doubt— these are all found in Satan's arsenal of deception.

3. SPIRITUAL BLINDNESS (II Corinthians 4:4)

The god of this world can blind the minds of unbelievers so that they cannot see the light of the gospel. Even your witness to a lost person is right in the thick of spiritual warfare. It is only as we learn to do battle scripturally that we can have success at breaking the satanic darkness that blinds the minds of unbelievers.

4. SPIRITUAL THIEVERY (Luke 8:12)

Satan can snatch the Word of God from people's hearts, keeping them from receiving Christ. The demonic forces are active, stealing our words of witness. We must learn how to be victorious over these spiritual thieves.

5. OPPOSITION (I Thessalonians 2:18; Revelation 2:13; Matthew 13:38, 39; Daniel 10)

Satan and his forces oppose everything that God's people do. Every spiritual victory that is won is won by doing spiritual battle. Even when we don't realize it, our daily walk with Christ is opposed by the devil's army.

6. PERSECUTION (Revelation 2:10)

The persecution of God's people originates with Satan himself. Persecution comes in many forms. Those who serve Christ can expect it.

7. ACCUSATION (Revelation 12:10)

Satan constantly accuses us before God, denying our position in Christ.

The operation of the satanic system is often subtle and able to get "positive press" at every turn. Believer, never attempt to judge something to be from God just because it appears good or because it "works" for others, even you. Just because something works doesn't mean it's from God. Satan and his organization of demons can and will counterfeit anything in order to lull you into a false sense of security. Don't fall for it! Remember that **God's Word, the Bible, must be the final authority in your experience, not the experience itself!**

(You might be wondering why we haven't included any discussion on "demon possession." We have omitted it because it is a rather complex issue and needs to be dealt with in detail. It is an important subject. If you would like to do further study in this area the following books are recommended: **Biblical Demonology**, M.F. Unger; **What Demons Can Do To Saints**, M.F. Unger; **Christian Counseling and Occultism**, Kurt E. Koch; **Demon Possession**, J.W. Montgomery.)

Satan and demons are behind the evil in the world. They operate behind the scenes in every facet of this earth's human arena. They are the instigators of all wickedness, all false religions and, yes, all false doctrines. The Bible specifically warns us about doctrines propagated by demons (**I Timothy 4:1**).

Our study thus far has given you some idea of who Satan is and how he operates his evil organization. But now we must look at the most important part of this subject.

THE CHRISTIAN'S WARFARE: OVERCOMING THE SATANIC SYSTEM.

The Bible makes it very clear that Christians are in constant warfare against the devil and his dark forces which work subtly behind the scenes of the world system. The Bible makes it equally clear that believers in Christ have the victory over Satan and demons through the person of Jesus Christ, through the indwelling Holy Spirit.

First, the victory is **POSITIONAL**, that is, we are in Christ who has the ultimate victory. Second, however, we must deal experientially with the devil's schemes during our time on this fallen earth, before the completion of our redemption (experientially) at Christ's return. But we do have the victory now, if we choose to live our lives in obedience to the Lord.

I John 4:4
"You are from God, little children, and have overcome them; because greater is He who is in you than he who is in the world."

James 4:7
"Submit therefore to God. Resist the devil and he will flee from you."

I Peter 5:8, 9
"Be of sober spirit, be on the alert. Your adversary, the devil, prowls about like a roaring lion, seeking someone to devour."

I Corinthians 10:13
"No temptation has overtaken you but such as is common to man; and God is faithful, who will not allow you to be tempted beyond what you are able, but with the temptation will provide the way of escape also, that you may be able to endure it."

II Peter 2:9
"...the Lord knows how to rescue the godly from temptation, and to keep the unrighteous under punishment for the day of judgment."

Hebrew 4:15
"For we do not have a high priest who cannot sympathize with our weaknesses, but one who has been tempted in all things as we are, yet without sin."

Hebrews 2:18

"For since He Himself was tempted in that which He has suffered, He is able to come to the aid of those who are tempted."

THERE IS VICTORY
OVER SATAN'S ATTACKS!

What is the key to overcoming the onslaught of Satan's forces in daily living? Paul gives us the complete answer. In the following verses we have God's outline for combat...

Ephesians 6:10-17

"Finally, be strong in the Lord, and in the strength of His might. Put on the full armor of God, that you may be able to stand firm against the schemes of the devil. For our struggle is not against flesh and blood, but against the rulers, against the powers, against the world forces of this darkness, against the spiritual forces of wickedness in the heavenly places. Therefore, take up the full armor of God, that you may be able to resist in the evil day, and having done everything, to stand firm. Stand firm, therefore, having girded your loins with truth, and having put on the breastplate of righteousness, and having shod your feet with the preparation of the gospel of peace; in addition to all, taking up the shield of faith with which you will be able to extinguish all the flaming missiles of the evil one. And take the helmet of salvation, and the sword of the Spirit, which is the word of God."

How will we overcome the devil?

PUT ON THE FULL
ARMOR OF GOD.

Note that Paul says, "the FULL armor." Not part of it. Not even most of it. But ALL of it! The indication is that if you only have partial armor you are vulnerable.

Let's look at this armor piece by piece.

TRUTH

Truth is light (**I John 1:5-7**). Jesus is the truth (**John 14:6**). In order to resist the devil you must walk in Christ, abiding in Him (**John 15:1-12**), and, therefore, you will be girding yourself with truth. The opposite of truth is deception—Satan's primary weapon. Walk in truth before God and men and you will not be defeated by deception.

RIGHTEOUSNESS

Remember, the fruit of righteousness is primarily related to conduct-your actions. As a believer, you are the righteousness of God in Christ Jesus (**II Corinthians 5:21**). Your protection from Satan's frontal attacks is righteousness living-being obedient to Jesus' lordship.

THE GOSPEL

A soldier without protective leggings was liable to be wounded in the feet or legs and therefore unable to stand and fight. The "preparation of the gospel of peace" refers specifically to the proclamation of the Gospel. Those who are always ready to share the message of Christ with others are more able to stand in spiritual combat because they are obedient to Jesus' most urgent command (**Matthew 28:18-20**).

FAITH

Faith could here be rendered "faithfulness" as well. The protection afforded by faithfulness is the ability to trust the Lord in all situations, knowing that, whether or not we can see the reasons or results of our obedience, He is able to protect and guide our every step. This faith causes us to keep marching forward in spite of Satan's flaming projectiles.

SALVATION

This is the hope (confidence) of salvation. Those who do not know for certain that their salvation is secure (**I John 5:11-13**) are wide open to Satan's attacks of doubt which cause one to stumble in the daily walk. To enter into battle without this vital piece of armor is to invite certain defeat.

THE WORD OF GOD

The Word of God, the Bible, is our only offensive weapon. Obedience to the Word causes Satan to flee. Ground yourself in the Word. Feed on it. Live in it. Act by it. God's Word is powerful and will cause you to advance on the battlefield of the Christian life (**Hebrews 4:12**). Read it. Study it. Memorize it. Meditate on it. Do these things to move forward for Christ!

God promises that all who put on His full armor will stand against Satan's attacks. Not only will you stand firm with the whole armor, but also you will attack and gain territory for God's kingdom by taking up the sword of the Spirit, God's Word. Don't just put on the armor to protect yourself, but to march into enemy territory with the gospel and claim souls in victory for God's glory!

Part Two

THE DYNAMICS OF
A SPIRITUAL LIFE

CHAPTER 12

THE HUMAN EQUATION

According to God's Word, the world has only two kinds of people—lost and saved. Those who have never received Jesus Christ as Savior and Lord are lost; that is, they are separated from God because they haven't personally accepted His forgiveness through Jesus' sacrifice for sin on the cross, and eternal life through His resurrection from the dead. Those who have accepted God's grace through faith in Christ are saved; that is, they have received forgiveness for sin and possess eternal life.

If you have never had a personal encounter with Jesus Christ and have never given your life to Him, you need not read any further into this book.

If you are a true believer in Christ, then what you'll learn as you study further may be used by God to bring about a radical transformation in your life. We say "may" because learning is never automatic. Living what you learn is certainly not automatic. If you don't have a deep desire to be a useful disciple of Jesus, you can't. Without a hunger for true spirituality, you'll never experience the abundant life. Just having a knowledge of what we're going to study does not guarantee that you'll become or experience what is taught.

How are these things applied to your life? How is true spirituality attained? This is what we'll discuss in this section. Right now it's important to understand how you can prepare yourself to learn and apply the teaching you're about to receive. Of course, there is the role of the human teacher (the one who is discipling you).

Ephesians 4:11-13
> "He gave some...teachers, for the equipping of the saints for the work of service, to the building up of the body of Christ; until we all attain to the unity of the faith, and of the knowledge of the Son of God, to a mature man, to the measure of the stature which belongs to the fullness of Christ."

Human teachers can bring spiritual truths to your mind for consideration, but **it is by the Holy Spirit that you are taught**, enabling the Word to penetrate into your inner man, where true spiritual learning is achieved.

John 14:26
> "...the Holy Spirit...will teach you all things."

I John 2:27
> "And as for you, the anointing which you have received from Him abides in you, and you have no need for anyone to teach you; but as His anointing teaches you

about all things, and is true and is not a lie, and just as it has taught you, you abide in Him."

I Corinthians 2:9, 10

"Things which eye has not seen and ear has not heard, and which have not entered the heart of man, all that God has prepared for those who love Him. For to us God has revealed them through the Spirit; for the Spirit searches all things, even the depths of God."

Ephesians 3:1 6-1 9

"...that He would grant to you, according to the riches of His glory, to be strengthened with power through His Spirit in the inner man; so that Christ may dwell in your hearts through faith; and that you, being rooted and grounded in love, may be able to comprehend with all the saints what is the breadth and length and height and depth, and to know the love of Christ which surpasses knowledge, that you may be filled up to all the fullness of God."

Stop right now and ask God to open your spiritual eyes to the truth of His Word.

Let's begin our spiritual journey. There's no better place to start than at

THE BEGINNING...

Genesis 2:7

"And the Lord God formed man from the dust of the ground, and breathed into his nostrils the breath of life; and man became a living soul." (KJV)

The first thing God produced in the creation of man was a physical **BODY**. Man's body contains the same elements that are found in the earth. The human body was created to live in the earthly environment along with the other living things God created.

The body provided man with mechanisms by which he could experience his environment—sight, hearing, touch, smell, taste—and a marvelous computer-like brain which would enable him to gather, store, comprehend, analyze and synthesize knowledge and information.

Without the body, communication, especially with other human beings, within the three-dimensional physical universe would be impossible. As you can see, the purely physical part of man serves a vital function.

The second thing produced in the creation of man was the human **SPIRIT**. Although **Genesis 2:7** doesn't explicitly state (in the original Hebrew) that the spirit of man was "breathed" into the body simultaneously with the "breath of life," it is obvious from other passages of Scripture that this is when it happened. (The reason that "breath of life" can't be equated entirely with "spirit" is that, although they don't have spirits, animals do have the breath of life, which is the Hebrew idiom describing the life-principle found in all living things. See **Genesis 6:17**, for example.) We know that at death the spirit is removed from the "earthly tent" and, for Christians, goes immediately into its resurrected permanent dwelling in the presence of Christ (**II Corinthians 5:1-8**). When physical life ends (when the breath of life expires) the believer's spirit leaves the present body to be where Jesus is. Therefore, it logically follows that, if the spirit leaves the body when physical life ceases (**Matthew 27:50; Mark 15:37; Luke 23:46; John 19:30; Acts 7:59**), then the spirit was, no doubt, given to Adam at the entrance of life into the body.

James 2:26
> "...the body without the spirit is dead...."

Your body has its specific functions. **What then is the function of your spirit?**

The body is the mechanism of operation and communication in the physical world.

THE SPIRIT IS THE MECHANISM
OF OPERATION AND
COMMUNICATION WITH GOD.

Your ability to have a personal relationship with God, to have fellowship with God, is brought about by your spirit. The human spirit was created to play a **dominant** role in the life of the individual and his or her relationship to God.

At this point the important distinction between the human spirit and God's Spirit, the Holy Spirit, must be made. **The Holy Spirit is God and is eternally self-existent. The human spirit is created.** Whereas the Holy Spirit is not confined by time and space, being omnidimensional, the human spirit is finite and is, being integrated with the body, spatially limited to three dimensions. God's Spirit and the human spirit are not made of the same "stuff." Our spirits are not a part of God. They are not little "divine sparks." God has created our spirits to allow us access to His person. Whenever we refer to God's Spirit, the word begins with a capital "S." When the human spirit is being referred to, the word begins with the lowercase "s." Most Bible translations make this distinction as well.

So then, the body is a physical mechanism. **The spirit is the mechanism provided for us by God allowing a personal relationship with Him.**

Now, the following equation is very important to our understanding:

SPIRIT + BODY = SOUL

When the spirit and body were integrated at the creation of man, the **SOUL** was formed. Note the important wording of...

Genesis 2:7
> "...the Lord God breathed into his nostrils the breath of life; and man became a living soul."

Man became a soul. The soul was the **product** of the interaction or reaction between spirit and body. The word "soul" (Old Testament Hebrew, "nephesh"; New Testament Greek, "psuche", from which we get the word psyche) basically means "being" or "person." However, the most accurate and descriptive terms in referring to the soul are **conscious life** or **conscious personality**. **Genesis 2:7** simply says, "man became a conscious personality."

You have a body. You have a spirit. You are a soul.

It has probably become apparent to you from our study thus far that many people confuse the terms "soul" and "spirit." In the Biblical view of things, they are not synonymous. The idea of the soul as the non-material real self comes from the Eastern religions and religions of that influence. The Biblical view of man is that he is a soul. In Scripture the soul, even when it is used poetically or in a figure of speech, is best understood as a reference to the entirety of the human being. "Soul" is the Biblical term for the physical-psycho-spiritual unity that constitutes a human being.

Because terminology and a correct understanding of it is so vital to the subject at hand, let's identify specifically how we will be using words and phrases in this and following chapters. The soul will also be referred to as **conscious life, conscious personality, and self.** Periodically we'll include the word "soul" in parentheses following these terms just to remind you that we're making reference to the soul [example: conscious life (soul)]. "Soul" itself will also be used. (We have avoided the term "ego" as a reference to the soul-although it is a good descriptive word and is used by many—primarily because it has connotations which are often limited by popular usage.)

It's also important to understand what is meant by the three terms "spirit," "soul," and "body," as they relate to one another **functionally**. Consider the following: You are a conscious personality (soul). Your conscious life (soul) is the product of the dynamic combination of spirit and body. Although there are only two basic elements involved (body and spirit), there are actually three functional parts of man—spirit, soul, and body. The soul isn't functional at all apart from either spirit or body, since it is a result of the merging of the two.

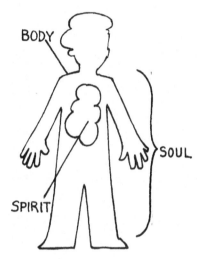

Both spirit and body retain their abilities to perform functions distinct from the conscious life which they produce as a result of their union. Your body's biological functions continue to operate on their own, and your spirit's function of communion with God continues regardless of your conscious state. For example, when a person becomes unconscious, even if comatose, both spirit and body continue to perform their functions. While a person in this condition may not be able to experience physical sensations or spiritual impressions consciously, they are operational nonetheless.

As we study further, don't look on yourself as being merely a combination of distinct parts, but as having three functional aspects which make up one distinct person—YOU!

The body is one element. The spirit is another element. Together they make a person, a soul. The soul, then, becomes the third functional aspect of the human creature, being comprised of all that a person is consciously (this includes any and all levels of consciousness). The soul, as the third functional part of man, has features which are identifiable apart from the purely physical (body) and spiritual (spirit) functions. These features are

MIND, WILL, and EMOTION.

So, while the term "soul" is not to be equated with the spirit, it does have two general uses in Scripture, both of which have already been described. The first use of the term identifies what man is in his totality—a living soul, a living person. The second use of "soul" is a reference to the function of conscious personality with its features of mind, will, and emotion. Certainly, the first use encompasses the second. But it's this second use—that of conscious personality—that predominates in the New Testament, especially when spirit and soul or spirit and soul and body are related to each other functionally. It's this second use of "soul" that's used in Scripture to describe the **old self** or the **flesh**, as we'll see a bit later.

Just remember, there are two basic elements—body and spirit— which were created and combined by God to form one unified being—soul—which can be described as having three functional parts—spirit, soul, and body. One of these functional parts—soul—has three conscious functions—mind, will, and emotion. That's simple enough!

Here's a little analogy that may help...

The light bulb's hardware—the glass, metal casing, wire, etc.—are analogous to your physical body. The electricity represents your spirit. The soul is represented by what happens when the electrical current and the light bulb interact to produce light and heat. When the electricity is absent, the bulb is "dead." If some vital part of the bulb's hardware breaks, the bulb is "dead." In either case, the bulb is unable to produce (or "be") that for which it was made. (They don't call it a LIGHT bulb for nothing!) No analogy is perfect, but you get the idea.

Just as the light bulb was designed to make visible the force of electricity in the form of light, so

GOD DESIGNED THE BODY TO EXHIBIT THE FUNCTION OF THE SPIRIT IN A PERSONAL RELATIONSHIP WITH HIM.

The created role for the conscious personality (soul) is the ability to have a voluntary personal relationship with God. Before sin entered the picture, the three basic functions of the soul—mind, will, and emotion—enabled man to experience fully an unhindered fellowship with the Creator. Adam and Eve walked with God. Their entire being—spirit, soul, and body—worked in perfect order, allowing them to experience a fully conscious relationship with the Lord God.

The basic reason for their ability to experience this intimate relationship with God was that they had spirit, soul, and body operating in the proper created order. The order is all-important. Spirit first, soul second, body third. It wasn't that God necessarily liked one part better than another, but simply that the spirit, as the mechanism of communion with God, was created to be in a position of **DOMINANCE**, allowing God access to their conscious lives.

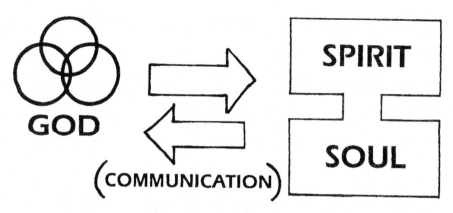

GOD (COMMUNICATION) SPIRIT SOUL

The conscious personality (soul) was to be tempered and directed by the human spirit. As a mechanism, or "organ" if you like, the God-sensitive spirit was designed to provide input from the Holy Spirit to the mind, will, and emotions of the conscious life. Just as the sense mechanisms of the body were made to send messages to the brain resulting in mental perceptions of the physical environment, so **the human spirit was specifically designed to transmit the dynamics of one's relationship to God into the mental processes, resulting in conscious perceptions of that relationship (spiritual insight).**

In their unfallen, innocent state, Adam and Eve experienced this process to its fullest potential. Their full conscious experience of the presence of God was possible because spirit, soul, and body were operating in the proper created order. As long as their spirits remained in the created position of dominance, Adam and Eve were able to know and experience the personal presence of God. This order—spirit first, then soul and body—was a primary feature of the fact that they had been created in the image of God (**Genesis 1:27**). God's relationship with them was initiated through their spirits. Their spirits reflected God—God is Spirit (**John 4:24**)—into their conscious personalities.

But something happened.

The third chapter of Genesis records the fall of man. As you study this passage carefully, you'll see that, for the first time in his life, Adam asserted his personality apart from the will of God. He acted on his own, separate from God's leadership. The created order of his own being was disrupted. The consequences were disastrous.

Satan deceived Eve and she ate of the forbidden fruit (**Genesis 3:13; I Timothy 2:14**). Adam, on the other hand, wasn't deceived at all. He knew clearly what God had told him about eating of that tree, even long before God brought Eve into his life.

Genesis 2:17

"But from the tree of the knowledge of good and evil you shall not eat, for in the day that you eat from it you shall surely die."

115

The warning was sure. Adam had God's direct and specific word on the matter. (Eve relied on information she obtained from Adam. Therefore, Satan's deceptive tactics were aimed not only at God's credibility, but Adam's as well.) Eve fell into sin by an attack on her mind and emotions. Adam was not attacked in the same way. He fell into sin by an exercise of his **will**.

In both cases, the conscious personality (soul) acted without reference to the spirit, therefore, without reference to God, because their relationship with God was spiritual (through their spirits). Their souls, acting apart from God, overcame their once-dominant spirits. At the very instant when the spirit of man was denied its proper function of communion with God—the moment that Adam asserted his conscious personality over his spirit's created role of dominance-he became separated from God.

When Adam chose to separate himself from God, God separated Himself from Adam. When the self (soul) rose in rebellion against God's will, God withdrew His Spirit from the spirit of man. When this occurred, man was

SPIRITUALLY DEAD.

God's warning stood true. Adam and Eve began to die physically, but spiritual death was instantaneous and devastating—for the whole human race. **Immediately, mankind was without God.**

Romans 5:12, 16, 18, 19

> "...through one man sin entered into the world.. .the judgment arose from one transgression resulting in condemnation... through one transgression there

resulted condemnation to all men. ..through the one man's disobedience the many were made sinners ...."

I Corinthians 15:21, 22

"...by a man came death.. in Adam all die...."

Romans 3:23; 6:23

"...for all have sinned and fall short of the glory of God. ..For the wages of sin in death...."

Pretty serious stuff, to say the least. Because of SIN (the action of the conscious personality—mind, will, emotion—apart from God) man's spirit ceased to function in its primary and most vital capacity. At the moment of sin, the Spirit of God withdrew from the spirit of man. Without the Spirit of God in union with it, the human spirit is dormant and unresponsive to God. This is the lost condition of mankind as a result of the fall. Paul, in **Ephesians 2** describes the lost as

WITHOUT GOD, DEAD IN TRESPASSES AND SINS, FAR OFF, SONS OF DISOBEDIENCE, SEPARATE FROM CHRIST, CHILDREN OF WRATH, EXCLUDED, STRANGERS AND ALIENS.

All people are born into this condition. It's inherited from Adam, the first man. The lost person operates only in the realm of the self (soul). Because his spirit is non-functional (spiritual death), the unregenerate person has absolutely no personal relationship with God. Because his spirit can't operate in its created role, being separated from God's Spirit, the lost person lives his life entirely on his own abilities. His own mind, will, and emotions are the only tools he possesses with which to confront life.

Paul graphically describes the **unsaved person** as a

NATURAL MAN.

1 Corinthians 2:14

"But a natural man does not accept the things of the Spirit of God; for they are foolishness to him, and he cannot understand them, because they are spiritually appraised."

The word "natural" in this verse is a translation of the Greek word "psuchikos," the adjectival form of the word "soul" (psuche). Psuchikos could be, and probably should be, translated "soulish" or "soul-dominated." It's a clear reference to the condition of man after the fall, that is, the unsaved. The "natural" or "soul-dominated" man is incapable of experiencing a personal relationship with God; spiritual things are completely out of his reach because they are only understood

117

as the Spirit of God reveals them through the human spirit (**I Corinthians 2:9-13; Romans 8:16**). But...

GOD HAS DONE SOMETHING ABOUT IT.

Only God could change the lost, unregenerate condition of Adam or any human being. God has provided a way for everyone to experience a personal relationship with Him. God came to earth in the person of the Lord Jesus Christ, bridging the gulf which separated man from God. Through the death and resurrection of Christ, restored communion and communication with God is available to every person! When, by faith, you receive Jesus Christ as Savior, fellowship with God is restored (remember that those in the Old Testament had the work of Christ credited to them because of their faith, as in the case of Abraham in Genesis 15:6).

Ephesians 2:17,18
> "And He [Jesus] came and preached peace to you who were far away, and peace to those who were near; for through Him we both have our access in one Spirit to the Father."

Romans 5:1
> "Therefore having been justified by faith, we have peace with God through our Lord Jesus Christ."

Through Jesus Christ the separation between God and man is removed. Peace with God is restored. The terrible spiritual catastrophe of the fall is put right again. In the next chapter we'll take a close look at your personal potential for true spirituality because of what Jesus Christ has accomplished by His crucifixion and resurrection from the dead.

Before we go on, let's review what we've covered in this chapter.

1. The human race has two kinds of people, _____ and

   _____.

2. The true learning process for the Christian is performed by the

   _____.

3. What is the function of the body?

   _____

   _____

4. What is the function of the spirit?

   _____

   _____

5. When the spirit was united with the body, the _____ was produced.

6. "Soul" means _____ or

   _____.

7. The conscious human personality was created with the ability to have a

   _____ with God.

8. The three basic functions of the conscious life (soul) are

   _____ , _____ ,

   and _____.

9. Genesis chapter _____ records the fall of man.

10. Adam and Eve asserted their _____ apart from God's leadership.

11. When man exercised his mind, will, and emotions over his spirit, the result was

    _____.

12. Sin brought about spiritual _____ from God.

13. The spirit of man was created to _____ the soul and body.

14. In the fall, the _____ lost its place of dominance and gave

    way to the operation of the _____ apart from God.

15. How does Ephesians 2 describe a lost person?

_____

_____

_____

16. Because his spirit does not function in its created role of communion with God, the unsaved person operates entirely in the realm of the

_____.

17. Paul describes the unsaved person as a _____ man.

18. _____ is another way to translate the Greek word rendered "natural" in I Corinthians 2:14.

19. Describe how the lost, unregenerate condition of mankind is solved.

_____

_____

_____

CHAPTER 13
THE WAR WITHIN

So far, we've learned that there are two kinds of people—lost and saved; believers and unbelievers; unregenerate and regenerate. Those who haven't entered into a right relationship with God through Jesus Christ are lost. Those who have come to Christ through faith are saved. In this chapter we'll look at **TWO TYPES OF CHRISTIANS.**

In the last chapter we centered on the creation of man—spirit, soul, and body—and the result of man's rebellion against God. Now we'll examine the inter-relationships between and the functions of the spirit and soul in your life. We'll pay particular attention to the importance of having a **DOMINANT SPIRIT.**

Let's begin by talking about

REGENERATION.

As we learned, the natural (lost) man is spiritually dead. Before receiving Christ, every person is in this category. **Upon receiving Christ, the Holy Spirit re-establishes contact with the human spirit, restoring communion and communication with God.** The once-dead spirit is revived by the regenerating power of the Holy Spirit.

This is what it means to be "born of the Spirit," and "made alive in Christ." Study these passages carefully...

John 3:6
> "That which is born of the flesh is flesh, and that which is born of the [Holy] Spirit is [a human] spirit."

Titus 3:5-7
> "He [God] saved us, not on the basis of deeds which we have done in righteousness, but according to His mercy, by the washing of regeneration and renewing by the Holy Spirit, whom He poured out upon us richly through Jesus Christ our Savior, that being justified by His grace we might be made heirs according to the hope of eternal life."

John 6:63
> "It is the Spirit who gives life; the flesh profits nothing."

I Peter 3:18
> "For Christ also died for sins once for all, the just for the unjust, in order that He might bring us to God, having been put to death in the flesh, but made alive in the Spirit...."

Romans 8:9, 10, 16

"...you are not in the flesh but in the Spirit; if indeed the Spirit of God dwells in you. But if anyone does not have the Spirit of Christ, he does not belong to Him. And if Christ is in you, though the body is dead because of sin, yet the spirit is alive because of righteousness...The Spirit Himself bears witness with our spirit that we are children of God."

Romans 8:2

"For the law of the Spirit of life in Christ Jesus has set you free from the law of sin and of death."

1 Corinthians 6:17

"But the one who joins himself to the Lord is one spirit with Him."

As a believer in Jesus Christ, your spirit is **alive** and **functioning**. But although your spirit has been renewed, your conscious personality (soul) is still in full operation. Even though your spirit will never be dead (separated from God's Spirit) again, being in union with the Holy Spirit, your soul can assert itself over your spirit, resulting in sin.

Before we examine the actual operation of both spirit and soul in your daily life, let's become familiar with the terminology of God's Word in referring to the soul and its activity (remember, the soul is the conscious personality which functions in all people, lost and saved). Here are some examples of the two most common ways the soul is identified in Scripture:

THE OLD SELF

(See **Romans 6:6; Ephesians 4:22; Colossians 3:9**.)

THE FLESH

(See **Matthew 26:41; John 3:6, 8:15; Romans 7:5-25, 8:1-13, 13:14; I Corinthians 5:5; II Corinthians 10:2, 3, 11:18; Galatians 4:14-29, 5:13-24, 6:8-13; Ephesians 2:3; Philippians 1:22-24, 3:3, 4; Colossians 2:11, 13; I Peter 4:1-6; II Peter 2:10; I John 2:16; Jude 23**.)

The "flesh" and the "old self" refer to the operation of the conscious personality apart from the controlling influence of the Holy Spirit through a dominant spirit. A person who hasn't received Christ lives completely in the flesh because his spirit isn't functioning in its created role. But even though a Christian has a regenerated spirit, he can, by asserting his own conscious personality (soul) apart from God's direction, live according to the flesh. To live according to the soul—according to the dictates of one's own mind, will, and emotions—is to live according to the flesh, the old self.

The conscious life of a lost person, with its functions of mind, will, and emotion, operates entirely without direction from the spirit. Without the Holy Spirit's union with the human spirit, the personality is left to fend for itself apart from God's guidance. This is the "natural man."

But, as a believer, your spirit is alive. God, by the operation of the Holy Spirit, is able to commune with you and give guidance to your life through your spirit. Your soul, however, is still very much alive—you are still thinking, feeling, and making choices! Even though you have had fellowship with God re-established by personally accepting the finished work of Christ, you retain the soul (the "flesh," the "old self') and must deal with it continually. The soul is the residing place of the sin nature passed down from Adam.

So, now, you seem to be in quite a dilemma: On the one hand, you have a spirit which is alive and in union with the Holy Spirit, and which offers the potential of living wholly within the will of God; on the other hand, you retain your own conscious personality (soul/flesh) which inclines you to live according to your own capabilities, resulting in sin.

THERE IS A WAR GOING ON BETWEEN YOUR SPIRIT AND YOUR FLESH.

Just so you don't lose heart over this awful predicament, you can be assured that when Jesus returns, the old self will be completely eradicated and you'll become what God has made you in Christ.

I John 3:2
> "Beloved, now we are the children of God, and it has not appeared as yet what we shall be. We know that, when He appears, we shall be like Him, because we shall see Him just like He is."

I Corinthians 15:51, 52
> "Behold, I tell you a mystery; we shall not all sleep, but we shall all be changed, in a moment, in the twinkling of an eye, at the last trumpet; for the trumpet will sound and the dead will be raised imperishable, and we shall all be changed."

Until that day when you meet the glorious Savior face to face, you must deal with the struggle of the spirit versus the soul. When your spirit is dominant, functioning in its created capacity, the abundant life becomes a reality; when the conscious personality rises up apart from God's leadership and pushes the spirit into subjection, there is real trouble. Paul describes this ever-present contest for control in your life.

Romans 7:15-24

> "For that which I am doing, I do not understand; for I am not practicing what I would like to do, but I am doing the very thing I hate. But if I do the very thing I do not wish to do, I agree with the Law, confessing that it is good. So now, no longer am I the one doing it but sin which indwells me [the sin nature]. For I know that nothing good dwells in me, that is, in my flesh; for the wishing is present in me, but the doing of the good is not. For the good that I wish, I do not do; but I practice the very evil that I do not wish. But if I am doing the very thing I do not wish, I am no longer the one doing it, but sin which dwells in me. I find then the principle that evil is present in me, the one who wishes to do good. For I joyfully concur with the law of God in the inner man [the spirit], but I see a different law in the members of my body, waging war against the law of my mind, and making me a prisoner of the law of sin which is present in my members. Wretched man that I am? Who will set me free from this body of death?"

There is a war going on between the inner man, the spirit, and the sinful nature of the soul. You must realize that your conscious life—with its arsenal of mind, will, and emotion-has a basic desire, because of the inherited sin nature, to rule over your life to the exclusion of God's will. The old self wants to overcome the dominance of your Holy Spirit-directed spirit and take control. In the Romans passage above, Paul shows that the created function of the inner man, the spirit, is to dominate the soul so that God is able, through the spirit, to direct and empower your conscious life.

But the sin nature of the old man maintains its pattern of resistance. You genuinely desire to please the Lord, to follow His divine leadership, but the soul, like a wild stallion, bucks stubbornly and refuses to be broken. Your spirit is the saddle. The divine Rider, the Holy Spirit, cannot gain control unless the saddle is firmly in its proper position. If the saddle slips to the side or underneath the horses belly, the rider cannot be in control. Only when the saddle is restored to its proper position atop the horse can the rider begin to exercise full control. Unless your spirit assumes its created position of dominance, the Holy Spirit is unable to exercise His control over your life. The spirit is custom-made to fit the Rider; the wild stallion, the soul, is not readily inclined to cooperate.

At this point we must introduce the two types of Christians: **SPIRITUAL** and **CARNAL**.

When your spirit is in its created role of dominance, which allows the Holy Spirit access to and control over your conscious personality, that condition is called

SPIRITUAL.

When your spirit is moved out of its dominant role by the activity of the soul-mind, will, emotion—apart from a desire to please the Lord, that condition is called

CARNAL.

Note carefully that both spirituality and carnality are **CONDITIONS**. To some extent they are matters of degree. However, there is a definite point at which the spirit's dominant position is usurped by the conscious personality, resulting in a carnal condition. Likewise, there is a point at which the soul submits to the spirit's domination, resulting in a spiritual condition. Indeed, there are varying depths of carnality and varying heights of spirituality. But the dividing line, the deciding factor, between spirituality and carnality is always at the point of the spirit's domination.

Because both spirituality and carnality are conditions, it is possible for any believer to be one or the other. It's possible for a brand new Christian to be spiritual. It's possible for someone who has been a Christian for 40 years to be carnal. In fact, all Christians struggle with bouts of carnality. It's important, therefore, to distinguish between spirituality and spiritual maturity, carnality and spiritual immaturity. **When you are spiritual, the process of growing spiritually is enhanced.** It's logical that your spiritual growth would best progress when you're spiritual. It also follows that the carnal condition hinders the process of spiritual maturity. Certainly, as you mature spiritually, spirituality can become increasingly more consistent. But no one, no matter how mature they are in Christ, is immune to carnality. The battle between the weak flesh and the willing spirit is a reality for every believer. Remember Paul's words in **Romans 7:15-24**!

So, in order to help us mature in Christ as consistently as possible, what we need to know is how best to maintain a dominant spirit (spirituality), so that the Holy Spirit can direct and empower our conscious lives. This will be covered in detail in the next three chapters. Right now, let's look at what God's Word has to say about the conditions of spirituality and carnality.

I Corinthians 3:1-3

"And I, brethren, could not speak to you as to spiritual men, but as to men of flesh, as to babes in Christ. I gave you milk to drink, not solid food; for you were not yet able to receive it. Indeed, even now you are not yet able, for you are still fleshly [carnal]. For since there is jealously and strife among you, are you not fleshly, and are you not walking like mere men?"

Here Paul tells the Corinthian believers that they're still carnal when they should be spiritual. Because they're not spiritual men, their growth has been virtually nil. They're still like babes. Why are they still acting like spiritual infants? Because their condition has remained carnal. Only when they become spiritual will they begin to mature beyond their infancy and begin to life and act like spiritual adults. Again, **being spiritual doesn't bring instant maturity, but it does create the best possible condition for the process of maturing in Christ.**

It's significant how the word emphasizes the fact that God doesn't want you to walk as a "mere man." The "mere man" in **I Corinthians 3:3** is the "natural man" spoken of earlier. The natural (soul-directed) man lives according to self. When your soul become dominant and forces your spirit into a subordinate position, the Holy Spirit doesn't have access to your conscious life. The Holy spirit is able to direct and empower your life only when your spirit is in its created position of dominance over your conscious life by means of your spirit, your effectiveness as a disciple is little more than that of a lost person. When this condition exists, you are fleshly, carnal.

The spiritual man possesses a dominant spirit. When the spirit is allowed to fulfill its proper role, the functions of the conscious personality—mind, will, and emotion—are utilized in service to Christ.

II Corinthians 10:3-5
> "For though we walk in the flesh, we do not war according to the flesh, for the weapons of our warfare are no of the flesh, but divinely powerful for the destruction of fortresses. We are destroying speculations and every lofty thing raised up against the knowledge of God, and we are taking every thought captive to the obedience of Christ."

Now that you're familiar with the relationship between the spirit and soul, let's take a closer look at the **dynamics** involved.

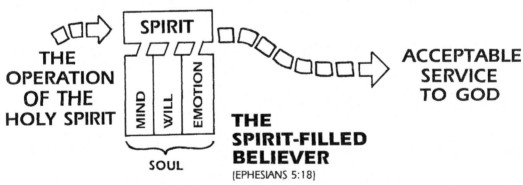

The spiritual believer (one who has a dominant spirit) is described in **Ephesians 5:18** as being **"filled with the Spirit."** The Holy Spirit fills your conscious life when the old self (soul) is in a position of submission. The preceding diagram will help you visualize the flow of the Holy Spirit through a properly ordered life.

1. THE MIND OF A CARNAL BELIEVER

The first major function of the soul is **MIND**. Many Christians possess acute mental capabilities. The conscious life often asserts itself by exerting intellectual prowess. It's not uncommon for carnal Christians to have at their command a great deal of Bible knowledge, facts, and superlative logic. They may take pride in their ability to "think through" matters, "prove" their point, or argue the finer points of "this or that" (**II Timothy 2:14-17**). God wants us to use our minds to their fullest, but under the influence of the Holy Spirit. The carnal believer has pushed the input of the Holy Spirit aside and thinks according to self.

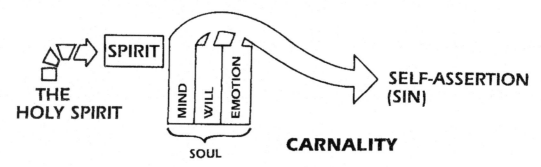

I Corinthians 8:1
"Knowledge makes arrogant…"

I Corinthians 2:5
"Your faith should not rest on the wisdom of men, but on the power of God."

Romans 8:5-7
"For those who are according to the flesh set their minds on the things of the flesh, but those who are according to the Spirit, the things of the Spirit. For the mind set on the flesh is death, but the mind set on the Spirit is life and peace, because the mind set on the flesh is hostile toward God...."

Colossians 2:18
"Let no one keep defrauding you of your prize by delighting in self-abasement and the worship of angels, taking his stand on visions he has seen, inflated without cause by his fleshly mind...."

When the mind gains prominence to the exclusion of the spirit, the access of the Holy Spirit to the believer's conscious life is blocked.

2. THE WILL OF A CARNAL BELIEVER

The second major function of the soul, the **WILL**, is also capable of blocking the operation of the spirit. The human will is bent on doing things its own way. The carnal Christian can't be obedient to God's will because God's will is transmitted to the conscious life only by the Holy Spirit's work within the human spirit. When your will receives priority, the function of your spirit in serving the will of God is diminished, or shut down altogether. Even Jesus, the sinless Son of God, didn't assert His own will, but submitted only to the will of the Father.

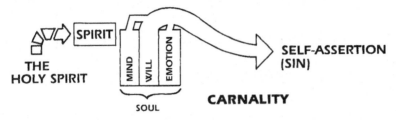

Luke 22:42

>"...not My will, but Thine be done."

John 5:30

>"I can do nothing on My own initiative. As I hear, I judge; and My judgment is just, because I do not seek My own will, but the will of Him who sent me."

John 6:38

>"For I have come down from heaven, not to do My own will, but the will of Him who sent Me."

If Jesus, who didn't have a sin nature (**Hebrews 4:15, 7:26; II Corinthians 5:21**), didn't exercise His own will, but followed only the will of God, think of how absolutely displeased the Lord is when we act out of our own will. Carnal believers have a self- assertive will. The free movement of the Holy Spirit in directing the entire conscious personality is restricted by the rise of the will.

3. THE EMOTION OF A CARNAL BELIEVER

EMOTION (or emotions) is the third function of the soul. The Christian whose emotional life is dominant isn't controlled by the Spirit of God, but by his environment. Whatever the emotional atmosphere, the emotion-controlled believer is likely to follow suit. When the situation is pleasant, he's happy. When the mood is melancholy, he's sad. When the emotional environment is charged with excitement, he's exhilarated.

Emotion-controlled believers are impulsive and often speak even without thinking. They're easily moved, easily angered, easily excited, easily depressed. They tend to gravitate toward anyone or anything that makes them feel good about themselves. They often flit from one "great idea" to another, never finishing what's begun. They may be drawn to "novel" or even heretical teachings, blown by one wind of doctrine, then another. These people often thrive on the exciting testimonies of other believers—often lacking a thrilling story of their own—and may spend a considerable amount of time reading devotional books instead of the Bible. Rarely probing the Word personally, they often travel about to hear special speakers; they love to be spoon-fed by others. Often talkative, they seldom hear the quiet promptings of the Holy Spirit through the inner man (the spirit).

Ephesians 4:14

> "We are no longer to be children, tossed here and there by the waves, and carried about by every wind of doctrine...."

II Timothy 2:16

> "But avoid worldly and empty chatter, for it will lead to further ungodliness...."

Study these passages which suggest the emotional capabilities of the conscious personality (soul): **Job 10:1; I Samuel 30:6; John 12:27; Matthew 26:38; Acts 2:43.**

The soul experiences love, hate, bitterness, happiness, sorrow, desire, exhilaration, and a wide range of other feelings and sensations. But, when the emotional faculty of the conscious life isn't under the domination of the spirit, an imbalance is produced, resulting in degrees of personal instability.

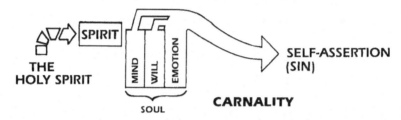

As we've seen, when the conscious personality (soul), by either mind, will, emotion, or any combination of these, rises to override the spirit's created role of dominance in the believer's life, the result is carnality.

Mind, will, and emotion are only capable of true spiritual service to God when each is under the domination of the spirit. Without the controlling factor of the spirit, self rages out of control and cannot please God.

As a Christian, you now know that your spirit must be allowed to take its proper position. When you develop a dominant spirit, you'll know and experience true spirituality-you'll begin to walk with God according to the power of the Holy Spirit, ensuring the process of spiritual growth.

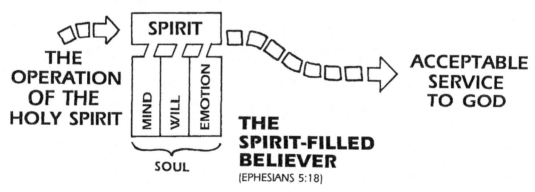

Before we go on, let's review...

1. What are the two types of Christians?

    _____

2. Explain regeneration.

    _____

    _____

    _____

    _____

3. As a Christian, your spirit is _____.

4. Your own personality (soul) can assert itself, resulting in

    _____

5. The soul is often referred to in Scripture as the _____

    or the _____.

6. The created capacity of the spirit is to _____ the soul.

7. The conscious personality is created to be dominated by the

    _____

8. The _____ is in union with the believer's spirit
    and is able to guide the whole person only when the spirit is

9. In _____ Paul describes the war between
    the spirit and soul.

10. What does it mean to walk like a "mere man"?

    _____

    _____

11. Mind, will, and emotion are available for service to God only when the spirit is dominant. Why is this so?

_____

_____

_____

12. So then, what is the difference between the spiritual Christian and the carnal Christian?

_____

_____

13. Spirituality and carnality are _____.

14. Spirituality (being spiritual, having a dominant spirit) provides the proper

condition for _____.

15. _____ is severely hindered
when carnality exists your life.

CHAPTER 14
A DOMINANT SPIRIT

So far, we've examined the three-fold division of man—spirit, soul, body—and the relationship of those three parts. We've seen that, in the original creation of human beings, the spirit of man was given the dominant position. The conscious personality (soul), with its functions of mind, will, and emotion, was intended to operate under the control of the God-directed spirit. We looked at the fall of man and the spiritual death that resulted. We've probed the subject of regeneration and introduced the battlefield within the life of every Christian, that is, the vying of the spirit and soul (flesh) for control (**Romans 7**). In this chapter, and the next, we'll discover how the believer gains a dominant spirit, that condition essential to the process of spiritual maturity and the abundant life.

As stated in the previous chapter, whenever the conscious personality, whether mind, will, or emotion, rises to the point of dominance in the believer's life, an imbalance results. This imbalance means that the believer has given way to the old man, the flesh, with its sinful nature, and has ceased to experience the guidance of the Holy Spirit.

Before we go on, there's something that needs to be very clear in your mind.

GOD WANTS THE WHOLE PERSON.

Every part of man has its proper function. The Bible doesn't present man as an irreconcilable dualism—the ancient Greeks saw man in this fashion—of good (soul or spirit) and evil (body). The Biblical view of man is that he is a unity; that is, a human being is not a human being apart from the integration of all the created parts, spirit, soul and body. In Scripture, the spirit is never called the "true man" or the "real person" because the spirit isn't the man. In fact, Biblically, the spirit of man wasn't created to exist apart from the body-and doesn't. This is Paul's entire emphasis in **II Corinthians 5:1-9**.

The spirit is rightly called the "inner man" (**Ephesians 3:16**) in Scripture, describing its function as a part of the total person. Both spirit and body, and their functional combination, the conscious personality (soul), make up the human being. The Bible makes it abundantly clear that salvation is not just for the spirit, but for the entire person, spirit, soul, and body (**I Thessalonians 5:23**). The reviving of the spirit in regeneration can be described as "phase one" of the redemptive process as we experience it. The final phase of our redemption (suggested in **Romans 13:11** and **I Peter 1:5**) is detailed by Paul in **I Corinthians 15** in his discussion of the resurrection.

The salvation of the soul—don't forget, you are a soul—is the salvation of the **whole person**. God saves complete people, not just parts of them. When the Lord returns, the entire person is freed from the sin nature which attends this present life. Our redemption guarantees us that we will spend eternity as glorified, complete people who will have become, by God's miraculous resurrection power, everything we were created to be in Christ Jesus. But even before the completion of our redemption at the Lord's coming, the whole person—spirit, soul, and body—can be used for the glory of God when brought under the control of the Holy Spirit.

II Thessalonians 5:23

> "Now may the God of peace Himself sanctify you entirely; and may your spirit, soul, and body be preserved complete, without blame at the coming of our Lord Jesus Christ."

This verse contains some very important insights. First, God is interested in the **entire person**. Second, God Himself **sanctifies the entire person**. Sanctify means "to make holy" or, literally, "to set apart." God wants your spirit, soul, and body set apart for His service. Third, the order—spirit, then soul, then body—is significant. Let's expand this third point.

A CRITICAL ORDER:
SPIRIT - SOUL - BODY

In order for the Holy Spirit to direct your life, the sequence must begin with the spirit. God's will isn't revealed first through your body; neither is it known through your mind, will, or emotion. The spiritual things of God are revealed through your spirit. Even your basic assurance of personal salvation is made known in your spirit by the Spirit of God.

Romans 8:16

> "The Spirit Himself bears witness with our spirit that we are children of God."

Spiritual truths are received through your spirit, that is, spiritually.

I Corinthians 2:14

> "...the things of the [Holy] Spirit.. .are spiritually [by your spirit] appraised."

Spiritual things are transmitted by the Holy Spirit to the human spirit. Your spirit is the mechanism by which God directs your life, and its dominance is essential if your conscious life is to be controlled and empowered by God. Once your spirit has received a direction or prompting from the Holy Spirit, it transmits that information to the conscious personality in the mind, will, and emotions. **The conscious life is in a position to receive and submit to spiritual guidance only when it is in subjection to a dominant spirit and, therefore, the Holy Spirit.**

When your conscious personality is submissive, it's able to bring the body under the direction of the Spirit's desires transmitted through the spirit. Notice this important progression.

In an earlier chapter we saw what happens when your conscious life (soul) asserts itself over your spirit. Now, let's look at what results when your spirit is allowed to dominate each function of your conscious personality.

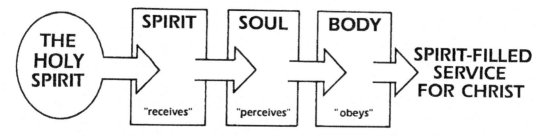

1. A SPIRITUAL MIND

When your God-sensitive spirit dominates your mind, your thought life is transformed according to patterns drawn by the Holy Spirit. No longer is your mind set on the world; it is now able to be used for God's divine purposes. Notice how God's Word describes the mind of the spiritual Christian [The word "heart," Greek "kardia," is variously used to depict the different functions of the soul. Sometimes kardia emphasizes a particular function such as mind, will, or emotion. In other instances it represents the whole self (soul). In the following verses it refers to the mind, the thought-life.]:

Romans 8:6

"For the mind set on the flesh is death, but the mind set on the Spirit is life and peace...."

I Corinthians 2:16

"For who has known the mind of the Lord, that he should instruct Him? But we have the mind of Christ."

Hebrews 8:10

"I will put My laws into their minds; and I will write them upon their hearts."

I Peter 1:13, 4:1

"Therefore, gird your minds for action...since Christ has suffered in the flesh, arm yourselves with the same purpose [mind]...."

Philippians 4:7

"And the peace of God, which surpasses all comprehension, shall guard your hearts and your minds in Christ Jesus."

Romans 7:25

"...on the one hand I myself with my mind am serving the law of God...."

Romans 12:2

"And do not be conformed to this world, but be transformed by the renewing of your mind, that you may prove what the will of God is, that which is good and acceptable and perfect."

Ephesians 4:22, 23

"...lay aside the old self...and...be renewed in the spirit of your mind."

II Corinthians 10:5

"We are destroying speculations and every lofty thing raised up against the knowledge of God, and we are taking every thought captive to the obedience of Christ."

GOD WANTS YOUR MIND.

God doesn't want you to give up your mind in order to glorify Him! He wants you to use your mind to its fullest capacity. Your mind, in its correct position under the spirit's domination and, therefore, the Holy Spirit's direction, is capable of serving God and bringing glory to Christ. The mind without the influence of the spirit is blind to the truths of the Word. **The Spirit-controlled mind not only comprehends Scripture, but is keener intellectually.**

2. A SPIRITUAL WILL

When your spirit is dominant, your will is able to conform to the will of God. When this occurs, you are capable of choosing those things which are pleasing to the Lord. As stated in the last chapter, even Jesus was obedient to the will of the Spirit of God, not His own will.

Romans 15:3

"For even Christ did not please Himself...."

GOD WANTS YOUR WILL
TRANSFORMED BY HIS WILL.

The spiritual believer has bowed the will in service to Jesus Christ. When the believer's spirit is dominant, the Holy Spirit brings his conscious will under God's control. As a Christian, you're to have authority over your own will-this means that your spirit is in its proper place of control.

I Corinthians 7:37

"But he who.. .has authority over his own will.. .he will do well."

Ephesians 5:17

"So then do not be foolish, but understand what the will of the Lord is."

I Peter 4:2

> "...live the rest of the time in the flesh no longer for the lusts of men, but for the will of God."

I John 2:17

> "And the world is passing away, and also its lusts; but the one who does the will of God abides forever."

Your will is important because it is that part of your soul which allows you to be submissive to God's desires. A spiritual will readily aligns with the will of God because it is sensitive to the leading of the Holy Spirit through the inner man (spirit). When your spirit is dominant, your will is in its proper place—you're in control of it. When your spirit isn't in its controlling role, your will is either self-oriented or, worse, controlled by something or someone else, meaning that you're out of control. The important thing about having your life properly ordered, with your spirit in its proper place, is that that's the only condition under which you're truly free to choose to serve Jesus Christ. **A spiritual will is the key to freedom in Christ.**

3. SPIRITUAL EMOTIONS

Whereas a dominant emotional faculty results in instability, Spirit-controlled emotions are of great benefit. The spiritual believer reacts, not according to the state of his environment, but according to the influence of the Holy Spirit in the inner man. Notice the emotional character of the spiritual believer:

Luke 1:46, 47

> "My soul exalts the Lord, and my spirit has rejoiced in God my Savior!"

Psalm 33:21; 97:12

> "For our heart rejoices in Him...Be glad in the Lord, you righteous ones."

John 11:35

> "Jesus wept."

Romans 12:15

> "Rejoice with those who rejoice, and weep with those who weep."

Ecclesiastes 3:4

> "A time to weep, and a time to laugh....

Jesus' emotional life was characterized by His capacity for compassion (**Matthew 9:36, 14:14, 18:27, 15:32, 20:34; Mark 6:34; Luke 7:13, 10:33**).

The soul's capability for producing a great variety of emotions is brought under the control of the Holy Spirit when the spirit is dominant. Spirit-controlled emotions bring about appropriate responses to every situation.

Before we continue, study the following diagram carefully; it will serve as a brief review.

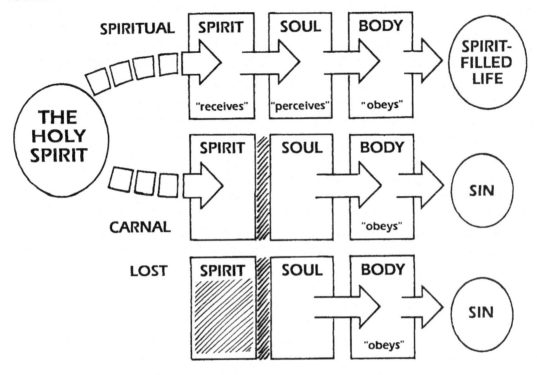

Now we must ask the question,

HOW IS A DOMINANT SPIRIT ACHIEVED?

How can you get your spirit, soul, and body properly ordered? How is the old self, with its sin nature, effectively dealt with in order to bring about true spirituality? In order to answer these questions, let's go the God's Word.

Hebrews 4:12

> "For the word of God is living and active and sharper than any two-edged sword, and piercing as far as the division of soul and spirit, of both joints and marrow, and able to judge the thoughts and intentions of the heart."

As if splitting joints and marrow, **the Word of God divides the soul and spirit**. There must be a division of soul and spirit—an unmistakable separation between the two.

What is meant by the division of soul and spirit? Simply this: When the conscious personality (soul) exercises control in your life, the spirit is suppressed by it. The soul must be made to release its suppressing grip on the spirit and allow it to assume its created position.

Your spirit must be at liberty to perform in its created role, but it cannot do so while it's being held captive by the soul. Until your spirit is cut free from the soul's domination and is itself allowed to dominate, your spirit's function of communion and communication with God is hidden from your conscious life.

SOUL AND SPIRIT MUST BE DIVIDED IF THE PROPER CHAIN OF DOMINANCE IS TO BE REALIZED.

It's essential that you be able to distinguish between what originates in your spirit by the Holy Spirit from what originates in your conscious mind, will, and emotions. (In the next lesson, we'll see how the flesh is often mistaken for the spirit.) That which is done by the Holy Spirit through your spirit is acceptable as service to the Lord. That which is carried out by the conscious personality alone is sin. More about this later. Right now, however, you must understand how your spirit is raised to the position of dominance in your life.

The spirit is "divided" from the soul by the **WORD OF GOD.**

A clear distinction between the work of God through the spirit and the work of the old man—the old man is the operation of the conscious life without direction from the Holy Spirit—is brought about only by the **SWORD OF THE SPIRIT**.

Ephesians 6:17
> "...the sword of the Spirit, which is the word of God."

The Bible, the Word of God, is inspired by the Holy Spirit (**II Timothy 3:16; II Peter 1:21**) and is His weapon for putting the conscious life in its proper place.

The Word is a sword. The word used in both **Ephesians 6:17** and **Hebrews 4:12** refers to the double-edged thrusting sword designed by the Romans and used with great success in the conquering of their empire. It was an important part of the Roman soldier's personal weaponry. This sword was not a delicate surgeon's scalpel, but a thrusting blade, capable of delivering lethal blows straight ahead or side to side. It was a killing sword able to hack clean through a joint or large bone with a single blow. In skillful hands, it was quick and powerful and deadly. This is the imagery behind the sword of the Spirit.

Certainly, this powerful sword of the Spirit is to be used against Satan and his evil forces. But it is to be used against the old self as well. In fact, it's the only thing that will put the old self to death in the believer's practical experience. Notice, as in the analogy of the "joints and marrow" (**Hebrews 4:12**), that a sword always pierces from the outside to the inside. In order for the inner parts to be exposed, the outer parts must be cut through. If the spirit is to be cut away from the domination of the conscious personality (soul), the conscious personality must first be pierced; it must take the initial killing blow from the sword of the Spirit.

THE OLD SELF MUST BE DEALT A DEATH BLOW BEFORE THE NEW SELF CAN ASSUME CONTROL.

We have already identified the old self, as that which existed before regeneration. When new birth is experienced, the **NEW MAN** is brought into being. The new man is the conscious personality (soul) under the domination of the spirit and, therefore, controlled and empowered by the Holy Spirit.

John 3:6
> "...that which is born of the Spirit is spirit."

John 6:63
> "It is the Spirit who gives life; the flesh profits nothing."

II Corinthians 5:17
> "Therefore if any man is in Christ, he is a new creature; the old things passed away; behold, new things have come."

Galatians 6:15
> "For neither is circumcision [being a Jew] anything, nor uncircumcision [being a Gentile], but a new creation."

Ephesians 4:24
> "...and put on the new self, which in the likeness of God has been created in righteousness and holiness of the truth."

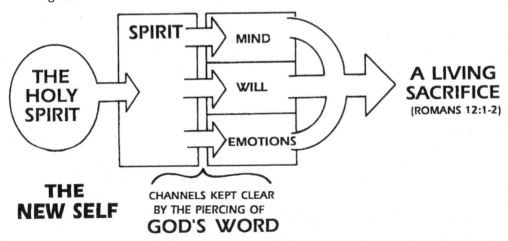

Colossians 3:9,10

> "...you laid aside the old self with its evil practices, and have put on the new self who is being renewed to a true knowledge according to the image of the One who created him."

The Word of God, the sword of the Spirit, is able to deliver the self-assertive old man to death, releasing the new man for spiritual service to Christ. Apart from the Word, the new self cannot be experienced. When the old self reigns, you are carnal and self-controlled; when the new self reigns, you are spiritual and Spirit-controlled.

So, how is a dominant spirit achieved? **A dominant spirit is achieved by the piercing activity of the Word of God which, in your practical experience, deals a death blow to the old self and releases the new self for service to Jesus Christ.** The dynamics of this process is the topic of the next chapter.

Before we proceed, a little review is in order.

1. Man, in the Biblical view, is not an irreconcilable dualism, but is a

   _____.

2. One part of sinful man-spirit, soul, or body-is no more acceptable to God than another. God doesn't love the spirit of man any more than He loves the soul of man. God loves the whole person as an integrated personality. Salvation is for the entire person-spirit, soul, and body. Explain, then, why the spirit is regenerated first, before the soul and body are transformed into the full image of Christ at the resurrection.

   _____

   _____

   _____

   _____

3. God is interested in the _____ person.

4. Explain the significance of the order, spirit-soul-body, in I Thessalonians 5:23.

   _____

   _____

   _____

5. Spiritual things are transmitted by the _____ to the human spirit.

6. Why is a dominant spirit necessary in order for a Christian to live according to God's will?

_____

_____

_____

7. Describe a spiritual mind.

_____

_____

8. Describe a spiritual will.

_____

_____

9. Describe spiritual emotions.

_____

_____

10. Explain what is meant by the division of soul and spirit.

_____

_____

_____

11. The division of soul and spirit is brought about by the

_____

12. Why is it necessary to be able to distinguish between what originates in the soul and what originates in the spirit by the Holy Spirit?

_____

_____

13. A sword cuts from the outside to the inside. Why is this important to our discussion?

_____

_____

14. The sword of the Spirit must strike the _____ first, before

the _____ can be released into dominance.

15. What is the old self?

_____

_____

16. What is the new self?

_____

_____

17. The Word delivers the _____ to death, allowing

the _____ to live the abundant life.

18. A dominant spirit is achieved by the _____ activity on the Word of God.

CHAPTER 15
THE PIERCING WORD

The Bible, the Word of God, is the instrument by which the old self is delivered to death in the believer's daily experience. The Word is the Sword of the Holy Spirit which cuts away the self (soul) and releases the new self for spiritual service to God. Without the Word, the conscious personality continues to assert control over the believer's life, quenching the activity of the Holy Spirit.

How does the Word act upon the conscious life in order to bring about the release of the spirit? To answer this question, its necessary to understand the nature of two basic facts: **1) the finished work of Christ**, and **2) the believer's experience**. Let's look first at Christ's finished work.

1 . THE FINISHED WORK OF CHRIST

The finished work of Christ is that which He has accomplished on our behalf in securing for us a restored relationship with God. This is the essence of the word **GRACE**. Because we are sinful and deserve eternal separation from Holy God, anything that He does for us is grace-His undeserved love toward us. He has every right to send us into everlasting punishment, but instead, because He loved us (**John 3:16**), He has done everything necessary in order for us to have abundant and eternal life.

Grace is God's free expression of divine love toward undeserving, unregenerate mankind. Salvation is by grace. We can't do anything to save ourselves.

Ephesians 2:8, 9
> "For by grace you have been saved through faith, and that not of yourselves, it is the gift of God; not as a result of works, that no one should boast."

II Timothy 1:8, 9
> "...God...who has saved us, and called us with a holy calling, not according to our works, but according to His own purpose and grace which was granted us in Christ Jesus from all eternity."

It's a common misconception that salvation is by faith. That's not so. The free gift of eternal life isn't given to you simply because you have faith. The very fact that God even allows you to approach Him in faith is granted by His grace. Know for certain that "by grace you have been saved **THROUGH** faith." Salvation is by grace. **GOD DID IT!** —not in response to your faith, but out of His absolute love. Salvation is God's work, not yours. Your salvation was secured before you ever knew anything about it. Faith means that you make a life-response to what God has already provided for you in Jesus Christ.

Even while you were an enemy of God, lost and without hope, God's salvation was in force.

I John 4:10, 19

> "In this is love, not that we loved God, but that He loved us and sent His Son to be the propitiation for our sins... .We love because He first loved us."

Romans 5:8, 10

> "...while we were yet sinners, Christ died for us.. .while we were enemies, we were reconciled to God through the death of His Son...."

Salvation is realized in your experience through faith. You don't bring it about, you simply receive the free gift as your very own.

God has done it all **IN CHRIST**. Truly, as **John 19:30** tells us:

IT IS FINISHED.

The finished work of our Lord was SUBSTITUTIONARY in nature, that is, what you could not do for yourself, Jesus did for you. Jesus is your substitute in every sense. There are two primary aspects of Christ's substitutionary work, **THE CROSS AND THE RESURRECTION**.

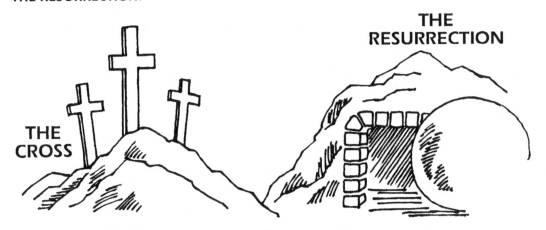

THE
RESURRECTION

THE
CROSS

a.) THE CROSS

The death penalty for sin is absolute—it had to be paid (**Romans 3:23; 6:23**). All have sinned; therefore, all must die. Many people think that in salvation God somehow waived the death penalty for every person. That is astoundingly false. Anyone who thinks this has missed the awesome gravity of Jesus' death on Calvary. Learn the truth of the Word on this subject! And be sure you don't take the cross lightly.

Isaiah 53:4-6

> "Surely our griefs He Himself bore, and our sorrows He carried; yet we ourselves esteemed Him stricken, smitten of God, and afflicted. But He was pierced through for our transgressions, He was crushed for our iniquities; the chastening for our

well-being fell upon Him, and by His scourging we are healed. All of us like sheep have gone astray. Each of us has turned to his own way; but the Lord has caused the iniquity of us all to fall upon Him."

II Corinthians 5:21

"He made Him who knew no sin to be sin on our behalf...."

Hebrews 9:26

"...He has been manifested to put away sin by the sacrifice of Himself."

Hebrews 10:10

"By this we have been sanctified through the offering of the body of Jesus Christ once for all."

1 Peter 3:18

"For Christ died for sins once for all, the just for the unjust...."

The death penalty was not dismissed! Jesus died every person's death; He took our place. Believer, that cross was not meant for Jesus Christ, it was meant for you. Look upon the dying Savior! That is your death being suffered by the Son of God. No, the death penalty for sin was not waived—**Jesus died in your place.**

b.) THE RESURRECTION

We have no life in ourselves. The life you have is Christ's. Jesus is your life. He lives in your place! There's only eternal death separation from God) within ourselves. Eternal life is found in Christ alone. By His resurrection from the dead we have eternal life—Jesus' eternal life.

John 11:25

"I am the resurrection and the life."

John 14:6

"I am the way, and the truth, and the life...."

I John 5:11, 12

"And the witness is this, that God has given us eternal life, and this life is in His Son. He who has the Son has the life; he who does not have the Son of God does not have the life."

I Peter 1:3

"Blessed be the God and Father of our Lord Jesus Christ, who according to His great mercy has caused us to be born again to a living hope through the resurrection of Jesus Christ from the dead."

Romans 6:23

"...the free gift of God is eternal life in Jesus Christ our Lord."

True life is only found in Christ. As a believer in Jesus Christ, the finished work of Christ has been placed to your account: therefore, when God views your life, He sees not a sinner deserving of death, but one having the righteousness of Jesus Himself.

II Corinthians 5:21

> "He made Him who knew no sin to be sin on our behalf, that we might become the righteousness of God in Him."

God sees the death of His Son as your death. He sees the life of His Son as your life. Because of this, the Spirit of Christ, the Holy Spirit, has re-established communion and communication with you in your spirit. This is why we are called the "body of Christ (**Romans 12:5; I Corinthians 12:12, 13, 27; Ephesians 4:12; Colossians 1:18**). When Jesus was on earth, He was filled with the Holy Spirit (**Luke 4:1, 14**). As we studied earlier, Jesus did not rely on His own power, but on the Spirit of God. Because He was sinless, Jesus was totally empowered by the Holy Spirit. Because of Jesus' substitutionary work, Christians, the body of Christ, have the Holy Spirit within them in the same manner Jesus did (**John 14:12-20**). The Holy Spirit is united with your spirit based on the finished work of Christ, and nothing else. This is why sin in your life grieves the Holy Spirit.

Now, let's look at the second basic fact-the first being the finished work of Christ-necessary to an understanding of how the Word of God accomplishes the division of soul and spirit in the believer's daily life.

2. THE BELIEVER'S EXPERIENCE

This second basic fact is your experience. Until you see Jesus face to face (**I John 3:2; I Corinthians 15:51, 52**), at which time your old self will be changed from sin nature to Christ-likeness, you must deal with the old self on a day-to-day basis.

We've already introduced the fact that the Word of God is the instrument by which the soul is dethroned in the believer's life. The new self-the conscious personality under the control of the Holy Spirit-must be released from suppression by the old self before the entire personality can be utilized in acceptable spiritual service to the Lord. How does the Word accomplish this?

It does so by **APPLYING THE FINISHED WORK OF CHRIST TO YOUR DAILY EXPERIENCE.**

Jesus died in your place. He lives in your place. In Christ you were crucified and raised to life again. These two facts are true of every believer. **The Word takes the facts of finished substitution and brings them consciously into the believer's present-tense experience.**

Although your death in Christ on the cross is an accomplished fact, positionally, it must be applied daily. Your life in Christ is a fact; but it must be realized in your daily experience. Spirituality is the result of this daily experience of Jesus' finished work.

Let's look at the dynamics of the work done by the Word in bringing this about.

As we studied earlier, the Word is the sharp two-edged sword of the Spirit which cuts from the outer man (the conscious life, soul) to the inner man (the spirit). The direction of the cut is important. Before the Word can pierce to the division of soul and spirit (**Hebrews 4:12**), it must cut through the conscious life itself. The piercing action of the Word is lethal to the continued operation of the old self (the conscious personality in domination over the spirit). It's so because the Word reminds the old self of death with Christ.

The Word causes you to view, in the death of Jesus, your own death. Not only does the Word recall your death, but also your life in Christ. You must be reminded that it's not your own life, but Christ's life that pleases God. The Bible records the facts of Jesus' substitutionary work and brings them consciously to your mind. Your spirit knows the work of the Lord because of the indwelling Holy Spirit. **Your mind, will, and emotions must be made, by the Word, to witness the death of self on the cross of Christ, and to see your new life in Him as a result of His resurrection.**

You must count these things as true in your daily living.

Romans 6:5-11

> "For if we have become united with Him in the likeness of His death, certainly we shall be also in the likeness of His resurrection, knowing this, that our old self was crucified with Him, that our body of sin might be done away with, that we should no longer be slaves to sin; for he who has died is free from sin. Now, if we have died with Christ, we believe that we shall also live with Him, knowing that Christ, having been raised from the dead, is never to die again; death no longer is master over Him. For the death that He died, He died to sin, once for all; but the life that He lives, He lives to God. Even so consider [count it as an absolute fact] yourselves to be dead to sin, but alive to God in Christ Jesus."

The old self must be made to admit its death. This is the death of self. The death of self in your daily experience is brought about by the piercing activity of the Word which brings to your mind the reality of the cross.

The mind realizes the fact of death, the will submits voluntarily to it, and the emotions record visibly the force of the piercing Word of God when you

CONSIDER YOURSELF DEAD TO SIN, BUT ALIVE TO GOD IN CHRIST.

The Word of God strikes with an accuracy devastating to the old self. When the Word is allowed to deal this death-blow to your soul, your spirit is freed to take its proper position of dominance. The spirit, thus liberated, is able to bring the empowering of the Holy Spirit into the conscious life. With spirit, soul, and body in proper order, you are able to serve God.

Be sure, you must never be allowed to forget your position of death. You must encounter the Word daily and be reminded of this death. You must be made to gaze upon your dying Lord and see your own death therein! You must understand that the life you are living is not your own life, but the very life of the risen Lord!

When the Sword of the Spirit is encountered on a daily basis and allowed to perform its piercing operation, you can shout aloud with the Apostle Paul...

Galatians 2:20
"I have been crucified with Christ; and it is no longer I who live, but Christ lives in me; and the life which I now live in the flesh I live by faith in the Son of God, who loved me and delivered Himself up for me."

Consider yourself dead to sin, but alive to God in Christ! This "considering" means "to count it as a fact" and "to reckon it so." This reckoning is a daily process. The self dies hard; it struggles to assert itself and is struck down to its position of death only by the sword of the Spirit, the Word of God. **You must experience this death every day.**

Luke 9:23
"If anyone wishes to come after Me, let him deny himself, and take up his cross daily, and follow Me."

I Corinthians 15:31
"[Paul said]...I die daily."

Romans 6:11
"Even so consider [keep on considering] yourselves to be dead to sin...."

So, how do you gain a dominant spirit? By allowing the soul to be put in its place of death by the quick and powerful sword of the Spirit. But remember...

A SWORD CANNOT CUT
WHEN IT'S IN THE SCABBARD.

Take the sword of the Spirit out of its sheath! Open it. Let it perform its powerful work in putting your life in order-spirit, soul, body. Let the Word keep before your mind the finished substitutionary work of Jesus Christ. The answer to Paul's searching question is found in Christ...

Romans 7:24, 25
"Wretched man that I am! Who will set me free from the body of this death? Thanks be to God, through Jesus Christ our Lord!"

The struggle between the weak flesh and the willing spirit (**Matthew 26:41**) is resolved in Christ. Through the Word you know that you must consider the finished work of Christ as your very own. When this occurs, your spirit becomes dominant and the Holy Spirit is able, therefore, to guide your conscious life.

Before you became a Christian, you had no choice but to serve the old self, the flesh-that's all you had to work with. But as a believer in Christ, you have been made a new creature (**II Corinthians 5:17**) with the Holy Spirit of God residing in your spirit. You're no longer a slave to sin. You're free to serve God. You must simply let the sword of the Spirit divide your soul and spirit in order to produce the condition of spirituality. Let the Word sever the old self from any domination within your life, and allow your Holy Spirit-controlled spirit to have its created role of dominance over your mind, will, and emotions.

Remember, the key to the process of spiritual maturity is the condition of spirituality, that is, having a dominant spirit. But while spiritual growth is a life-long process, spirituality is the condition God desires for your Christian life no matter where you are along the road to maturity-whether you have just received Christ or have been a believer for 50 years.

YOU DON'T GROW INTO SPIRITUALITY.

Spirituality isn't gained by doing. It is gained by **realizing what Jesus Christ has done for you**, and surrendering yourself to it. When you submit to the Word of God and count the Lord's death and life as your very own, a dominant spirit will result.

You received Christ through faith. You must also live by faith, knowing God will perform, through His Word, that which He has promised. But realize that the sword of the Spirit cannot cut until it's taken from the scabbard and thrust forth. Keep the Word before you continually.

Psalm 119:11

"Thy word I have treasured in my heart, that I may not sin against Thee."

151

The Word will train you to consciously distinguish between good (that which is produced by the Spirit through your spirit) from evil (that which is of the self alone). Every attitude and motive is meticulously examined by the Word.

Hebrews 4:12

> "For the word of God is...able to judge the thoughts and intentions of the heart [mind]."

Hebrews 5:13, 14

> "Anyone who lives on milk, being still an infant, is not acquainted with the teaching about righteousness. But solid food is for the mature, who by constant use have trained themselves to distinguish good from evil." (NIV)

The condition of spirituality produced by the piercing Word becomes stronger the more it's maintained. The more spirituality is maintained, the more active the maturing process. Just as your body needs physical food in order to thrive, your spirit needs the spiritual food of the Word in order to grow strong. The stronger your spirit grows as a result of feeding on the Word, the better it will be able to maintain its position of dominance in your life. So, spirituality and spiritual maturity do go hand-in-hand. **Spiritual growth occurs on the basis of spirituality; spirituality is strengthened by the process of spiritual maturity.**

Having learned the dynamics of the sword of the Spirit in producing true spirituality, in the next chapter we'll take a close look at the characteristics of a Spirit-controlled life. We'll also examine carnal counterfeits of true spiritual qualities.

Before we do, let's review what we've learned in this chapter...

1. The _____ is the instrument by which your

   _____ is delivered to death in your daily life.

2. The two primary aspects of the finished work of Christ are the

   _____ and the

   _____.

3. What does "finished" mean in reference to what Jesus has done?

   _____

   _____

   _____

4. What does "substitutionary" mean?

_____

_____

5. Describe briefly the substitutionary death of Christ on the cross. How does it affect you?

_____

_____

_____

_____

6. Describe how the substitutionary nature of Christ's resurrection applies to you.

_____

_____

_____

_____

7. The Holy Spirit has re-established fellowship with your spirit on what basis?

_____

8. How does the finished work of Christ contrast with your daily experience? Is there any difference between the two? When will the difference finally be resolved?

_____

_____

_____

_____

9. Explain how the Word is able to bring about a dominant spirit.

_____

_____

_____

_____

10. What is "reckoning"?

_____

_____

11. The Word cases the _____ to realize the fact of

death in Christ, the _____ submits voluntarily to it, and the

_____ are a visible record of the power of the piercing Word.

12. How often must you encounter the Word, and why?

_____

_____

_____

CHAPTER 16

TRANSFORMED TO OBEDIENCE

The importance of the Word of God in your life cannot be minimized. Without it a dominant spirit is never achieved and, therefore, the Holy Spirit is not able to control your conscious life. When your spirit is in its proper position, your conscious personality, with its functions of mind, will, and emotion, is able to be used for God's purposes. By the Word, the old self is delivered to death in your daily experience so that the Spirit- controlled new self is free to serve the Lord.

So far, we've concentrated mainly on the transformation of the mind, will, and emotion through maintaining a dominant spirit. But what about the **BODY**? Can the body be used in service to Christ? Absolutely **YES!** You can

GLORIFY GOD IN YOUR BODY.

When the Holy Spirit is directing the activities of your conscious life through a dominant spirit, the activities of the body are also controlled by the Spirit. The physical appetites can be brought under the direction of the Holy Spirit, and they must be if you're going to be a living testimony to the transforming power of Christ. Remember, your body is what the world sees. There can be no witness to the lost without the body! **The message of the gospel cannot be confined to the mind; it must be conveyed by the body in speech and service.**

Romans 12:1
> "I urge you therefore, brethren, by the mercies of God, to present your bodies a living and holy sacrifice, acceptable to God, which is your spiritual service of worship."

Romans 6:12, 13
> "Therefore do not let sin reign in your mortal body that you should obey its lusts, and do not go on presenting the members of your body as instruments of unrighteousness; but present yourselves to God as those alive from the dead, and your members as instruments of righteousness to God."

I Corinthians 6:13
> "...the body is not for immorality, but for the Lord...."

II Corinthians 4:10-11
> "...always carrying about in the body the dying of Jesus, that the life of Jesus also may be manifested in our body. For we who live are constantly being delivered over to death for Jesus' sake, that the life of Jesus also may be manifested in our mortal flesh."

155

Philippians 1:20, 21

> "...Christ shall.. .be exalted in my body, whether by life or by death. For me to live is Christ, and to die is gain."

Your body is holy (set apart) for the Lord's service. In fact, **your body is a sacred dwelling place of God's Spirit**...

I Corinthians 6:19, 20

> "...do you not know that your body is a temple of the Holy Spirit who is in you, whom you have from God, and that you are not your own? For you have been bought with a price; therefore, glorify God in your body."

When the spirit is dominant, the entire person, including the body, is available for service to God.

ACCEPTABLE SERVICE TO GOD

To this point, we've examined the dynamics of spirituality as it's developed and maintained within your life. As we've seen, spirituality is the proper ordering of spirit, soul, and body, so that the Holy Spirit is able to exercise control over the whole person. But how is spirituality manifested outwardly? What are the recognizable results of a dominant spirit?

The Bible refers to these visible results of the Spirit-controlled life as

THE FRUIT OF THE SPIRIT.

Galatians 5:22-25

> "But the fruit of the Spirit is love, joy, peace, patience, kindness, goodness, faithfulness, gentleness, self-control; against such there is no law. Now those who belong to Jesus Christ have crucified the flesh with its passions and desires. If we live by the Spirit, let us also walk by the Spirit."

The fruit of the Spirit consists of a variety of **character qualities** produced by the presence of the Holy Spirit who, through your spirit, controls the activities of your mind, will, and emotions, and your body.

The fruit of the Spirit is in diametric opposition to the natural works of the unaided conscious personality (flesh). This is made clear in the verses which precede **Galatians 5:22**. Notice that the flesh always works against the Spirit when the flesh is not in the position of death. Whatever the conscious life produces on its own is not pleasing to God.

Galatians 5:16, 17

> "But, I say, walk by the Spirit, and you will not carry out the desire of the flesh. For the flesh sets its desire against the Spirit, and the Spirit against the flesh; for these are in opposition to one another, so that you may not do the things that you please."

Paul then proceeds to list the deeds of the flesh (**Galatians 5:19-22**). It's obvious that the flesh is capable of producing every kind of evil, and the believer is happy when he gains victory over such things. With the absence of the "obviously sinful," the believer delights in the good things he's now able to perform. It is precisely here that the danger lies.

For what many Christians fail to understand is that, while the old self is adept at practicing evil, it is equally capable of producing very attractive works and noble qualities. But know for certain that if the flesh is still producing "good," it has not yet been put entirely to death in the daily walk.

The mere absence of transgression does not mean that the conscious personality has given way to the Spirit's control. If you're living "righteously" on your own power, it's a sure sign that the old self is yet enjoying dominance over your life. Self masquerades subtly as being somehow "spiritual" in order to avoid the piercing death blow of the sword of the Spirit.

What you must comprehend is that sin isn't simply what's bad, but WHATEVER THE SELF DOES, GOOD OR BAD.

Romans 14:23

> "...whatever is not from faith is sin."

Whatever is not produced by your personal faith-relationship with Jesus Christ is sin. Period.

Even an unregenerate man is capable of doing "good" deeds (**Matthew 1 9:16-22**), but they're not acceptable to God.

Isaiah 64:6
> "All our righteous deeds are like a filthy garment...."

You must be careful that you don't mistake fleshly righteousness for true spirituality. For every character quality of the fruit of the Spirit, there's a carnal counterfeit. What appears on the surface as spirituality may actually be the self-righteousness of the natural personality. Let's look at some of these

CARNAL COUNTERFEITS...

- Natural compassion is often mistaken for love.

- A happy expression may seem to be the joy of the Spirit. Self-confidence is easily misconstrued as true peace.

- What appears as Spirit-produced patience may well be a form of natural determination, stubbornness, or even procrastination.

- What may seem to be spiritual kindness is often mere human graciousness.

- To the observer, natural moral sensitivity may be misinterpreted as goodness, and noble fleshly character as faithfulness.

- The self may have tendencies toward tenderness viewed as gentleness.

- What seems to be spiritual self-control may only be a strong human will.

Yes, it's much easier to parade the "good" qualities of the flesh rather than commit it ALL to death. Besides, why kill something with such marvelous potential? Why? Because whatever the self does, good or bad, is sin.

Think back for a moment: Do you recall, from a purely human point of view, anything horribly bad about Adam's and Eve's eating the fruit of the tree of the knowledge of good and evil, except for the fact that God had forbidden it? In commanding them not to eat from that tree, God simply opened up the possibility for them to exercise their free choice. But in order for them to eat that particular fruit, they had to do so apart from God's leadership. And that's what **SIN** is all about. Remember, it all looked good to Eve. **But just because it looks, tastes, smells, feels, sounds, or does "good," don't be deceived into believing that it must be OK with God.**

Don't forget, whatever is not from faith is sin.

The believer who is satisfied with the general absence of evil in his life is in real trouble-study the lives of the Pharisees! The old self must be put to death absolutely. When properly dead in the daily life, the old self cannot do anything, good or bad. The capability of producing "good" means that the flesh is still alive. Believer, count it dead, **crucified with Christ!** Encounter your own death in the Word of God and consider it a reality.

You died with Christ on the cross centuries ago! You also rose to life in Him. Now you must experience these facts in daily living. Let the sword of the Spirit perform its work in your life—let it divide your soul and spirit so that you may recognize what is of the flesh and what is of the Spirit.

True spirituality is the result of realizing what Jesus Christ has done for you, and surrendering yourself to it. When you study the Word, the Holy Spirit is able to bring about the proper sequence of domination—spirit, then soul, then body—by which He is able, from the Word, to transmit spiritual truths into your conscious personality. When this occurs, you are made aware of what things must be done in order to please the Lord, and you submit thankfully and joyfully. When your spirit is dominant, your will is able to submit to the leadership of the Holy Spirit.

The action of a spiritual will in obedience to the Lord is called

DISCIPLINE.

The action of the flesh in attempting obedience to God is called

LEGALISM.

Many confuse legalism with discipline; however, there is a profound difference. The Lord requires **OBEDIENCE** from every believer. The spiritual believer responds to the Lord's call to obedience through personal discipline. The carnal believer responds to that call—if he responds at all—legalistically.

DISCIPLINE IS SPIRITUAL.
LEGALISM IS CARNAL.

Discipline is the spiritual attitude which allows you to be trained by the Word, leading to orderliness and efficiency in your life.

Legalism is the carnal attitude which insists upon strict adherence to laws, rules, regulations, and traditions, in an attempt to bring about godliness.

LEGALISM IS BASED ON REWARD AND PUNISHMENT...

...DISCIPLINE IS BASED ON LOVE AND GRATITUDE

Note the contrast between spiritual discipline and carnal legalism:

- Legalism is the self-life; discipline is dying to self.

- Legalism leads to hypocrisy; discipline leads to consistency.

- Legalism expects a reward; discipline serves without thought of gain.

- Legalism brings pride; discipline brings humility.

- Legalism is applied externally through the outer man, the soul; discipline originates within the inner man, the spirit, by the Holy Spirit.

- Legalism is conformation; discipline is transformation.

- Legalism requires from others; discipline teaches others in love.

- Legalism is works-oriented; discipline is by grace.

- Legalism brings bondage; discipline is the true expression of the believer's freedom in Christ.

- Legalism makes time for duties; discipline gives time for service.

- Legalism says "no" to protect its appearance of piety; discipline says "no" because of spiritual insight.

- Legalism is religion; discipline is relationship.

The development of a dominant spirit by the activity of the Word of God brings about true spirituality. The spiritual life is a **disciplined life** characterized by the fruit of the Spirit. Your entire being—spirit, soul, and body—can bring glory to God. Make this your most fervent prayer.

Now for a brief review...

1. How is the body able to glorify God?

_____

_____

_____

2. The outward manifestation of the Spirit-controlled life is called the

_____

3. What is the fruit of the Spirit?

_____

_____

4. List the character qualities of the fruit of the Spirit.

_____

_____

_____

5. What is a carnal counterfeit?

_____

_____

6. The flesh is capable of doing "good." When it does, what is that a sign of?

_____

7. What is the basic difference between discipline and legalism?

_____

_____

_____

Part Three

THE DYNAMICS OF
MAKING DISCIPLES

CHAPTER 17
DEFINING DISCIPLESHIP

The reason you're on this earth, as a believer is so you can carry out the plan of Jesus Christ to reach other men and women with the gospel. It is with this understanding in mind that you have been called out to follow Christ as His **disciple**. Jesus expressed this to the first twelve followers.

Matthew 4:19
> "Follow Me, and I will make you fishers of men."

Someone has appropriately said that there is only one thing we can do here on earth that cannot be done when we get to heaven—win the lost for Christ. Truly, there is but one ultimate purpose for the life of every believer which brings glory to God. That is proclaiming His gospel. This was Jesus' most fervent desire for His Church.

Acts 1:8
> "But you shall receive power when the Holy Spirit has come upon you; and you shall be My witnesses both in Jerusalem, and in all Judea and Samaria, and even to the remotest part of the earth."

You might be thinking, "What does that have to do with discipleship?" That's an excellent question. And the answer is...

DISCIPLESHIP HAS EVERYTHING TO DO WITH REACHING THE UNSAVED FOR CHRIST.

When most people hear the word "discipleship" they think of things like spiritual growth, Bible study, and the need for discipline in the daily walk with Christ. While all of these things are a part of it, the New Testament concept of discipleship is not, in a primary sense, equated with these. Discipleship is much more, as we shall see.

Discipleship is, without a doubt, Jesus' highest priority for the believer. Pray earnestly that God will open your eyes to the truth of His Word concerning these matters. Satan will do everything in his power to keep you from applying these things to your life. But stand firm! God wants to use you in His magnificent, divine mission to reach this world for His glory!

We'll begin our study by

DEFINING DISCIPLESHIP.

The word "disciple" has been used in various ways. We could say that it means "pupil," "learner," or "adherent"–that is, one whose life of thinking is patterned after or significantly affected by another person. That is what the word means in Latin. The English spelling of the word "is" is also derived from Latin. But although our spelling is Latin in origin, the full meaning of "disciple" in the English language is–interestingly and quite conveniently for our study–derived from Greek, specifically the New Testament.

The Greek word translated "disciple" is "mathetes" (the "e" is pronounced as a long "a"). It is used well over 200 times in the first five books of the New Testament. It's this use of "disciple," mainly by Jesus, that gives us the basis of our English definition. As the authoritative Oxford English Dictionary points out, the English definition is gained primarily from the relationship of Jesus Christ to the Twelve—the first Christian disciples.

The New Testament and English definitions of "disciple" are identical. We're fortunate in this because it isn't often that a Greek word from the New Testament can be translated with an English word of precisely the same meaning. But because the meaning of "disciple" isn't merely a one or two-word definition, it will take us several hours of study to develop an adequate understanding of what a disciple is. The meaning of "disciple" and, therefore, "discipleship" is so profound that the failure to comprehend and apply it means that God will not be able to use you to His fullest desire.

Let's start building our understanding of discipleship with this...

DISCIPLESHIP MEANS WHAT JESUS MEANT BY IT.

Nothing more, nothing less. No matter how badly some people might want to give discipleship a simple, short definition, it just can't be done. In order to know what being a disciple truly is, we must carefully examine what Jesus meant by it. That will be our definition. Whatever "disciple" meant before Jesus got hold of it is not adequate because Jesus transformed the concept of discipleship into His complete, perfect divine plan for reaching men and women around this globe with the good news of salvation in Him.

In coming to an understanding of what discipleship is, we must look at Jesus' relationship to the Twelve. **The principle of discipleship involves that which Jesus exemplified in His relationship to His personal disciples, nothing less.**

Before we go any further, let's organize our thoughts like this:

1. **A disciple is what Jesus meant by "disciple."**

2. **Discipleship is the act of being what Jesus meant by "disciple."**

3. **Any other definition or concept of discipleship is incorrect and irrelevant.**

Later we'll do a detailed examination of what Jesus did to turn the Twelve into disciples. For right now, we can make at least three general observations about Jesus' concept of discipleship Being a disciple involves...

1) an intimate **personal relationship** with a disciplemaker;

2) a **personal commitment** to be made into a disciple; and

3) **personal instruction** by a disciplemaker.

Viewed from another standpoint, these can be stated like this:

1. Disciplemaking cannot be accomplished by impersonal means.

2. Disciplemaking cannot be done without personal commitment.

3. Disciplemaking cannot take place apart from personal instruction.

An indispensable element in everything we've said thus far is that

DISCIPLES CAN'T BE MADE WITHOUT A DISCIPLEMAKER.

Obviously, a disciplemaker is one who makes disciples—not just any old way, but in the same manner that Jesus made disciples of the Twelve. This is another important point. (As you'll see later, disciples must be made; they don't happen accidentally.) In one sense, every believer is a disciple of Jesus just like Peter, James, and John. But in a practical sense, Jesus, when He ascended back to heaven, turned the job of making disciples over to His followers. And He gave them the Holy Spirit to empower their disciplemaking efforts.

So, we can add this bit of understanding to our growing definition:

A DISCIPLE IS ONE WHO HAS BEEN DISCIPLED BY A DISCIPLER.

The next question that must be answered is: **HOW DO YOU MAKE A DISCIPLE?**

Answer: **THE SAME WAY JESUS DID!**

Every new believer—and every old one, too, if he or she hasn't been properly disciple—must be discipled by a disciplemaker who applies Jesus' personal discipling methodology.

WHO IS A DISCIPLEMAKER?

In order to answer this question, we must turn to what is known as

THE GREAT COMMISSION.

When Jesus' ministry on earth came to an end, He went back to heaven. He was no longer physically present to make disciples of the many who would come to believe in Him as the gospel continued to be proclaimed by His followers. Did this mean that disciplemaking as Jesus established it was ended? **ABSOLUTELY NOT!** Before Jesus ascended, He said something very important to His disciples...

Matthew 28:18-20
> "And Jesus came up and spoke to them, saying, 'All authority has been given to Me in heaven and on earth. Go therefore and make disciples of all the nations, baptizing them in the name of the Father and the Son and the Holy Spirit, teaching them to observe all that I commanded you; and lo, I am with you always, even to the end of the age."

One of the great Christian scholars of our time commented on these final words of Jesus on earth:

You can often get a pretty good idea of a man's basic concern from his last words. This isn't always the case, to be sure, for there have been famous people whose last words are of no more profundity than 'May I have a glass of water.' But in the case of our Lord, since His last word was given before ascending into heaven, when He was fully aware of what He was doing, we can be quite sure that He was saying something that He wanted emphasized above everything else in His church. (J. W. Montgomery, **Damned Through the Church**, pp. 41-42)

The Great Commission stands at the pinnacle of everything Jesus said in His earthly ministry. It stands in the ultimate place of emphasis. He gave it on the basis of His divine authority. Everything Jesus said and did while on earth led up to this climactic statement. His meaning was unequivocal. It was an absolute command with no options implied.

Matthew 28:18
> "All authority has been given to Me in heaven and on earth."

In essence, Jesus was saying, "What I am about to say to you is grounded in My absolute authority over all things, so you must listen carefully and do exactly as I say!"

Having stated His authority, Jesus gave His great command:

Matthew 28:19, 20

> "Go therefore and make disciples of all the nations, baptizing them in the name of the Father and the Son and the Holy Spirit, teaching them to observe all that I commanded you...."

In this command, in Greek, there is one subject, one **imperative verb**, and three temporal participles. This is crucial to our understanding. Why? Because most people think that the command, the imperative, in verse 19 is "go." But that's completely wrong. The command in **Matthew 28:19** isn't "go." The imperative verb—the subject "you" is understood—is **"MAKE DISCIPLES"** (in Greek it's the aorist active imperative of "matheteuo").

So, the emphasis of the Great Commission is not "go" but "make disciples." (The King James Version, although generally a good translation, badly mistranslates the passage "Go.. .and teach all nations." But matheteuo should never have been translated "teach." Because it was, and because the KJV has been used by most Christians in the English-speaking world since its publication in 1611, the true meaning of the Great Commission has been hidden from many believers. Teaching alone is not making disciples, as we will see from our study.) And the record must be set straight on this if a proper understanding of the Great Commission is to be gained. Jesus said, in the most unequivocal manner possible, **"MAKE DISCIPLES."**

If we use a more diagrammatic form to view these important verses, you can see the meaning clearly:

Go (participle)...

MAKE DISCIPLES (imperative verb)...

baptizing (participle)...

teaching (participle)...

Properly rendered from the Greek text, the Great Commission reads:

"As you go [wherever and however you go in the course of your lives], [I am commanding you to] **MAKE DISCIPLES of all peoples** [of every race], **baptizing them** [those who believe] **in the name of the Father and the Son and the Holy Spirit, teaching them to observe** [to be obedient to] **all that I have commanded you; and, yes, I am with you always, even to the end of the age."**

What a tremendous command! There are many implications here, and we'll discuss them in the coming chapters. But for now, it's important to concentrate on the primary imperative of the Great Commission—**"MAKE DISCIPLES."**

WHAT DID JESUS MEAN BY "MAKE DISCIPLES," AND DID HIS DISCIPLES COMPREHEND WHAT HE HAD COMMANDED?

Jesus had spent three years personally discipling the Twelve (now only eleven). Everything they heard from Him, every moment He spent with them, led up to the giving of this command. But did they **understand** what Jesus meant?

The fact is, they understood precisely what He meant. Jesus spent three years making disciples of them, and now He was commanding them to do the same. Did they know how to go about it? Without a doubt. There was no doubt in their minds that Jesus was commanding them to individually and personally implement His disciplemaking methodology and strategy in the lives of others—now they were to become the "fishers of men" He had talked about from the very start. He had discipled them to be fishers of men. They didn't get that way by some accident of evolution! It was all a planned and scheduled process.

Jesus' **methodology** was specific. His **strategy** was obvious. And His disciples knew exactly what He wanted them to do...

MAKE DISCIPLES OF OTHERS JUST AS HE HAD MADE DISCIPLES OF THEM.

And Jesus gave to them—and this has been given to all believers—the same disciplemaking power that He had possessed during His ministry...

Acts 1:8
> "But you shall receive power when the Holy Spirit has come upon you; and you shall be My witnesses both in Jerusalem, and in all Judea and Samaria, and even to the remotest part of the earth."

Jesus closed the Great Commission by saying "and lo, I am with you always, even to the end of the age." This was the promise of the Holy Spirit, the Spirit of Christ, which came to fulfillment on the Day of Pentecost. Jesus had told them...

John 14:16-18
> "And I will ask the Father, and He will give you another Helper, that He may be with you forever; that is, the Spirit of truth, whom the world cannot receive, because it does not behold Him or know Him, but you know Him because He abides with you, and will be in you. I will not leave you as orphans; I will come to you."

John 15:26, 27
> "When the Helper comes, whom I will send to you from the Father, that is the Spirit of truth, who proceeds from the Father, He will bear witness of Me, and you will bear witness also, because you have been with Me from the beginning."

Upon the vertical arrival of the Holy Spirit, the stage was set. They had not only been taught how to make disciples, they also had the **power** to do it.

Their (and our) task of disciplemaking involved two basic things according to **Matthew 28:18-20** and **Acts 1:8**. First, they were to be **BAPTIZING**. Baptism is the outward sign of successful evangelism. Disciplemaking first means proclaiming Christ to the lost and, once they have received Him, baptizing them as their first step of obedience to the living Lord. Baptism isn't **for** salvation, but **because of** salvation. Baptism is **for** sons, not to **become** sons.

Jesus was baptized as the one and only, unique Son of God.

Matthew 3:16, 17

"And after being baptized, Jesus went up immediately from the water, and behold, the heavens were opened, and he saw the Spirit of God descending as a dove, and coming upon Him; and behold a voice out of the heavens, saying, This is My beloved Son, in whom I am well pleased.'"

John 1:32-34

"And John bore witness saying, 'I have beheld the Spirit descending as a dove out of heaven; and He remained upon Him. And I did not recognize Him, but He who sent me to baptize in water said to me, "He upon whom you see the Spirit descending and remaining upon Him, this is the one who baptizes in the Holy Spirit." And I have seen, and have borne witness that this is the Son of God."

We are baptized, having become sons, children of God, through faith in THE SON.

John 1:12

"But as many as received Him, to them He gave the right to become children of God, even to those who believe in His name."

Romans 8:15-17

"For you have not received a spirit of slavery leading to fear again, but you have received a spirit of adoption as sons by which we cry out, 'Abba! Father!' The Spirit Himself bears witness with our spirit that we are children of God, and.. .fellow-heirs with Christ, if indeed we suffer with Him order that we may also be glorified with Him."

Galatians 4:4-7

"But when the fullness of the time came, God sent forth His Son, born of a woman, born under the Law, in order that He might redeem those who were under the law, that we might receive the adoption as sons. And because you are sons, God has sent forth the Spirit of His Son into our hearts, crying 'Abba! Father!' Therefore, you are no longer a slave, but a son; and if a son, then an heir through God."

So then, baptism—new believers following the command to identify with Jesus' death and resurrection as adopted sons through water baptism—is evidence of evangelism accomplished.

Second, disciplemaking involves **TEACHING**. Teaching what? "...teaching them to observe all that I commanded you..." Disciplemaking involves instruction, specifically, in "all that I commanded you," that is, the Word of Christ, the Word of God.

Colossians 3:16
> "Let the word of Christ richly dwell within you...."

II Timothy 3:16, 17
> "All Scripture is inspired by God and profitable for teaching, for reproof, for correction, for training in righteousness; that the man of God may be adequate, equipped for every good work."

Those who receive Christ must be personally instructed, for a measured and definite period of time, in the fundamental principles of Christian living. They must be nurtured in the Word until they are able to stand on their own feet spiritually, feed themselves, and continue to mature in Christ as a result. This **must** occur. If this period of disciple-training is missed, a weak and unproductive "church goer" will result (if they go to church at all!).

It's crucial to the whole subject of disciplemaking for one to comprehend the fact that

THE GREAT COMMISSION IS NOT AN IMPERATIVE TO EVANGELIZE.

To be sure, evangelism is the initial phase of the Commission. But the command is not merely to proclaim the gospel to unbelievers, but rather to make disciples; and not according to one's own whims, but according to Jesus' own divine plan. He told us to do it. He told us how to do it. He gave us the power to do it. Disciplemaking isn't just a way to fulfill the Great Commission...

DISCIPLEMAKING IS THE GREAT COMMISSION.

Now we must ask: Who is responsible to carry out the task of making disciples? Know for certain that the imperative is universal to **all** believers because Jesus gave a **perpetual command**... "...teaching them to observe all that I commanded you..." **Matthew 28:20**.

Who is "them"? Whoever receives Christ. And if every person who receives Christ is to "observe all that I commanded you," then the Great Commission, Jesus' final marching orders, must be included in "all that I commanded." The logic is flawless. The Great Commission is to be included as part of one's fundamental training as a Christian. And the Great Commission is disciplemaking. Therefore, every believer must become a disciplemaker if the Great Commission is to be taken seriously.

172

And we had better take it seriously! Jesus has made it abundantly clear: As you go, make disciples ... baptizing ... teaching ... and, when you have made disciples of them, deliver to them the same command which you received—**MAKE DISCIPLES!**

THE GREAT COMMISSION APPLIES TO EVERY BELIEVER WITHOUT EXCEPTION.

Christians who are not making disciples must not rationalize and think that the Great Commission can be fulfilled outside their personal involvement.

When Jesus gave the command to make disciples, He implied only the methodology and strategy which He Himself specified through His personal ministry. Anything else is a counterfeit!

As you can easily see, merely to be a disciple is not what Jesus had in mind. Jesus wants, then and now. When Jesus gave the Great Commission, He gave the definition of "disciple" a new element that changed it radically. And we must include it in our understanding as well. For every believer...

DISCIPLE = DISCIPLEMAKER.

A "disciple" who never becomes a disciplemaker isn't what Jesus intended a follower of His to be. To be a disciple in the sense that Jesus desires is to become a maker of disciples. In fact, because becoming a disciplemaker is directly commanded, the Christian who doesn't become a disciplemaker is in the deepest kind of spiritual rebellion, no matter how fine his church attendance record, his involvement in Bible studies, or his ingratiating personality.

Believer, you must not only become a disciple, but also you must become a disciplemaker. That's the reason God left you here on earth after you received Christ. **MAKE DISCIPLES!**

Just for review...

1. In the light of our study so far, give a definition of discipleship.

    _____

    _____

    _____

2. What is the ultimate goal of becoming a disciple?

    _____

3. Basically, being discipled involves three things. They are:

_____

_____

_____

4. Why is a disciplemaker necessary in discipleship?

_____

_____

5. Christians are born; disciples are _____.

6. Who is a disciplemaker according to the Great Commission?

_____

7. Write the Great Commission as a personal affirmation, using the first person...

As I go, _____

_____

8. What did Jesus mean by "make disciples"?

_____

_____

9. What is the power source for carrying out the Great Commission?

_____

10. Baptism is evidence of _____ accomplished.

11. In disciplemaking, teaching involves instruction in what?

_____

12. Why must you become a disciplemaker?

_____

_____

CHAPTER 18

THE DIVINE PLAN

In the last chapter we looked at some of the elements of the definition of New Testament discipleship. Thus far, discipleship has been described generally as **God's plan for reaching the world with the gospel.** And that it is. We have seen that discipleship must be defined in terms of Jesus' Great Commission (**Matthew 28:18-20**), and not merely in terms of spiritual growth, although growth is involved. In the Great Commission we see that discipleship demands that one become a **disciplemaker**, not just a disciple. There comes a time in the experience of each disciple when the learner becomes the teacher, the receiver becomes the giver, the follower becomes the leader, the served becomes the servant.

Let's now take a little closer look at Jesus' personal practice of discipling, focusing more clearly on just what He did as a disciplemaker—for we must use the same basic principles that He used. As a disciplemaker, Jesus utilized

THE DIVINE METHODOLOGY.

The Great Commission is an imperative that applies to **all** believers in Christ, and it contains a built-in **methodology**. Jesus, as in everything He taught, gave us the divine example of how disciplemaking works.

There is only **ONE** divine methodology. There aren't two or three or ten different ways to make disciples. The Lord has provided one gospel of salvation—there is only one way to be saved—and He has sanctioned disciplemaking as **THE WAY** to spread that gospel to the ends of the earth.

Disciplemaking is the sole divinely-authorized means of propagating the gospel given in Scripture. Evangelism (of any kind) is the first step in the process of making disciples. The goal of evangelism is to reach people for Christ. The goal of disciplemaking is to insure that those who receive Christ are able not only to lead others to Christ, but also to make disciplers (disciplemakers) of them, and so forth. Evangelism all by itself is a dead-end street as far as the Great Commission is concerned.

Discipling is the way that the gospel is to be spread, according to Jesus. This doesn't mean that Biblical discipling as set forth by Jesus is in any way static or narrow. On the contrary, the principle of disciplemaking is a universally applicable concept, as we'll see in another chapter.

In order to discover the methodology in Jesus' command to make disciples, one need only examine how He went about the task of discipling the Twelve. That is the Biblical model. When we ask the question "How shall we make disciples?" we must look to the Master to discover the components of His divine example. When Jesus' discipling ministry is studied carefully, several outstanding principles come to light. There are at least **TEN BASIC PRINCIPLES OF DISCIPLESHIP** evident in Jesus' ministry to His first disciples. We'll discuss these in detail in later chapters. For now, suffice it to say that all ten discipling principles, or factors, have a singular common element...

PERSONAL RELATIONSHIP.

If one could formulate an iron-clad rule concerning the nature of disciplemaking, it might be something like this: "Discipling requires a personal relationship between the disciple and the discipler." Disciplemaking cannot occur outside this most basic element.

The requirement of intimacy in discipling manifests itself in the limitation of group size. Jesus didn't neglect the masses; however, when implementing His plan to spread the gospel throughout the earth, He concentrated His efforts upon a mere handful of men. Why? Because

DISCIPLING DEMANDS INTIMACY.

Discipling cannot be accomplished through impersonal means. Jesus didn't choose a throng of men. He selected a few individuals who were willing to follow Him. Jesus knew all about small-group dynamics—and so He should have, since He created man in the first place! Jesus knew that a larger number wouldn't allow for the adequate development of interpersonal relationships both between the disciples and their discipler and between the disciples themselves.

Teaching such a large number of people that personal relationships cannot be formed is not discipling. The very nature of the word "disciple" demands intimacy. Discipling requires that the discipler maintain a close personal relationship with those being discipled until the desired objective is reached.

WHAT IS THE OBJECTIVE?

The objective in disciplemaking is to grow each disciple to a level of spiritual stability which transforms the disciple into a disciplemaker.

Jesus divine methodology is designed to take an unregenerate person, transform him by the power of the gospel implanted through faith, ground him in essential principles for abundant living through the Word, and release him into the world to win and make disciples of others.

The Great Commission wasn't a surprise to the first disciples. They knew full well what Jesus meant. They had been discipled by Jesus, now it was their turn. Not only did they know precisely how to make disciples, but also they knew what the result would be. They didn't just know the methodology, they knew the STRATEGY as well. Let's look at this

DIVINE STRATEGY.

Concerning the absolute necessity for a well-thought-through strategy for reaching the lost with the gospel, R. E. Coleman says,

> We must know how a course of action fits into the overall plan God has for our lives if it is to thrill our souls with a sense of destiny. This is true of any particular procedure or technique employed to propagate the gospel. Just as a building is constructed according to the plan for its use, so everything we do must have a purpose. Otherwise, our activity can be lost in aimlessness and confusion.
>
> **(The Master Plan of Evangelism**, p. 12)

How important this is to realize! God doesn't do anything willy-nilly. God never works by haphazard randomness, confusion or chaos. His divine, orderly plan for disciplemaking is designed to impact this planet with the eternal gospel of salvation in Jesus Christ.

The **methodology** and **strategy** inherent in the Great Commission are perfectly conceived for the purpose of fulfilling that Commission.

The hard fact of the matter is that if there has been a failure to fulfill the Great Commission, it must be directly attributed to the failure of Christians to properly apply the divinely ordered plan to bring about its fulfillment. **THE FAULT LIES NOT WITH THE PLANNER, BUT WITH THE WORKERS.**

Soldiers are schooled in combat techniques. Their combat methodology, however, is useless unless an adequate battle strategy is conceived, through which their combat methods may be effectively applied. Without an overall battle plan, all combat knowledge and abilities are ineffective. Without a proper strategy, an advance cannot be made.

The Biblical disciplemaking methodology, likewise, is to be utilized within the framework of an equally Biblical strategy. When these are rightly meshed, the lost are reached with the gospel and are trained as victorious and effective disciplemakers.

THE TRAGIC TRUTH...

But, are the lost being reached? Just how serious is the failure of Christians to win the lost to Christ? Examine any set of statistics you wish. Based on the number of church-goers (in any given year since records have been kept) it takes, depending on whose statistics you use, from 50 to 500 "Christians" to produce one convert in a year's time. That means only one-in-fifty to one-in-five hundred professing Christians ever leads anyone to Christ! Tragically, world population growth has been outstripping the numerical growth of Christianity for centuries. These facts are obvious—and painful to the believer who truly understands the Word of God.

One can only conclude this: The general failure of the Church to reach the lost for Christ is a direct result of the **failure to properly employ the divine methodology and strategy** inherent in the Great Commission.

Jesus' command to make disciples has not only an intrinsic methodology, but also a built-in strategy which must be followed if the Great Commission is to be carried out successfully. What is this strategy? It's very simple. The strategy behind that Great Commission can be described as

REPRODUCTION.

Whereas the purpose of the ten-point methodology is spiritual growth and stability, the goal of the strategy is

NUMERICAL INCREASE.

Many have used the term "multiplication" to describe the discipling strategy, but multiplication carries with it an impersonal connotation.

Reproduction denotes intimacy—the most fundamental element of discipling. The strategy of disciplemaking, as a spiritual reproductive process, can be simply explained in the following manner: A disciple—a believer who has already been disciple—leads unsaved persons into the experience of the new birth (evangelism), thus becoming a "spiritual parent." The discipler then, through the application of Jesus' discipling methodology, trains the new believers, personally guiding them in their walk with Christ. When the group of disciples has been sufficiently grounded in the Word and equipped to the point of spiritual stability, they are commanded to carry out the Great Commission by doing with others what has been done with them. They become disciplers themselves.

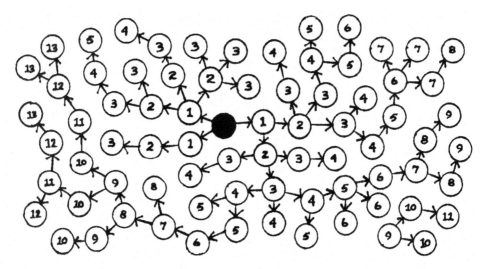

Disciplers produce disciplers, who produce disciplers who produce disciplers. From every discipler the gospel radiates concentrically through generation after generation of believers. **Reproduction!**

For decades, even centuries, believers have been taught to sit. The first thing most new Christians learn is how to sit in a worship service. Next, they learn to sit in a Sunday school class. Eventually, some learn to sit in Bible study groups. Let's face it! Churches spend a great deal of time and energy and money conditioning people to sit.

Now, there's nothing fundamentally wrong with sitting. But, in most cases, church-related sitting involves a lot of input and very little output—many being fed, but few actually learning to and becoming feeders.

Disciplemaking strategy has a **front door** and a **back door**. One enters as an infant believer and emerges as an empowered worker. In many ways, discipling is much like military boot camp. Recruits enter as soft civilians and come out as toughened soldiers, ready for combat.

Have you ever watched a mother bird raise her young? She spends many long days and nights brooding over her eggs. When the eggs hatch she immediately begins to feed her babies, working tirelessly to gather enough food to feed hungry mouths that never seem to be satisfied. As the baby birds grow, they eat more. Until, one day, they reach a point in their maturing process when the mother bird knows it's time for them to be about being birds themselves. One by one, she maneuvers them out of the nest and forces them to try their wings. Finally, they are on their own, freeing themselves, and the mother, to reproduce even more of the species.

In a similar way, the strategy of disciplemaking is designed to produce disciplers—via the methodology—and to increase the number of believers greatly over time, efficiently and systematically. We'll detail the strategy of disciplemaking in a coming chapter.

God wants to use you to make the Great Commission work! Pray that you will be obedient to His command!

Let's review...

1. How many ways are there to fulfill the Great Commission?

    _____

2. How is the Commission fulfilled?

    _____

3. Diagram and discuss the divine plan of the Great Commission.

    _____

    _____

    _____

    _____

    _____

    _____

    _____

CHAPTER 19

THE EARLY DISPLEMAKERS

The question that follows logically from the giving of the command to "make disciples" is this: **Did the disciples carry out the divine plan according to the training they received during their discipling by Jesus?** Did they employ the divine methodology and implement the discipling strategy as they had been instructed to do?

In order to discover the answer to this question, one must turn to the **book of Acts**. If they carried out their "marching orders" correctly, Acts, which chronicles the first thirty years of Church history, should reveal this and give us some key insights into their perceptions of the Great Commission.

In dealing with the book of Acts, it's important to realize that its narrative spans some 30 years and that its accounts are compressed and often skeletal. Thoughtfully written and carefully researched, Acts serves to highlight those aspects of Church development which the Holy Spirit saw fit to emphasize through the writing talents of Luke.

Having been personally discipled by the apostle Paul, Luke had an excellent grasp of Church doctrine and polity and was in a particularly good position to witness the principle of discipleship in operation through Paul's ministry, having actually accompanied the apostle on several missionary excursions. As we shall see, the book of Acts is quite revealing concerning the subject of disciplemaking. But we must

TAKE A CLOSE LOOK.

A casual reading of Acts often results in misconceptions about early Church growth. A careful study, however, brings to light the fact that the early believers took the Great Commission literally and performed the task of making disciples exactly as Jesus had commanded.

As one would expect, the first chapter of Acts includes the closing moments of Jesus' earthly ministry (**Acts 1-11**). Among the "parting shots" is a re-statement of the Great Commission with specific emphasis on the strategy involved.

Acts 1:8

> "But you shall receive power when the Holy Spirit has come upon you; and you shall be My witnesses both in Jerusalem, and in all Judea and Samaria, and even to the remotest part of the earth."

Jesus revealed the basic **concentric expansion** of the gospel proclamation. And it happened exactly that way—Jerusalem first, then Judea, Samaria, and on into the whole world.

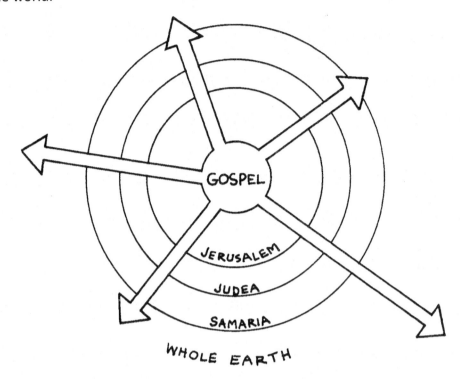

Acts follows this pattern.

After He gave His final words, Jesus departed into the heavens and the disciples returned to Jerusalem as the Lord had commanded. They entered the upper room and waited for the promised Holy Spirit. In all, there were about 120 persons gathered together. Soon the promise came.

The Day of Pentecost is an event often explored-at least the first 13 verses of **Acts 2**. These verses (**Acts 2:1-13**), however, mark only the beginning of what happened, and began to happen on that historic day. When the Holy Spirit arrived, indwelling and empowering the disciples, the wheels of the divine strategy began to turn. (It's often said that the reason for the great expansion of Christianity in the first century was the presence of the Holy Spirit. While this is true, it isn't the whole story. If Jesus hadn't made disciples first and established the guidelines for the systematic expansion of the Church by that method, nothing would have happened. The Holy Spirit gave power to those who were obedient to the command "make disciples.")

Shortly, Peter got up to proclaim the gospel to the assembled multitude, which included a great number of "foreign" Jews from throughout the Roman Empire (verses 14-40). They responded to Peter's message and about 3,000 became believers in Christ. But this was only . . .

THE BEGINNING.

The story does not stop there. It merely begins there. Verses 41-47 are often passed over lightly but are, in reality, the most important part of Acts 2. For it is in these verses that we first encounter disciplemaking in operation. Look at this passage very carefully, and put aside any preconceived notions you may have had about it.

The first element of disciplemaking, evangelism, is evident in verse 41. A great multitude of people were saved. But what happens, beginning in verse 42, is often overlooked. Read this passage carefully...

Acts 2:42-47

>"And they were continually devoting themselves to the apostles' teaching and to fellowship, to the breaking of bread and to prayer. And everyone kept feeling a sense of awe; and many wonders and signs were taking place through the apostles. And all those who had believed were together, and had all things in common; and they began selling their property and possessions, and were sharing them with all as anyone might have need. And day by day continuing with one mind in the temple, and breaking bread from house to house, they were taking their meals together with gladness and sincerity of heart, praising God, and having favor with all the people. And the Lord was adding to their number day by day those who were being saved."

These 3,000 people began to be trained in the apostles' teaching (the teaching Jesus had committed to them). They had fellowship, shared in the Lord's supper, prayed and ate meals together...

BUT WAIT...

C'MON.... ALL 3,000 OF US ARE INVITED TO PETER'S FOR LUNCH!

Are we to understand that all of these people—at least 3,120—went together as a single group from house to house?

Absolutely not! That would be absurd, and impossible, especially when one considers the small houses and narrow streets in Jerusalem. Then what was really happening?

All we have to do to gain an adequate understanding of this passage of Scripture is to be realistic, and to keep in mind the Great Commission itself. Obviously, because the disciples knew Jesus' disciplemaking methodology and strategy, the

3,000 converts were divided up into as many as 120 discipleship groups, led by the 120 original disciples. This would mean, if all 3,000 remained in Jerusalem for a period of training, that they could have been placed into groups of 30 or less. When you realize that most of the 3,000 were from out of town, the situation becomes even more apparent.

Jewish people from all over the Roman Empire-that is, those who could afford it—often made the journey to Jerusalem in order to celebrate the Passover. Many of them, especially if they came from a long distance away, would not make the trip for just a few days, but would plan an extended stay to include the Pentecost celebration as well. **Acts 2:8-11** makes it quite clear that a great number of the Jews present at the scene of events in **Acts 2** were from out of town. Most likely they had originally come for the Passover feast and were, therefore, at the tail-end of their "vacation." This means that great numbers of these Jewish travelers had been in Jerusalem for at least seven weeks, and had been gone from their homelands for eight or more weeks. Surely, since the majority of them planned to return home immediately after the feast of Pentecost, they were near the end of their financial provisions by the time the events of **Acts 2** occurred. No doubt many of them who were of lesser means had saved for a long time, possibly a lifetime, for such a pilgrimage.

Now 3,000 of them had responded to the proclamation of the gospel by Peter. Suddenly the first 120 disciples were faced with the responsibility of making disciples of this large group of people. But even if the entire 3,000 converts remained in Jerusalem for a period of discipleship training they could, as has already been pointed out, be placed into manageable groups of about 25 people. Realistically, however, it's safe to assume that many of those who became followers of Messiah Jesus on that day had to leave almost immediately in order to begin their journeys home. Depending on how many remained in Jerusalem, the size of the discipleship groups could have been reduced to as few as five or ten individuals.

One must also recognize that verses 42-47 span at least **several months** and possibly as much as a **year** or more. So the great number of converts from the Day of Pentecost, at least those whose finances had become depleted, were broken up into groups and taken into the homes of local believers. Although some of the 120 local disciples were people of means, most certainly were not. But, because of the responsibility to make disciples of as many of these converts as possible, the 120 had a tremendous financial burden placed upon them. Feeding and housing several hundred or thousand people for the necessary length of time would have created an emergency financial situation that called for some drastic measures.

But they were committed to making disciples, no matter what the cost. They began to sell their property and possessions in order to meet the financial need.

Scripture indicates that these early days of making disciples—supporting so many foreign guests for the period of disciplemaking—a caused such a financial depletion of the Jerusalem believers that they never recovered. Recall that Paul, in his missionary travels, took up numerous offerings for the "poor saints at Jerusalem." Making disciples was so important to them that they literally gave it everything they had.

In spite of the financial hardship, the results of the discipling ministries of the 120 and those they discipled were significant to say the least! Day by day, people were being saved and added to the community of believers (verse 47).

What was taking place?

DISCIPLEMAKING.

As a result of being discipled, they were sharing their faith with the lost and personally discipling those who came to Christ. They were obeying Jesus' imperative to make disciples. The tremendous growth of the Jerusalem church cannot be attributed to the efforts of the apostles alone. The people, **average citizens**, were primarily responsible for this growth because they realized their personal responsibility to spread the gospel by making disciples.

"But," you might say, "how do you know that **Acts 2:41-47** is in reality a description of disciplemaking methodology and strategy in action?" This question is answered conclusively in **Acts 6**.

Acts 6:1, 7

> "Now at this time...the **disciples** were increasing...the word of God kept on spreading...the number of the **disciples** continued to increase greatly in Jerusalem..."

You must remember the force of the meaning of the word "disciple." Luke was well aware of what disciplemaking entailed and what a disciple was. Had he been describing anything less than the divine disciplemaking plan as instituted by Jesus, he could have used any one of several other words to refer to these believers. Luke, under the inspiration of the Holy Spirit, uses the word "disciple" as a direct indication that the early believers took the Great Commission seriously—they were making disciples.

WITHOUT DISCIPLEMAKING THERE CAN BE NO DISCIPLES.

The use of the word "disciple" in any context demands the occurrence of disciplemaking. If the Great Commission is to be taken literally and seriously there is no other possible way to interpret it. In the book of Acts, if anyone is called a "disciple" it is because, and only because, he or she has been discipled according to the Great Commission plan, nothing less. As we move through Acts, the evidence of disciplemaking is abundant and irrefutable. Let's look at some of these passages....

Approximately two years after the events of Pentecost—possibly as many as five years, depending on the date of Christ's ascension—we find Saul of Tarsus on the road to Damascus.

Acts 9:1

"Now Saul, still breathing threats and murder against the disciples of the Lord, went to the high priest...."

Saul was deeply threatened by this new movement and he did everything within his power to stop it. But disciplemaking cannot be stemmed. You can kill preachers and evangelists, burn down church meeting places and disperse believers to the four winds, but **DISCIPLEMAKING CANNOT BE STOPPED**. Saul's persecution of the early disciples was like throwing gasoline on the fire. Remember, a disciple is a disciplemaker. When believers have been made into disciples, they'll make disciples wherever they go.

Through the book of Acts, whenever and wherever disciples pop up, you can bet your life that someone has trained them according to Jesus' plan.

Acts 9:10

"Now there was a certain disciple at Damascus, named Ananias; and the Lord said to him in a vision, 'Ananias.' And he said, 'Behold, here am I, Lord.'"

Ananias had been disciple—he was a discipler. His next project: Saul of Tarsus. Paul—he carried both names, Saul (Hebrew) and Paul (Greek) from birth—spent many days with the disciples in Damascus after his conversion (A.D. 34) before departing to Arabia where he was personally instructed by the Lord for about two years (A.D. 34-36) (**Galatians 1 : 15-17**). Certainly Paul heard the Great Commission directly from Jesus Himself, for he became a vocational disciplemaker, as we shall see.

Paul received his first discipleship training under someone in Damascus, probably Ananias. Paul was evidently an energetic and rapid learner—after all, he had studied to become a rabbi—and soon began to make disciples of others. Because of Paul's activities of disciplemaking and preaching the gospel in the synagogues, the Jews plotted to kill him. (Having a "favorite Pharisaic son" jump over to the side of the opposition didn't sit well with the Jewish officials!) Paul found out about the plot against his life and decided that it was in his best interests to leave town. But notice who helped him escape...

Acts 9:25

> "...but his disciples took him by night, and let him down through an opening in the wall, lowering him in a large basket."

Notice carefully that these people are called "his disciples." Now why do you suppose they'd be called that? Because they had been personally discipled by Paul. The concept of personal disciplemaking was taken seriously by Paul. In fact, it was one of the first things that he learned. Just look how soon he began to do it. **Disciplemaking is part of the basic training for all believers—that's the Great Commission.**

Paul soon went home to Tarsus where he continued his discipling ministry. After about five years (AD. 37-42), Barnabas came to Tarsus looking for Paul and, having found him, they both went to Antioch to make disciples there (**Acts 11:25-30**).

Acts 11:26

> "And when he had found him, he brought him to Antioch. And it came about that for an entire year they met with the church, and taught considerable numbers; and the **disciples** were first called Christians in Antioch."

The disciples first began to be called "Christians" in Antioch. And where there are disciples, disciplemaking is in full operation.

Paul's first disciplemaking journey—some call these missionary journeys, but Paul's method and strategy for missions was to make disciples according to the plan of the Great Commission—is recorded in **Acts 13:4-14:26** (about A.D. 46-47). This record of Paul's activities is highly significant in its reflections of disciplemaking methodology and strategy.

Acts 14:21

> "And after they had preached the gospel to that city and **had made many disciples**, they returned to Lystra and to Iconium and to Antioch."

The importance of this statement can't be overstated. The Greek verb translated "had made disciples" is the same verb used by Jesus in the Great Commission. In the Commission (**Matthew 28:19**), the verb "make disciples" is a translation of an aorist active imperative. The form of the verb in **Acts 14:21** is an aorist active participle, correctly rendered "having discipled" (or literally, "having disciplized"). Paul precisely fulfilled the imperative of the Great Commission in his ministry. Why? Because he made disciples according to the divine plan. "Having made disciples" is the specific expectation of the command "Make disciples"!

Acts 14:21, 22

> "And after they had preached the gospel to that city and **had made many disciples**, they returned to Lystra and to Iconium and to Antioch, strengthening the souls of the **disciples**, encouraging them to continue in the faith, and saying, 'Through many tribulations we must enter the kingdom of God."

At this point, nearly 15 years after Jesus gave the command to make disciples, the divine plan is still being carried out with such **fidelity** to the original imperative that the Holy Spirit directs Luke to use the aorist active participle of **matheteuo** in the only appearance of the verb in the New Testament after the giving of Great Commission itself. What were Paul and other believers doing throughout the book of Acts? They were making disciples just like Jesus told us to!

Acts 14:25-28

> "And when they had spoken the word in Perga, they went down to Attalla; and from there they sailed to Antioch, from which they had been commissioned to the grace of God for the work that they had accomplished. And when they had arrived and gathered the church together, they began to report all things that God had done with them and how He had opened a door of faith to the Gentiles. And they spent a long time with the **disciples**."

When Paul arrived back in Antioch, the local believers are still called "disciples" by Luke, not "Christians," even though the word "Christian" was coined there. And, yes, where there are disciples, disciplemaking must have taken place—Luke doesn't use the term loosely! When Luke uses "disciple" he means "one who has been discipled by a disciplemaker according to the divine plan." In the light of the Great Commission, and Jesus' ministry of discipleship which logically preceded it, it is abundantly clear that the early Christian community did not use the term "disciple" in any sense other than that which the Lord intended.

Acts 16:1-3

> "And he came also to Derbe and to Lystra. And behold, a certain **disciple** was there, named Timothy, the son of a Jewish woman who was a believer, but his father was a Greek, and he was well spoken of by the brethren who were in Lystra and Iconium. Paul wanted this man to go with him...."

Paul wanted Timothy to go with him, to assist him in the ministry of disciplemaking (second journey, A.D. 49-51). Paul was very selective about his partners in ministry (**Acts 15:36-40**). Timothy had been properly discipled by his mother (**II Timothy 3:14-15**). And as result of both Paul's and Timothy's discipling ministries the churches were increasing numerically.

Acts 16:5

> "So the churches were being strengthened in the faith, and were increasing in number daily."

On his third disciplemaking journey (A.D. 52-57), Paul continued to make disciples, and re-visited many groups of disciples, no doubt to make sure that they also had become disciplemakers.

Acts 18:23

> "And having spent some time there, he departed and passed successively through the Galatian region and Phrygia, strengthening all the disciples."

As you can easily see, throughout his description of this third journey—throughout Acts for that matter—Luke often uses "disciple(s)" in referring to believers, emphasizing the fact that these people weren't merely Christians by virtue of having received Christ, but that they had been made into disciples by the Great Commission process of disciplemaking, and were continuing to win and disciple others in their respective communities.

Paul thought in terms of Jesus' disciplemaking methodology and strategy and operated accordingly. Paul, in every city, concentrated on a small group of converts. When he had discipled them adequately, he left them with the responsibility of advancing the gospel in their own communities by making disciples themselves. Paul knew that the Great Commission was meant for every believer. Paul taught so that others might teach. He knew the principle of discipleship well and reflects this knowledge in his instructions to his "son" in the ministry, Timothy.

II Timothy 2:1-2

> "You therefore, my son, be strong in the grace that is in Christ Jesus. And the things which you have heard from me in the presence of many witnesses, these entrust to faithful men, who will be able to teach others also."

As you can see, the most important thing about the book of Acts is that **THE EARLY BELIEVERS FOLLOWED DIRECTIONS. THEY WERE DISCIPLEMAKERS.**

The same explosion of the gospel can happen today if you and others will simply

MAKE DISCIPLES.

Disciplemakers are the only people in the world who are obedient to the Great Commission. Become one!

Let's review...

1. Discuss how disciplemaking applies to your life.

_____

_____

_____

_____

_____

_____

2. In the book of Acts, to what does "disciple" refer?

_____

_____

3. What's the difference between "believer" and "disciple"?

_____

_____

4. Briefly explain the explosion of the gospel in the book of Acts, in the light of the Great Commission.

_____

_____

_____

_____

_____

_____

CHAPTER 20

THE MINISTRY
OF DISCIPLESHIP

The word "disciple" is used well over 200 times in the four Gospels and Acts. Interestingly enough, it isn't found in any of the remaining 22 books of the New Testament. Why is there a complete elimination of the word "disciple" beyond the first five books of the New Testament?

The answer to this question has intrigued and puzzled scholars for centuries. Some explain the "sudden disappearance" as merely a change in the word-preference of Paul and others who chose to speak of believers as "brothers and "saints" rather than "disciples." Others have suggested that the New Testament writers suspended the use of "disciple" because it gave the connotation of a commitment beyond that which Jesus required from "ordinary" believers other than the apostles.

Neither of these explanations is valid for at least two reasons.

First, Matthew, Mark, Luke, John, and Acts were written comparatively late in the writing order of New Testament books. The letters of Paul, at least, were all written before the Gospels and Acts (except possibly for Mark which was written sometime in the A.D. 50's). Obviously, "disciple" was used historically by Jesus and His first followers as recorded in the narratives of the Gospels and Acts, which tell of the beginning of the development of the Church. In the days of Jesus and the early Church, "disciple" was used freely in reference to followers of Christ.

But the actual writing of the narratives of the Gospels and Acts didn't occur until rather late in the historical sequence of events in the early Church. This means that "disciple" was commonly used by the writers of the Gospels and Acts which were all penned after the historical period recorded in the book of Acts itself. It also means that, in the book of Acts, Luke—whose vocabulary was highly influenced by Paul, who discipled him—used "disciple" to refer to believers when writing of time periods concurrent with the writing of Paul's own letters. Luke wrote after Paul had trained him. Luke uses the term "disciple" throughout his writings; yet Paul, writing before Luke, never uses it at all. Luke, when writing about Paul's life, refers to believers as "disciples," and even speaks of Paul's own disciples.

What does this tell us? It tells us quite plainly that "disciple" was used by the Church from the beginning of Jesus' ministry right on through the time contemporaneous with the writing of the last Gospel (probably the Gospel of

John). The fact is that there isn't a time in the history of the New Testament Church when believers weren't called "disciples," clearly as a reference to those who had been made disciples in fulfillment of the Great Commission.

So, did the word "disciple" give way to allegedly synonymous terms like "brother" and "saint," and thereby account for the absence of "disciple" in the New Testament beyond the Gospels and Acts? Absolutely not. Logically, such a conclusion is absurd.

Second, there is simply no evidence in Scripture to indicate that Jesus or the early Church ever lowered the standards of discipleship for those who would come after the initial twelve men (or the 120). In fact, as His prayer shows us (**John 1 7:1 8-23**), Jesus considered all (future) believers as equal in scope and commitment with His first disciples...

John 17:18-23

'"As Thou didst send Me into the world, I also have sent them into the world. And for their sakes I sanctify Myself, that they themselves also may be sanctified in truth. I do not ask in behalf of these alone, but for those also who believe in Me through their word; that they may all be one; even as Thou, Father, art in Me, and I in Thee, that they also may be in Us; that the world may believe that Thou didst send Me. And the glory which Thou hast given Me I have given to them; that they may be one, just as We are one; I in them, and Thou in Me, that they may be perfected in unity, that the world may know that Thou didst send Me, and didst love them, even as Thou didst love Me."

Jesus' desire is for every one of His followers to be made a disciple. The level of commitment that He requires has been the same since the day He called out His first disciples: "He who loses his life for My sake shall find it." No, the commitment level of discipleship hasn't changed since the beginning, and the early Church didn't lessen it to any degree. To think such a thing is to condemn Christians to an un-Christ-like mediocrity.

So why does the word "disciple" not appear outside the Gospels and Acts in the New Testament? In order to answer this question—and the answer will play a significant role in our understanding of discipleship—we must ask, **"What is the fundamental difference between the Gospels/Acts and the rest of the New Testament that might account for the absence of 'disciple' in the latter?"**

The answer is quite obvious when you stop to think about it. The Gospels and Acts share a common theme that's distinct from the epistles and Revelation. Likewise, the epistles and Revelation possess a common denominator which sets them apart from the Gospels and Acts. What is this basic difference in the character of these two divisions of the New Testament?

The Gospels and Acts are the record of the **inception**, **development**, and **expansion** of the Church into the world. They tell us how the gospel is spread from Jesus to the first disciples, to Jerusalem, to Judea and Samaria, and to the Gentile world.

The epistles and Revelation were written to (or about) **established churches** and the ministry of the **functioning local body**. They deal with matters of doctrine, church leadership and organization, and the spiritual functions of the church, individually and collectively.

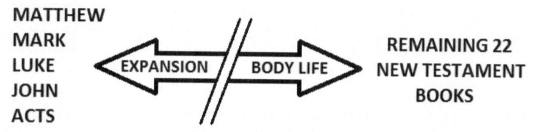

MATTHEW
MARK
LUKE
JOHN
ACTS

EXPANSION // BODY LIFE

REMAINING 22
NEW TESTAMENT
BOOKS

Look at it this way: The word "disciple" is an **expansion** term which explicitly reflects the process of taking the gospel to the world. Disciples are those who proclaim the gospel to others and make disciples of those who respond to the gospel. Therefore the expansion books, the Gospels and Acts, most often use the word "disciple" to describe believers. However, when local churches—and these exist only after disciplemaking has occurred—are addressed, believers are called "brothers," "sisters," and "saints" because the writers are dealing with the dynamics and problems of the body ministry. The Gospels and Acts treat the subject of **KINGDOM EXPANSION**. The remainder of the New Testament deals with **BODY MINISTRY**. The difference can be diagrammed like this...

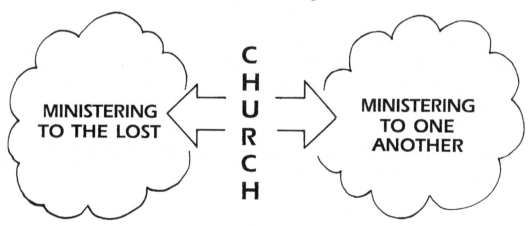

MINISTERING TO THE LOST

CHURCH

MINISTERING TO ONE ANOTHER

So, "disciple" is the term used when describing kingdom expansion—this reflects "Go.. .make disciples of all peoples" (**Matthew 28:19**) and "having made many disciples" (**Acts 14:21**) which refer to the practice of disciplemaking which produces disciples. When the context of "local church matters" prevails, as in the epistles, the word "disciple" is absent.

"Disciple" specifically relates to the evangelization of the lost and the initial grounding of new converts in the faith prior to their ability to function as members of a local church body.

To the local church, believers are brothers and saints who exercise spiritual gifts and abilities for the building up of the body. To the lost, believers are disciples (disciplemakers) who carry out disciplemaking as witnesses of Christ, proclaiming the gospel to the unsaved and training new believers in the Word until they are able both to make disciples and to function as effective members of the local church.

This is the pattern of Acts, and should be the pattern of Kingdom expansion for all church and mission endeavors without exception: **Disciplemaking (evangelism and discipleship training) guides the spiritual development of believers until they are able to be integrated into a local church body; when an adequate level of maturity is reached, church leaders (elders, deacons, etc.) are appointed to give spiritual guidance and structure to the functioning body.**

Acts 14:21-23

"And after they had preached the gospel to that city and had made many disciples, they returned to Lystra and to Iconium and to Antioch, strengthening the souls of the disciples, encouraging them to continue in the faith...And when they had appointed elders for them in every church, having prayed with fasting, they commended them to the Lord in whom they had believed."

Titus 1:3

"For this reason I [Paul] left you in Crete, that you might set in order what remains, and appoint elders in every city as I directed you."

When disciplemaking was completed and the disciples in a given city were spiritually mature enough to function as a unified local body, then leaders were appointed and the new church was 'commended to the Lord" as an autonomous body.

Whether a church is established or newly planted, the only method and strategy of numerical growth authorized by Scripture is **DISCIPLEMAKING**. It's the Great Commission.

What, then, is the relationship between discipleship and the local church? (Remember that "discipleship" and "disciplemaking" are interchangeable. Discipleship includes everything that's involved in being a disciplemaker.) How does discipleship operate relative to a local church body?

Disciplemaking is the responsibility of the believer, **individually**. The local church is comprised of believers collectively united for the purpose of body ministry, by which the body itself is strengthened. While each believer has one or more spiritual gifts and/or abilities to exercise within the context of the local body (**Romans 12; I Corinthians 12; Ephesians 4**), disciplemaking is not a gift, neither is it an option. The responsibility to make disciples is given to each and every believer without exception. No one believer has any more or less responsibility to make disciples than any other believer.

Disciplemaking is your individual responsibility to proclaim the gospel to unbelievers and to train those won to Christ in the essential principles of the Christian life. As a disciplemaker, your job is to disciple people into the local church body once you have led them to Christ.

Believers have a **two-way ministry**—in the direction of the **world** and in the direction of the **church**. It is not a function of the church, collectively, to make disciples. The essence of the local church is fellowship, not discipleship. Of course, the successful fellowship of a local church is predicated upon making disciples of each member. Disciplemaking must be accomplished by individual believers as they personally encounter unbelievers in the world.

Fellowship occurs when the church is gathered together. Discipling occurs when individual believers are dispersed into the world by the circumstances of daily living – "as you go, make disciples."

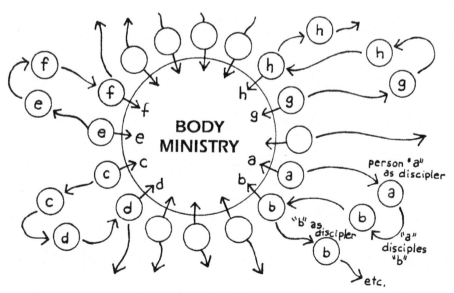

This isn't to say that new believers can't meet with and experience the benefits of the local church body; certainly they must. After all, they are being discipled into the body. But it is to say that new believers must be personally attended to by a discipler in the context of daily living, until they are spiritually stable enough to relate to the church body in a **knowledgeable** and effective way, and also to carry on their own personal ministries of disciplemaking to those they meet in the world.

DISCIPLEMAKING IS LIKE PARENTING.

New converts can't be shuffled into the local church and be expected to grow adequately in the Faith. Just as an infant must be closely supervised until a certain level of maturity is reached, so a new Christian must be personally discipled until he or she can relate to the local body in a meaningful and significant manner. What would happen if you took a newborn baby, dressed him in a coat and hat and escorted him out the front door of the hospital, then left him on his own? He would die in a matter of hours. Babies can't fend for themselves. They need the protection and nurture that only loving parents can offer.

And that's exactly what happens to new Christians who aren't properly discipled—for all practical purposes they die to the cause of Christ. Oh, they're still saved, but their ability to affect the world around them for Christ is severely hindered, even nonexistent. Whose fault is it? Theirs? And several years later we're griping about their lack of maturity and participation in the ministry of the church. Who's fault is it? It's the fault of whoever failed to disciple them. It's the church's fault for not making sure that every new believer is properly discipled. (Is it any wonder that most churches have a majority of members who never, or almost never, get actively involved in the church?)

Unless the divine plan for disciplemaking is rightly comprehended and pursued, churches will continue to be filled with spiritual infants who are incapable of impacting the world for Christ, individually or collectively.

Let's stop for a moment and reflect on what we've learned about discipleship so far...

1. Disciples are _____ not born.

2. Why must you be discipled?

_____

_____

_____

3. Is discipleship optional? For what reason?

_____

_____

_____

4. What happens to believers who aren't properly disciple?

_____

_____

_____

5. From everything you've learned thus far, write the fullest definition of discipleship that you can.

_____

_____

_____

_____

_____

It's tragic that most believers today have abandoned the Great Commission and are not making disciples. Even though many use the word "discipleship" very few know what its real meaning is.

WHATEVER HAPPENED
TO DISCIPLEMAKING?

Jesus made disciples. He established the divine methodology and strategy (discipleship) by which the gospel was to be taken to the entire planet. He gave the Great Commission, commanding His disciples to carry on the work of disciplemaking as the primary task of the Church. When the age of the indwelling Holy Spirit dawned on the Day of Pentecost, the early believers were set in motion, fulfilling, with a precise zeal, the imperative of Jesus. But what of the succeeding generations of Christians? How long did the Church continue to follow her orders to make disciples?

The answer to these questions is, indeed, a sad one, for the history of the Church reveals a steady decline in disciplemaking until, finally, no evidence can be found of its existence, at least in the written records, much beyond the first century. Certainly Christianity experienced remarkable growth until about A.D. 300, and even became the state religion of the Roman Empire by virtue of an edict of Constantine in the year 313—an act which in itself proved disastrous. But the reality of the disappearance of disciplemaking by the end of the third century must not be taken as evidence of a sudden demise of the divine plan.

Disciplemaking had been in the process of abandonment for two centuries, which attests to its dynamic nature—discipling, even when partially applied, was successful enough to overspread the entire Roman Empire within a relatively short period of time. Nevertheless, to the same degree that disciplemaking was abandoned, the Great Commission failed to be carried out. (Remember, disciplemaking is the Commission!)

What brought about the decline and eventual disappearance of discipling? At least three factors were involved...

1. HUMAN NATURE

Human nature is opposed to disciplemaking. This is so because the fundamental essence of discipling is intimacy. Discipling means that one must get personally involved in the lives of those being discipled. Relationships must be developed. But relationships mean vulnerability, and it's the nature of the human species to seek that which offers the least possibility of injury. Human nature desires comfort, protection, and most of all, convenience. The Church began to turn away from disciplemaking for the same reason that most believers today refuse to return to it—the cost is just too high.

ONLY SPIRIT-FILLED BELIEVERS BECOME DISCIPLEMAKERS.

Whenever the old self dominates, disciplemaking is not practiced, but shunned. Discipling necessitates personal responsibility and sacrifice. The Church, in time, began to give in to the inward pressures to conform to the old nature, choosing comfort over commitment, protection over personal involvement, convenience over command.

2. "CLERGY" VS. "LAITY"

Slowly but surely, the Church began to recognize a division between "clergy" and "laity," a distinction foreign to first century Christians. This was a devastating blow to the fulfillment of the Great Commission. The first century believers were disciples, therefore disciplemakers. The success of early Church expansion is directly attributable to the fact that everyone was a witness, every believer was proclaiming the gospel and making disciples. Tragically, satanic influences began to eat away at this vitality. J. E. Conant correctly observes that:

> The one thing, aside from the divine power, that made the program such a sweeping success was that every disciple was a witness; they were all propagandists. It was right here that Satan struck his blow. The first thing he did was so to overemphasize the distinctions in the divinely appointed division of service as finally to get an entirely equal witnessing brotherhood divided into two companies, with the great majority in one, and the small minority in the other. The small company came to be called 'clergy' and the large company 'laity.' And then he worked the witnessing out of the hands of the 'laity' until it was finally regarded as the exclusive right of the 'clergy.
>
> (**Every Member Evangelism**, pp. 41-42)

Once the concept of the personal involvement of all believers in disciplemaking had been eroded away, the ministry of the Church began to slip from the grip of "everyday" people. Eventually, not only was the missionary imperative lost, but also the body ministry crumbled beneath the feet of men clothed in ecclesiastical garb. It was the logical conclusion of the attitude "someone else will do it." Relationships gave way to religion—vertically and horizontally.

3. INSTITUTIONALISM

The inevitable consequence of the first two factors, institutionalism, like an icy rigor mortis, crept over the Church with rigid formality and traditionalism. Grandiose cathedrals, like ornate tombs, housed what remained of a once vibrant and glorious movement of the Spirit of God. And the Dark Ages came.

> This was the most terrific blow Satan ever dealt the Church, and one from which she has never recovered. It stunned the Church and all but killed her, and although the Reformation gave some promise of returning health and vigor, yet the recovery of her normal functions was only partial, and she is today slowly but surely losing out to the powers of darkness. The fact is that there are multitudes in the Church today who are still living in the Dark Ages, at least so far as obedience to the Great Commission isconcerned.
>
> (Conant, **Every Member Evangelism**, p. 42)

DEAR BELIEVER, IT'S TIME FOR YOU TO COME OUT OF THE "DARK AGES" AND DETERMINE TO FULFILL THE GREAT COMMISSION IN YOUR OWN LIFE—NO MATTER WHAT EVERYONE ELSE IS, OR ISN'T, DOING.

There is no optional course for your life. Any detours at this point will lead you away from God's plan for your life...

MAKE DISCIPLES!

CHAPTER 21
GETTING BACK
TO DISCIPLEMAKING

Matthew 28:18-20

> "And Jesus came up and spoke to them saying, 'All authority has been given to Me in heaven and on earth. Go therefore and make disciples of all the nations, baptizing them in the name of the Father and the Son and the Holy Spirit, teaching them to observe all that I commanded you; and lo, I am with you always, even to the end of the age.'"

DISCIPLEMAKING IS
UNIVERSALLY RELEVANT.

Jesus' command to make disciples was a perpetual one. Every believer, throughout all ages, is personally responsible for it. Because the Great Commission applies to every Christian in every era and every culture, it was, and is, necessary for the methodology and strategy of the Commission to be universally applicable.

To make disciples is the Great Commission-this is the divine imperative. The Commission itself is not only of divine origin, but its inherent methodology and strategy are also of divine design. God's great plan of disciplemaking is the only Biblically-authorized means of reaching our entire planet with the gospel of Jesus Christ.

As the only divinely-authorized plan for the spread of the gospel, disciplemaking is a universally relevant and timeless principle. When Biblical discipling is employed, the result is always the same-an explosion of the gospel concentrically expanding into the world.

DISCIPLING WORKS.
IT ALWAYS WORKS.

Properly applied, the principle of disciplemaking fulfills the expectations of the Great Commission powerfully and precisely. And well it should-it is the Commission.

Before we study the reasons for the universal relevancy of disciplemaking, an examination of some other "methods" of gospel propagation will enhance the dramatic supremacy of disciplemaking.

One of the most common methods of spreading the salvation message is mass evangelism. There is nothing wrong with reaching thousands of people at one time. There is a Biblical precedent for mass evangelism-the events of the Day of Pentecost, for example-but one must remember that evangelism alone is only the first phase of the Great Commission. Evangelism—communicating the gospel to the lost—must be followed by a period of discipleship training, during which individuals are personally discipled by a discipler. This must happen if the requirements of the Great Commission are to be met. As we said previously, evangelism without disciplemaking is a dead-end street as far as the Great Commission is concerned. New believers—and old ones if they've never been properly disciple—must be transformed into disciplemakers so that the gospel continues to be proclaimed beyond the "meeting hall." True, evangelism is better than nothing at all. But

WHY SETTLE FOR LESS THAN WHAT JESUS COMMANDED?

Personal (one-on-one) evangelism is the responsibility and privilege of every believer. But, again, why stop short of what Jesus truly desires? Jesus wants that person who is led to Him to be discipled so that he, too, becomes a disciplemaker.

DON'T STOP SHORT OF THE GREAT COMMISSION!

Sunday School evangelism is often hailed as a great tool in winning the lost to Christ. And it does produce more significant results than most methods of evangelism. But, as is the case with any form of evangelism, if it stands alone apart from full-blown disciplemaking, it is fundamentally flawed.

It's often stated by church leaders, "Most of the people who make professions of faith in Christ come through the Sunday School." Assuming this to be an indication of the evangelistic potential of the Sunday School many conclude that, since the great majority of new converts are related to the Sunday School in some way, an effective plan for Sunday School growth will enhance evangelistic possibilities, resulting in an increase in church membership.

True, many churches realize most of their growth in relation to the Sunday School (or similar programs). But to draw a conclusion such as the one just stated is a subtle and convenient way to avoid the major issue! If we take a close look at this kind of approach, it isn't difficult to see just how it is flawed as far as the Great Commission is concerned.

Consider this analogy:

A prospector discovers a stream from which, to his delight, he is able to pan an ounce of gold a day. However, a mile upstream, and unknown to him, lies the source of the tiny nuggets—a hill so laden with gold that whenever it rains, millions of gold particles are washed into the stream.

The hill contains so much gold that one shovel-full would yield several times more gold than a week of panning. But the prospector concludes, "If such a small stream produces an ounce a day, then just think what would happen if the stream were larger!" So the prospector buys a dredge and proceeds to make a bigger stream.

Having made the stream bigger, he happily discovers that now he is able to pan two ounces of gold per day. Yet the hill of gold remains unknown to the prospector who gleefully continues to spend countless hours picking minuscule gold flakes from the sand and mud. As you watch the whole procedure, it makes you want to grab the old prospector by the nape of the neck, march him up to the gold-laden hill and say, "Wake up, buster, and get a clue! Save yourself a lot of time, energy and money and dig here!"

A church with 100 in Sunday School may baptize ten or so people in a year. A church with 500 in Sunday School may baptize 50 or 100. A church with 2,000 in Sunday School may baptize 200 or more. And, for most churches, any of these ratios would be considered almost extraordinary, especially when the real figures are exposed (most evangelical churches baptize far, far fewer).

The point is this: Larger Sunday Schools, or churches in general, may have more baptisms, but the average ratio of members-to-converts remains unchanged—and even pathetic! Even in the most evangelistic churches in the world the ratio of members-to-converts is approximately 10%. The fact is that most church members never, ever, on their own, lead anyone to Christ in their entire lives. And most of the converts who come via the Sunday School aren't led to Christ outside the church building. This is not the Great Commission in action.

But what would happen if the methodology and strategy of the Great Commission were put into action in the life of each and every church member, as commanded by our Lord? **If each church member became obedient to the Great Commission by becoming a disciplemaker, church growth would be greatly accelerated.** That's a divine fact.

Don't just make the stream larger—GO WHERE THE GOLD IS!

Why wait for the unsaved to filter through the Sunday School (or any other program, for that matter) as the primary means of reaching people for Christ? Why not, as a church, become obedient to the Great Commission and train every member as a disciplemaker! Only when believers are properly discipled will they lead others to Christ and make disciples as a daily responsibility.

Don't be a sub-Great Commission believer. Don't be a sub-Great Commission church.

DON'T SETTLE FOR LESS
THAN GOD'S BEST.

Disciplemaking, as compared with all other concepts of church growth, is divinely superior. Anything less than fully-implemented Great Commission disciplemaking is sub-Biblical and, therefore, inadequate for the fulfillment of Christ's imperative. No other "method" of spreading the gospel is universally applicable.

DISCIPLEMAKING IS RELEVANT
IN EVERY CONTEXT.

The principle of discipleship is relevant in any culture or social setting, under any political system, in war or peace, in areas of poverty or wealth. There is no life-context in which disciplemaking does not apply. Disciplemaking requires no special place, no meeting house, no advertisement, no special organization, no special programs. It applies equally at home or on the mission fields of the world. In fact, any missions effort is sub-Biblical if it doesn't fully utilize disciplemaking as its primary means of reaching the unsaved.

There's only one kind of situation in which discipling isn't immediately applicable— a lone person shipwrecked on a desert island; a prisoner in solitary confinement; a hermit who completely avoids any contact with other people. Disciplemaking cannot take place in the context of one. There has to be someone else to make a disciple of. **But wherever there are people, the divine plan of disciplemaking can be put into action.**

Disciplemaking can be employed in any cultural setting and always with maximum results. This was Paul's personal method and strategy. Paul didn't just plant missions, he made churches comprised of nationals (locals) whom he and his team personally discipled. The first thing that Paul did in any location was to communicate the gospel to those in the community using various kinds of evangelism. Each person who received Christ was then discipled by Paul and/or his traveling companions. When the period of disciplemaking was completed, he appointed elders (leaders) from among them and left them to carry out the work of the Kingdom on their own, under the guidance of the Holy Spirit.

Paul's goal as a missionary—Biblically, a missionary is a vocational disciplemaker—was always to work himself out of a job in any given city. The sure sign of failure to utilize the Great Commission methodology and strategy in missions is when missionaries stay in a single location for years without moving on to another area. If an autonomous church led by nationals doesn't result from a missions effort, lack of proper disciplemaking is the most likely cause. Paul experienced marvelous success because he followed the Great Commission. He planted churches by means of disciplemaking. And because the people in those churches were properly discipled, they themselves became disciplemakers to their communities and capable members to their respective local fellowships.

Disciplemaking fulfills the Great Commission in the city and in the country, in the suburbs and in the ghetto, in the primitive village and in the technological society. It works for adults and young people. It works for doctors and plumbers, carpenters and teachers, politicians and students, homemakers and salespersons. Disciplemaking is viable under democracy or communism. Yes, the principle of discipleship is the universally applicable means of spreading the universal gospel of Jesus' saving power!

Now think about this: Baptism is the first step of obedience for every believer—it is the outward expression of sonship. Who would think of ignoring baptism as unimportant? Yet the Great Commission imperative for making disciples is almost wholly ignored. The process of making disciples demands not only baptizing new believers, but also training them as disciples and disciplemakers. You cannot rationalize this away. You cannot get around the fact that Jesus has commanded us not just to evangelize and to baptize, but to **MAKE DISCIPLES**. It's wonderful that we have such a divinely powerful, universally applicable plan for spreading the good news of eternal life in Christ and for providing a solid foundation for the growth of churches, both spiritually and numerically. Yet, tragically, it remains virtually untouched.

We must get Jesus' imperative to make disciples back into the lives of believers. Can this be done? If so, how can it be accomplished? Let's look at

DISCIPLEMAKING AND THE CONTEMPORARY CHURCH.

There is no segment of our global society in which the methodology and strategy of disciplemaking cannot be effectively applied. According to the Great Commission, disciplemaking is the vehicle to take the gospel to the ends of the earth—to every culture and every level of society. Because this is so, the contemporary Church, as much as the Church of the first century, is directly responsible for making disciples of all peoples. In order for this to be accomplished, the present-day Church must re-discover its two-fold responsibility—to the world as disciplemakers, to the local church as ministering body members.

This is precisely where the great difficulty lies. We must

GET BACK TO BASICS.

Whereas the early Church began by obeying the Great Commission exactly as Jesus had given it—every person becoming a disciplemaker—today we find ourselves caught in the dilemma of attempting to "revive" disciplemaking from nearly 1,900 years of oblivion. And, from all indications, that appears to be an extremely difficult task.

WHY?

Why should it be that the Church of the present day knows little or nothing of disciplemaking? It is absent from the Church today for the same reasons that the early Church eventually lost it. Human nature dislikes the thought of it. The making of disciples lies generally outside our comfort zone, now as in the past. Whenever people are called upon to press beyond themselves into relationships which demand levels of vulnerability exceeding routine "normalcy," they have an innate tendency (the old self) to shrink back into their protective personal spaces.

This phenomenon is complicated in our society by an excessive emphasis upon leisure time. Coupled with poor time-management, which plagues most people, these factors combine to militate against disciplemaking which, by nature, requires the pouring of one's life into another. Doing this takes both interpersonal involvement and quality time.

Unfortunately, most churches throughout history have molded and structured themselves to fit the mind-set of convenience and comfort. Certainly, there's nothing categorically wrong with convenience and comfort. There's nothing wrong, basically, with an attractive and, hopefully, functional church facility. There's nothing wrong with making services and programs conveniently accessible to church members. But for the most part, Christians have forgotten their responsibility to

"SEEK AND SAVE..."

The problem arises when a church fails to emphasize the individual believer's responsibility to the world and to train each person to carry out that responsibility. Can we justify a statement like, "Our church is so dynamic—we have something for everyone going on all the timer? Shouldn't we be saying, "Our church has become so corporately self-oriented that we measure our success based on how many activities can be conceived to get our people involved, preventing our members from developing their own personal disciplemaking ministries to those in the world!"?

Churches spend mountains of time, energy, words, and money getting people to "come." Then, almost ironically, many churches spend more time, energy, words, and money trying to get people to come so that they can get motivated to do some "going" in between all the "coming," which, characteristically, often ends with a host of people who don't know whether they're "coming" or "going." And besides, there are only so many hours in a day. There are only so many nights in a week. Make disciples? WHEN?

This isn't to imply that meeting together doesn't require depth and vulnerability; it does—if and only if it's done for the right reasons (See **Ephesians 4:11, 12; Hebrews 10:24, 25**). But it must be emphasized that while assembling together has never passed out of vogue, disciplemaking has all but vanished. Even the church at Laodicea (**Revelation 3:14-21**) met

together; but they turned inward upon themselves and became "lukewarm." The Ephesian church, great as it was, lost the primal love (**Revelation 2:4**) which Jesus proclaimed (**John 3:16**) and which was the very reason for the Great Commission.

When disciplemaking is ignored, the unavoidable result is lukewarmness—something that's sickening to the Lord...

Revelation 3:15, 16

> "I know your deeds, that you are neither cold nor hot; I would that you were cold or hot. So because you are lukewarm, and neither hot nor cold, I will spit you out of My mouth."

This fact must be reckoned with: If a local body of believers is comprised of individuals who, in their personal lives, are not pouring themselves into others who have come to know Christ as a result of their witness, then that church, no matter how much it gives the appearance of an exciting, thriving fellowship, is in a precarious position indeed. All the activity in the world can't make up for failure to be obedient to the Great Commission.

IT'S TIME TO GET DOWN
TO BRASS TACKS.

What contemporary local church will dare defy centuries of tradition and adopt the two-fold ministry of the New Testament for its members, not as an option, but as a divine imperative? Every member must be trained to minister both to the church and TO THE WORLD. Churches that don't are destined to be vomited from the Lord's mouth (**Revelation 3:15, 16**).

We must be willing to face the reality that the edifices constructed by the Church over the last nineteen centuries—buildings, liturgies, modes of worship, programs, boards, societies, auxiliaries, unions, conventions, synods, conferences—are not the essence of the Christian life, nor necessarily a sign of it. The day may soon come when, by bombs or persecution, the tides of the world will dash all these things to pieces before our eyes. Then what will remain amidst the rubble of pews, spires and Sunday School quarterlies? Only the essence of Christian living will survive—the two-fold ministry...

Matthew 28:19

> "Go therefore and make disciples of all the nations...."

and

Hebrews 10:23-25

> "Let us hold fast the confession of our hope without wavering; for He who promised is faithful; and let us consider how to stimulate one another to love and good deeds, not forsaking our own assembling together, as is the habit of some, but encouraging one another; and all the more, as you see the day drawing near."

And neither the ministry to the church nor the ministry to the world require the frills of formality. They demand only the very basic life of the believer, which is Christ (**Galatians 2:20**). Believers, fed by the Word and empowered by the Holy Spirit, need little else in order to fulfill the Great Commission in their personal lives. If that sounds radical it's because, somewhere in our doing of Christian "things" and massive accumulation of Christian "stuff," we've lost our basic reason for being.

We've got to get back to disciplemaking, no matter how radical it sounds, no matter what the cost. Disciplemaking is the only way the Church can be relevant in the world. Making disciples never becomes obsolete. It's never replaced by something else. The Great Commission is either obeyed or disobeyed. Not to make disciples is for the Church, individually or collectively, to become an irrelevant relic—displayed, but of little practical value to the lives of real people.

Concerning the relevancy of the Church in the modern world, Francis Schaeffer has said,

> A revolution is coming and is here. If we don't have the courage in Jesus Christ to take a chance of getting kicked out of our churches and being ostracized today, what are we going to do when the revolution comes in force? If we don't have the courage to open our homes and begin to enter these things into the churches, slowly begin to make the changes that can be brought within the forms of the polity of the New Testament, then don't be concerned about having courage when the pressure comes.
>
> **(The Church at the End of the 20th Century**, p.111)

The world is constantly changing. Society is changing. More and more the Church is having to battle secularism and humanism.

How can the Church, how can Christians, maintain a relevant presence in the world capable of making an impact for Christ? Plan all the activities and programs you want. Eat all the hotdogs and play all the games you want. Contrive every gimmick and spout every cliché you can think of. But your church, or individual, ministry will only be pleasing to the Lord if it's fulfilling the Great Commission by making disciples. Let's not fool ourselves. The Holy Spirit empowers disciplemakers. That's what we're here for, and that's why He came.

Concerning disciplemaking, as well as body ministry, some changes must be made if the desires of the Lord are to be carried out. Not only must the body ministry of the local church be kept in line with Scriptural norms, but also disciplemaking must be re-established as an essential in the life of each individual believer. The gospel will never begin to reach maximally into local communities, and into the world, until the Great Commission methodology/strategy is practiced in the lives of believers—like **YOU!**

In order for this to happen, attitudes of complacency, convenience, and comfort must be shattered. To ignore the issue is to invite the disciplining hand of the Master.

Revelation 2:5; 3:19

"Remember therefore from where you have fallen, and repent and do the deeds you did at first; or else I am coming to you, and will remove your lampstand out of its place- unless you repent...Those whom I love, I reprove and discipline; be zealous, therefore, and repent."

Before you go on to the next chapter, discuss together the need to be obedient to Jesus' call to discipleship. How is it affecting you personally?

CHAPTER 22

THE METHOD AND STRATEGY OF DISCIPLEMANKING

Jesus ministered to the multitudes. He preached to hundreds, even thousands, yet His divine plan for spreading the gospel throughout the world involved the special training of 12 men. As we know, Jesus' plan for reaching the world with the gospel can be called **THE PRINCIPLE OF DISCIPLESHIP**. Let's take a close look at this important principle and discover its exciting application to your life as a believer in Jesus Christ. Look again at the Great Commission...

Matthew 28:18-20

> "And Jesus came up and spoke to them, saying, 'All authority has been given to Me in heaven and on earth. Go therefore and make disciples of all the nations, baptizing them in the name of the Father and the Son and the Holy Spirit, teaching them to observe all that I have commanded you; and lo, I am with you always, even to the end of the age."

Jesus gave this command to make disciples on the basis of His absolute authority. His lordship compels us to seek out and make disciples of others.

Later, just before His ascension, Jesus re-emphasized the Commission.

Acts 1:8

> "...you shall receive power when the Holy Spirit has come upon you; and you shall be My witnesses both in Jerusalem, and in all Judea and Samaria, and even to the remotest part of the earth."

The order of the movement of the gospel into the world is significant.

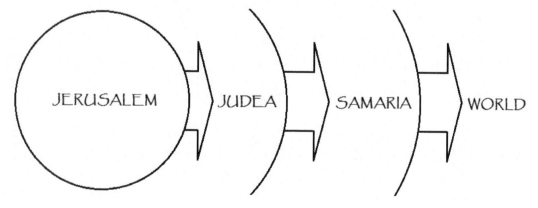

Jesus' plan for reaching the world with the gospel is a systematic, strategic combination of saturation and outward **momentum**. This simply means that when His divine plan is followed correctly, the movement of the gospel expands outwardly from any point of concentration.

When the gospel had effectively saturated Jerusalem, its natural and ever-widening influence moved outward through Judea and Samaria and, ultimately, into every part of the world.

How does this apply to you?

YOU MUST MAKE DISCIPLES!

You must become committed to follow the divine plan. If the gospel isn't expanding outward from a concentration point involving your life, then you need to discover why Jesus' Great Commission isn't being fulfilled through you.

The devil isn't stupid. He's got your number. He may have you, and countless other Christians, thinking that good fellowship, singing, cookies and Kool-aid, activities and programs are somehow—you never could figure out just how—carrying out the Great Commission. Some of these things may be important, but

ONLY DISCIPLEMAKING FULFILLS THE GREAT COMMISSION.

Now, let's look at Jesus'

METHODOLOGY

point-by-point, and apply it to the present. As in everything He taught, Jesus provides Himself as the prime example for the principle of discipleship.

Jesus' method of making disciples isn't haphazard. On the contrary, the process of discipling one or several people has an identifiable methodology designed specifically for that purpose. The basic pattern for making disciples is the Lord

Jesus Himself. He has provided, by way of His personal example, the formula necessary for the proper development of disciples. These are the things the first disciples learned as they were being discipled by Jesus. When He commanded them (us) to make disciples, they knew that He wanted them to do with others just as He had done with them.

As we examine the discipling ministry of Jesus, several elements come to light. In His relationship to the Twelve, Jesus utilized at least **TEN FACTORS** which, together, form His disciplemaking methodology. Well spend the remainder of this chapter talking about the first factor, **EVANGELISM**.

FACTOR ONE: EVANGELISM

From the outset of Jesus' ministry, many "followed" Him. Thousands of people flocked to hear Jesus of Nazareth speak. Indeed, He spoke as no man had ever spoken. And Jesus didn't neglect the masses. However, when it came to the task of taking His gospel to the world, Jesus didn't appeal to the great throngs of people who followed Him about. Jesus concentrated His disciplemaking efforts on the lives of a mere handful of men.

Luke 6:12, 13
> "And it was at this time that He went off to the mountain to pray, and He spent the whole night in prayer to God. And when day came, He called His disciples to Him; and chose twelve of them, whom He also named as apostles."

Jesus prayed earnestly about those who would be His disciples—not disciples in the general sense, as in the case of the hundreds who followed Him around, but as men who would undergo the kind of training necessary to accomplish the fulfillment of the Great Commission, His ultimate directive.

The men He chose weren't necessarily the most intelligent, the most talented, the best educated, or the most finely cultured. But whatever they were—and they were a motley lot, to be sure—they possessed a common and crucial characteristic:

THEY WERE WILLING
TO FOLLOW JESUS.

But why select only a few? Why not start with a hundred, or even a thousand?

Why? Because Jesus wasn't interested in attracting a crowd. He was, by a preconceived plan, initiating a great

MOVEMENT.

Isn't it odd that we usually approach things from the opposite direction, and almost always attempt to start big? But Jesus knew that the **FEW**, properly discipled, would become **MANY**.

Jesus also knew the dynamics of the human personality. He was aware of the fact that a large number of people would prevent the creation of a proper "high-yield" environment for learning. Jesus wanted to produce an explosion of the gospel into the world. And explosions occur only when the conditions are exactly right. By concentrating on a small group, Jesus was able to control the reaction, making sure that it took on the appropriate form and proper direction at the correct time.

The effective outward movement of the gospel begins by concentrating disciplemaking efforts in the lives of a few willing people. Selecting those to be discipled must be done under the guidance of the Holy Spirit. The Christian disciplemaker must be sensitive to the Lord's direction in communicating the gospel to unbelievers. In witnessing, what we're actually doing is allowing Christ, through the presence of His Spirit in our lives, to call men and women unto Himself. Those who are willing to follow Christ are to be

discipled immediately. When you lead someone to Christ, begin discipleship training as soon as possible (the next two chapters will detail what to do when making a disciple).

Don't procrastinate. Those who are willing to receive Christ are, at that moment, willing to be discipled. It's only when spiritual babes are left alone—for even a relatively short period of time—that the diseases of disinterest and waning desire set in. If this happens it can, and probably will, result in a life-long pattern of carnality and marginal church involvement.

The Greek word from which our word "evangelism" is derived means "to bring (or announce) good news," or "to proclaim the gospel." In the early days of the Church, while disciplemaking was still being carried out in fulfillment of the Great Commission, every believer became a proclaimer of the good news.

Acts 8:1, 4

> "...And on that day a great persecution arose against the church in Jerusalem; and they were all scattered throughout the regions of Judea and Samaria...Therefore, those who had been scattered went about preaching the word."

The early Christians were proclaiming the gospel and, as we've seen, were making disciples.

EVANGELISM IS BRINGING THE GOOD NEWS OF SALVATION IN CHRIST TO THOSE WHO ARE LOST.

Today, the average Christian isn't involved in evangelism. Statistics tell us that the vast majority of Christians never lead anyone to Christ—ever. Many reasons can be given for this very negative fact. But among all the reasons or rationalizations that could be given, one stands out at the bottom line:

FAILURE TO PROCLAIM THE GOSPEL IS THE INEVITABLE RESULT OF THE FAILURE TO MAKE DISCIPLES.

Every believer who is discipled, who becomes a disciplemaker, will do the task of evangelism. Disciplemakers are sensitive to evangelistic opportunities in daily living because they see the calling of men and women to follow Christ as fundamental to their way of life. When properly discipled, the disciplemaker knows and understands the no-options nature of making disciples.

MAKING DISCIPLES IS NOT OPTIONAL!

Becoming a disciplemaker isn't just a matter of choice. The believer who isn't involved in making disciples is living outside God's will by way of disobedience to Jesus' most fervent command.

The new believer must be discipled from day one. The new believer's perception of the Christian life must be formulated according to Biblical standards, not according to the watered-down versions of Christianity so common in the world today. Present-day Christians will never begin to evangelize until they are taken back to square one and properly discipled in the truth of the Word concerning their responsibility, as followers of Christ, to fulfill the Great Commission in the first person singular.

Simply to teach methods and techniques of evangelism is to fall woefully short of the New Testament standard. Evangelism isolated from full-blown disciplemaking perpetuates the near-extinction of personal evangelism—which has been in a steady process of decline since the close of the apostolic era. A person won to

Christ, if not adequately discipled, will not evangelize. Is not the state of Christianity today proof enough of this fact? It is, and more.

Remember, the Great Commission is to make disciples, not merely to evangelize. Evangelism is only the **first** factor in the fulfillment of Jesus' imperative. The evangelism factor is lost if the other factors of personal discipling aren't carried out to the fullest. The Great Commission is the mechanism for reaching the world with the gospel, and evangelism is, so to speak, the cutting edge of the arrow. But an arrow is much more than an arrowhead.

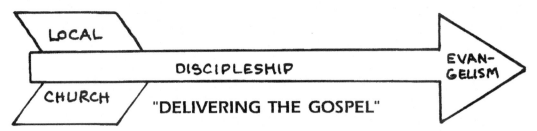

Without the support of the shaft (discipling) the point fails to reach the mark. And, for stability, guide-feathers are necessary—this represents the ministry of the local church body. Without the support and direction of the shaft and the stabilizing action of the guide-feathers, the arrowhead would tumble haphazardly through the air. If an unattached point reached the target at all, it would stick purely by accident. And that's just how most evangelism happens—almost by accident, if at all.

Disciplemaking develops Christians who have a proper sense of direction—to take the gospel to others. The local church contributes stability to the believer's life through the teaching of the Word and the ministry of fellow Christians.

This is one way to visualize disciplemaking. But, no matter how you choose to picture it, disciplemaking is the most fundamental principle in the expansion of the Church-not evangelism alone.

So, how is the evangelism factor applied in contemporary situations? In the same way it was applied in the first century—in the daily life of each believer. "But," you might be saying, "what kind of an answer is that? Aren't there some slick techniques that can be learned in order to make a person a more effective witness? Doesn't, one need to take a course in personal evangelism? Isn't it true that most people just don't know how to share their faith and don't do it for fear of embarrassing themselves?"

Now, back up for a moment. How did the first Christians (**Acts 8:1, 4**) learn to proclaim the gospel? How did they learn this without evangelism seminars? What was their secret?

No secret. No seminars. Then what?

DISCIPLEMAKING.

Disciplemaking means approaching the Christian life on a no- options basis. In the early expansion of the Church, when the Great Commission was literally being followed, if people weren't willing to take up the cross in discipleship, they didn't follow Christ at all. First and foremost, there were no cheap decisions to follow Christ in some loosey-goosey manner. And to follow Christ often meant severe persecution. Not a situation for the faint-of-heart or -faith. To them, the call to follow Christ was a call to discipleship—nothing less.

For the Church of the first century, the call to faith in Christ was to repent and turn from one's former life and become obedient to Christ. The Greek word translated "believe" denotes entering into a personal union with Christ, therefore submitting to His commands and desires. In those early years, those confronted with the claims and call of Christ knew that to follow 'The Way" was to make a radical commitment which, of course, included becoming a disciplemaker.

They also knew there was a very good chance that, in the process, their physical lives would be terminated by opponents of gospel. In Paul's day, a Christian was a proclaimer of the gospel. Those who were faced with the opportunity to follow Christ knew that if they did, they too would become proclaimers and would, most likely, be subject to the attacks perpetrated against the Faith by the enemies of Christ. And great numbers of them did die for the cause of Christ.

But this kind of commitment isn't the norm for Christians today. Christianity is generally offered as a basic fire insurance policy with a number of options to be selected at the recipient's convenience. There is no counting the cost. There is no explanation of the demands of discipleship. And, in almost all instances, there is no disciplemaking at all.

If evangelism according to the New Testament pattern is to be re-established today, uncompromised disciplemaking must also be re-established. The "options" must be emphasized for what they really are—the characteristics of a normal Christian life.

DISCIPLEMAKING IS BASIC.

Disciplemaking and, therefore, evangelism can only be re-introduced through the bold application of discipleship methodology and strategy by believers who are willing to fulfill the Great Commission in their own lives.

WILL YOU START?

217

Disciplemaking can begin with one. The road will be hard and long, but the result will be the salvation of men and women who will otherwise be passed over as believers pursue more comfortable and convenient enterprises.

You are called upon to share the gospel with those who fall within the context of your life—whomever you meet in the course of daily living. You are Christ's personal representative...

II Corinthians 5:17-20

"Therefore if any man is in Christ, he is a new creature; the old things passed away; behold, new things have come. Now all these things are from God, who reconciled us to Himself, not counting their trespasses against them, and He has committed to us the word of reconciliation. Therefore, we are ambassadors for Christ, as though God were entreating through us; we beg you on behalf of Christ, be reconciled to God."

How are you to share? Two words suffice:

IN LOVE.

We share the gospel because the love of Christ within us compels us to reach out to those who so desperately need Him.

WHAT DO I SHARE?

The **GOSPEL!** You already know what the gospel is. You became a Christian, didn't you? Then you know what the gospel is because you accepted its message for yourself (see Chapter 1). You not only already know what the gospel is, but you also know enough to share your faith effectively. But

BE SPECIFIC!

There's no reason to beat around the bush. When God provides the opportunities- and He will-let people know that:

1. God loves them and desires to enter into a personal relationship with them (**John 3:16**) and that's why they were created (**Genesis 1:27**).

2. But all people have sinned (**Romans 3:23**) and are, therefore, separated from God (spiritual death) (**Romans 6:23**) and cannot enter into a right relationship with God based on their own efforts or merits (**Ephesians 2:8, 9**).

3. Yet God still loves them, and has provided the way, His way, for them to be forgiven of all their sins through the death of Jesus Christ, His Son (God in human form), on the cross (**Romans 6:23, 5:8**), and to receive eternal life by Jesus' resurrection from the dead (**I Corinthians 15:3-6**).

4. Only by receiving Christ (**John 14:6, 1:12**) through faith (**Ephesians 2:8, 9; Romans 10:9, 10**) can they experience a personal relationship with God; this must be done personally by opening up the door of their lives to Christ (**Revelation 3:20**), following Him with unreserved commitment (**Matthew 16:24, 25**).

5. God's Word, the Bible, promises eternal life to all who have received Christ through faith (**I John 5:11-13**), and they can receive Him now if they truly desire to follow Him (**I Corinthians 6:2**). They can express the desire of their life to God through prayer, and He will not turn them away (**Romans 10:13**).

Once these things have been shared in love, people should be encouraged to give their lives to Christ—before it's too late.

When a person receives Christ as a result of your witness, it immediately becomes your personal responsibility to disciple that person (or find a disciplemaker who is appropriate for them; its best for men to disciple men and women to disciple women, for example). Don't wait even one day to begin, if at all possible. You don't need a group. You can disciple someone one-on-one. In fact, that's an extremely good way to do it. The important thing is to avoid any delay.

Before we look at the other nine factors of disciplemaking, it will be helpful for you to do the following review and applications...

1. Why did Jesus disciple only a few men instead of a multitude?

2. What happens when evangelism is done without disciplemaking?

3. Why should a new believer be discipled beginning the day of his conversion?

_____

_____

_____

_____

_____

4. If you feel that you need some practical help in sharing the gospel, ask your discipler to go with you to see someone you know who needs Christ, and let him/her show you by example how to present the gospel. You may want to do this several times until you feel comfortable on your own. But remember, the best preparation and motivation to witness is that you love people and don't want them to spend eternity without Christ. You have what it takes! The Holy Spirit will empower you. Do it!

5. There are many good books that offer excellent help in sharing the gospel. **How to Give Away Your Faith**, by Paul E. Little, is very helpful.

6. From time to time you will encounter legitimate questions from unbelievers that stand in the way of their coming to Christ. There are many books that provide excellent help in this area. Josh McDowell has written several helpful books; among these are: **Answers to Tough Questions, Reasons Skeptics Should Consider Christianity, The Resurrection Factor, and Evidence That Demands a Verdict I & II**. John W. Montgomery's **Faith Founded on Fact and History** and **Christianity** are very helpful.

7. Make it a point to look for opportunities to present Christ. Pray that God will use you to reach many for His glory!

See the Handbook section of the manual, Chapter 28, for further help in the area of personal evangelism.

CHAPTER 23

THE METHOD AND STRATEGY OF DISCIPLEMAKING

(Continued)

In the last chapter we examined evangelism as the first factor of disciplemaking. As we've seen, evangelism alone isn't able to fulfill the Great Commission. In making disciples, there are several other factors which must be included in order for Jesus' imperative to be satisfied.

Once one has received Christ (evangelism), a period of discipling should begin immediately. This discipling period, through which the new believer is trained in the basics of the Christian walk, will include the same kinds of things Jesus did in making disciples. As we study Jesus' personal disciplemaking ministry, we discover nine discipleship factors beyond evangelism. If your personal disciplemaking is to meet the requirements of the Great Commission, each of the following discipleship factors must be met.

FACTOR TWO: PROXIMITY

One of the most important things Jesus did for the Twelve was to allow them close proximity to Himself. Jesus didn't call weekly meetings or merely schedule convenient times to meet. What He did do is significant to the whole process of making disciples: **THEY WERE WITH HIM.**

Luke 8:1

> "...He began going about from one city and village to another, proclaiming and preaching the kingdom of God; and the twelve were with Him...."

Mark 3:14

> "And He appointed twelve, that they might be with Him...."

Jesus, the Master Disciplemaker, made certain the disciples were able to view and experience His life on a daily basis. They watched Him eat. They watched Him deal with people. They watched how He reacted to frustrating situations. They watched Him minister, pray, and teach. And, whether they consciously realized it or not, the Twelve were learning a great number of things simply as a result of being around Him.

Jesus, through this principle, was stressing the importance of being as the basis of doing. This close personal contact provided the disciples with a picture of the continuity and harmonious orchestration of the various elements of Jesus' life. No matter what the tone of the environment-serious, light, tense, joyful, sorrowful-or the type of situation at hand, the Twelve experienced the stability of Jesus' life. They saw what He was. Jesus practiced

VISIBILITY.

When discipling others, the discipler must be visible and accessible. The disciples must see more than the "spiritual" side of the discipler. They must experience a demonstration of the discipler's spirituality in as many different contexts as possible. Life isn't lived in a church building or in someone's living room.

An effective movement of the gospel requires that disciples gain a first-hand view of the discipler's ability to apply the Christian Faith in the real world. This demonstrates that the disciplemaker is what he teaches.

I CAN HARDLY WAIT TILL I CAN GET OUT OF HERE...

The main element in the factor of proximity is time-quality time. For the disciplemaker to do an adequate job of training disciples, he must be willing to make the sacrifices necessary to be with them, not only for teaching, but also for them to see him as he encounters various aspects of life-decision-making, joy, stress, morality, ethics, family life, prayer, evangelism, etc.

Again, those being discipled need to experience the Christianity of their discipler in the broad spectrum of **REAL LIFE**. This subjects the discipler to a great deal of vulnerability. This, however, isn't an unjust pressure on the discipler. It simply requires that he live what he teaches. Disciplemaking leaves no room for hypocrisy.

But in an age characterized by the phrase, "There isn't enough time to do what has to be done, much less what one wants to do," how can enough time be found in order to pour one's life into others? This is a problem, but it isn't insurmountable. The following words speak to the heart of this issue:

> Step aside and sit down. Let your motor idle down for a minute and think for a change. Think about your pace.. .your busyness. How did you get trapped in that squirrel cage? What is it down inside your boiler room that keeps pouring the coal on your fire? Caught your breath yet? Take a glance back over your shoulder, say, three or four months. Could you list anything significant accomplished? How about feelings of fulfillment-very many? Probably not, if you're honest...
>
> Busyness rapes relationships. It substitutes shallow frenzy for deep friendship. It promises satisfying dreams but delivers hollow nightmares. It feeds the ego but

starves the inner man. It fills the calendar but fractures a family. It cultivates a program but plows under priorities.

Many a church boasts about its active program: 'Something every night of the week for everybody.' What a shame! With good intentions the local assembly can create the very atmosphere it was designed to curb....

WANT TO CHANGE? HERE'S HOW: First, admit it. You are too busy...

Second, stop it. Starting today, refuse every possible activity which isn't absolutely necessary....

Third, maintain it.

(C. Swindoll, Killing Giants, Pulling Thorns, pp. 78, 79)

Once superficial busyness has been checked, there will be ample time for family, church, business, and **DISCIPLEMAKING**.

It's a matter of setting priorities-and not just for individuals. Churches that desire to help members become involved in fulfilling the Great Commission MUST re-evaluate their priorities. Church members must be freed to pursue individual ministries to the world. And, indeed, it may be more difficult to get pastors and church leaders to transform "come and get it" ministries into the "go and share it" kind than for the average believer to re-order his approach to life.

TRADITIONS DIE HARD.

This fact is unavoidable: If disciplemaking is to be re-established, there must be adequate time for the proximity factor to take effect. For disciples to see only the "sacred" side of the disciplemaker is to give them a distorted view of reality and to set them up for serious disappointments and disillusionment. The disciple's proximity to the actual life of the discipler is a critical part of the discipleship process. And it takes **TIME**.

FACTOR THREE: FRIENDSHIP

Jesus' relationship to the Twelve went beyond that of teacher/pupil. He was their friend.

John 15:15

> "No longer do I call you slaves, for the slave does not know what his master is doing; but I have called you friends, for all things that I have heard from My Father I have made known to you."

Jesus was concerned not only with their education, but also with their personal problems. They knew they could count on Him when they had no one else to turn to.

Certainly Jesus enjoyed being with His disciples. They socialized together, laughed together, cried together. They were friends.

Those being discipled must be able to sense true friendship in their relationship to the discipler. A sense of acceptance is important to the overall disciplemaking process. The failure to allow the development of friendships seriously hampers the effectiveness of discipleship by undermining the aspects of mutual trust and intimacy which are crucial to the discipling process.

Friendship involves several things, but possibly the two most important ingredients in friendship are **TRUST** and **LOVE**.

TRUST between friends is developed as the relational knowledge of each individual grows. Knowing leads to trusting. This, however, is a most difficult thing for the disciplemaker. For how can a discipler experience this kind of relationship with each disciple, especially when the discipler is working with a larger group of, say, six to eight people? Is the disciplemaker to entrust himself to every person he trains? No, not exactly.

What must occur in the area of trust is the confidence of the disciples in their discipler. The disciples must be able to trust their leader, knowing that he is a person of his word, that he is honest, and that his leadership is worthy of their "followship." The disciplemaker may not implicitly trust every disciple. There may be much spiritual growth to be had before some of the disciples themselves are trustworthy. However, each disciple must sense that his discipler is trustworthy.

LOVE is a powerful agent. If a would-be discipler does not have love, he will fail at the task of making disciples. The very love of God, born through the believer by the Holy Spirit (**Galatians 5:22**) is the motivation for the discipler's work. One will have no desire to make disciples if love isn't found within.

We must remember that Jesus' disciples were not altogether a lovable lot. Yet, because of His great love for them, they responded to Him. He knew what they could become. He saw their potential.

And that's precisely the kind of love a disciplemaker must have for those he trains. Paul's tremendous passage describing this agape love is highly instructive for the discipler.

I Corinthians 13:1-8
"If I speak with the tongues of men and angels, but do not have love, I have become a noisy gong or a clanging cymbal. And if I have the gift of prophecy, and know all mysteries and all knowledge; and if I have all faith, so as to remove mountains, but do not have love, I am nothing. And if I give all my possessions to feed the poor, and if I deliver my body to be burned but do not have love, it profits me nothing. Love is patient, love is kind, and is not jealous; love does not brag and is not arrogant, does not act unbecomingly; it does not seek its own, is

not provoked, does not take into account a wrong suffered, does not rejoice in unrighteousness, but rejoices with the truth; bears all things, believes all things, hopes all things, endures all things. Love never fails...."

Through friendship, you are able to communicate Christ-likeness. After all, every disciplemaker is but an imitator of the Master Discipler.

FACTOR FOUR: EXAMPLE

This principle is similar to that of proximity (and requires it) but the emphasis here is on doing-which is the result of being.

John 13:15

> "For I gave you an example that you also should do as I did to you."

Jesus didn't teach in word only. He was never one to give orders without first providing Himself as an example. A notable instance of this is Jesus' teaching on prayer. He stimulated the disciples' interest by doing it Himself. Then they followed with the request, 'Teach us to pray." He then gave the model prayer (**Luke 11 :1-4**).

At every turn, Jesus provided a personal "how to." And these weren't examples of a secondary nature—they were examples woven into the fabric of daily living. Jesus' examples weren't merely simulated for the purpose of instruction. They were the real thing.

The disciplemaker must provide personal examples of what is being taught to the disciples. If there's a task or an activity which is better done according to a pattern, then a model will give impetus to the learning process. Examples should, ideally, be actual situations and not "staged." Disciples need to see how the variables of real life affect systematic approaches to ministry activities and personal disciplines.

The ministry of a discipler can't be all talk. Talk is easy. It's one thing to speak about the truths of Christian living; it's another thing altogether to live those truths.

Disciples may become discouraged or disheartened if all they acquire from their discipler is theory. They must be convinced that these principles of abundant living are actually livable. The discipler must demonstrate that the power of God to transform lives is a practical reality and not merely the stuff of clichés and hackneyed phrases.

This takes time. But, again, contemporary society seems to tie one's hands. Neither the discipler nor the disciples appear to have the time necessary to devote to such pursuits. But here is the beauty of disciplemaking:

DISCIPLEMAKING IS DONE "AS YOU GO."

This strongly implies that the strategy of discipleship is aimed primarily at one's peers, one's colleagues. The field of harvest for any person is his own sphere of activity. One need not make special trips outside of an established life-context in order to fulfill the Great Commission. On the contrary, the Great Commission makes every believer a missionary within his or her own circle of living. Whatever you do in the course of your life, you can make disciples.

Therefore, when you, as a disciplemaker, proclaim the gospel, it's in your own situation, within a familiar environment. When this results in the salvation of one or more persons, you will use the same environment as the discipling-ground, with the common experiences of that environment as examples of the Christian Faith in action.

Of course, this whole factor of example requires that you literally possess a life transformed by the Holy Spirit. The mediocre lifestyle displayed by many believers will not meet the demands of discipleship. Without a proper model, you cannot disciple others.

FACTOR FIVE: COMMITMENT

The level of commitment required to be a disciple of Jesus was high:

Matthew 16:24, 25

> "Then Jesus said to His disciples, 'If anyone wishes to come after Me, let him deny himself, and take up his cross, and follow Me. For whosoever wishes to save his life shall lose it; but whoever loses his life for My sake shall find it."

John 6:53-66

> "Jesus therefore said to them, 'Truly, truly, I say to you, unless you eat the flesh of the Son of Man and drink His blood, you have no life in yourselves. He who eats My flesh and drinks My blood has eternal life; and I will raise him up on the last day. For My flesh is true food, and My blood is true drink. He who eats My flesh and drinks My blood abides in Me, and I in him. As the living Father sent Me, and I live because of the Father; so he who eats Me, he also shall live because of Me. This is the bread which came down out of heaven; not as the fathers ate, and died; he who eats this bread shall live forever.' These

things He said in the synagogue, as He taught in Capernaum. Many, therefore, of His disciples, when they heard this said, This is a difficult statement; who can listen to it?' But Jesus, conscious that His disciples grumbled at this, said to them, 'Does this cause you to stumble? What then if you should behold the Son of Man ascending where He was before? It is the Spirit who gives life; the flesh profits nothing; the words that I have spoken to you are spirit and are life. But there are some of you who do not believe.' For Jesus knew from the beginning who they were who did not believe, and who it was that would betray Him. And He was saying, 'For this reason I have said to you, that no one can come to Me, unless it has been granted him from the Father.' As a result of this, many of His disciples withdrew, and were not walking with Him any more."

Jesus made each disciple count the cost. He required obedience and discipline. He rebuked them when they acted according to selfish motivations. When a great number of His followers (disciples in the looser sense) were not willing to meet Jesus' demands for discipleship, the Twelve remained faithful. They were committed—committed to **the point of no return.**

The outward movement of the gospel requires that each disciple make a **LIFE COMMITMENT**. "Commitment" is often a nebulous term. We say that one is "committed" to Jesus Christ, generally meaning that there has been an acceptance of Christ as Savior, an acknowledgement of His divine lordship. But while this use of the word is somewhat accurate, it fails to place any emphasis on the proper thing, that is, a transformed life.

COMMITMENT IS A VERY PRACTICAL WORD.

Can there be a true inward commitment without changes being manifest in the whole personality? It's one thing to say, "I am committed to democracy," and quite another to take the time necessary to cast one's vote. A commitment to democracy without participation in its due processes is to enjoy the benefits of democracy as a parasite. Many believers are not unlike this in their relationship to Christ.

The world is full of parasitic Christians who have delighted to take the benefits of Christ's blood as a safeguard against eternal damnation, while rejecting the call to deny one's self, take up one's cross and follow Him.

227

Commitment is the practical result of faith. A true saving faith results in commitment. At this point, study **James 2:1 4-26**.

True faith leads to action. In sports, it's often said that a player "committed" himself too early—as in the case of a basketball player who misjudges a rebound and jumps too soon, or gets up in the air as the result of a head-fake, thereby committing a foul. The player may have reacted mentally to several split-second options, but the moment he reacted physically—jumping, turning, passing, shooting—he was "committed" beyond the point of no return. **COMMITMENT MEANS ACTION**.

In the life of a believer, commitment means the same thing—action. This must be communicated to the disciple. The true meaning of commitment will be learned by a disciple as the discipler relates it to daily living. For example, if a discipleship meeting is to be held at 7:00 p.m., Thursday, each disciple must know that true commitment means being there on time, ready to learn. The believer's somewhat nebulous desire to be discipled is translated into a concrete commitment the moment he actually walks through the door.

By making every conscious effort to communicate the tangible nature of commitment, you'll build within a disciple an attitude of action, service, and responsibility. Where there is commitment, there is accomplishment. A lackadaisical approach to life is an insult to Christ.

FACTOR SIX: RESPONSIBILITY

Jesus required His disciples to fulfill appointed tasks.

Mark 6:7
> "And He summoned the twelve and began to send them out in pairs...."

They were required to do what they had learned. Jesus knew that teaching which only went into a "notebook" could never reach the world with the gospel. What is learned must be lived.

The ultimate assignment of responsibility came with the articulation of the Great Commission. This was the final note sounded in the disciples' instruction.

The disciplemaker must see to it that those being trained are directed to become "doers" and not merely "hearers." Disciples must experience involvement in ministry. This kind of on-the-job training prepares them for their own future ministries as disciplemakers.

One thing that the disciplemaker must constantly avoid is the notion that the spiritual growth gained through discipling is an end in itself. Disciples are being trained as instruments for the fulfillment of the Great Commission.

In a successful discipling situation, there will be spiritual maturation. There will be fellowship. The experience will be an enjoyable one. But there is a danger here. Human nature seeks comfort, convenience, and security. Within a brief period of time the atmosphere surrounding the relationship between disciples and disciplemaker may become, in the minds of those involved, a kind of release from the stresses of daily living-a means of relaxation, a good change of pace. At this point the group may turn inward upon itself and lose any sense of outward momentum. The discipler cannot allow this to happen, but must maintain in the group environment an attitude of personal responsibility-of sacrifice. Along each line of teaching there must be some creative sort of assigned responsibility which directly relates to that teaching. (See Chapter 29 for more insight on this point.)

FACTOR SEVEN: KNOWLEDGE

Something must be known before it can be taught. The knowledge to be gained in discipleship training is that of God's Word. Jesus taught the Word (Old Testament truth and His truth as its fulfillment). What we have seen as fundamentally necessary in the area of knowledge has been produced in this manual, which is designed to aid you in discipling others. The teaching provided through this manual forms a groundwork for the development of disciplemakers. But don't forget to apply all the discipling factors as best you can.

As you personally begin to disciple others, you'll become increasingly more adept at teaching. The Holy Spirit indwells you and will teach God's truths through you. The materials we've produced in this manual are designed to help your teaching by providing a format that's easy to follow, with ample visual helps.

BE CREATIVE!

Teaching can take place almost anytime and anywhere.

The remaining three discipleship factors will be covered in the next chapter.

CHAPTER 24
THE METHOD AND STRATEGY OF DISCIPLEMAKING
(Continued)

The final three factors of disciplemaking emphasize the movement of the gospel into the world through the personal ministry of the disciplemaker.

FACTOR EIGHT: GOAL

Being discipled isn't an end in itself—it has an ultimate GOAL. Jesus never let His disciples forget the reason they were following Him....

Matthew 4:19
> "And He said to them, 'Follow Me, and I will make you fishers of men.'"

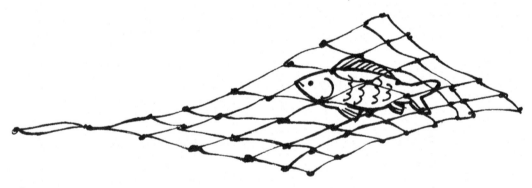

John 3:16
> "For God so loved the world, that He gave His only begotten Son, that whoever believes in Him should not perish, but have eternal life."

John 4:35
> "Do you not say, 'There are yet four months, and then comes the harvest'? Behold, I say to you, lift up your eyes, and look on the fields, that they are white for harvest."

Luke 19:10
> "For the Son of Man has come to seek and to save that which was lost."

Matthew 28:19
> "...Go therefore and make disciples of all the nations...."

The purpose of disciplemaking isn't spiritual growth, although that's part of it. The purpose of disciplemaking is to reach the world with the gospel. Disciplemaking is the plan by which the saving message of Christ is carried to the lost. Believers must be continually reminded of this. An integral part of discipleship training is to impress believers' minds and hearts with the fact that each is responsible to **FULFILL THE GREAT COMMISSION.**

FACTOR NINE: POWER

Jesus didn't send the disciples into the world under their own power, but sent the Holy Spirit to energize them with divine power—the power needed to carry out the Great Commission, the

POWER TO MAKE DISCIPLES.

Acts 1:8
> "...you shall receive power when the Holy Spirit has come upon you; and you shall be My witnesses both in Jerusalem, and in all Judea and Samaria, and even to the remotest part of the earth."

The Holy Spirit-given vertically to the Church at Pentecost and subsequently expanding horizontally to the Samaritans and all Gentiles (**Acts 8 and 10**)—provides the power for the propagation of the gospel through disciplemaking.

The Holy Spirit indwells every believer; therefore, every believer has the power necessary to be a discipler. There are no excuses!

There's an important point touched on in a previous chapter that needs to be re-emphasized here: Many credit the great expansion of the Church in the first century solely to the influence and activity of the Holy Spirit. But that's not entirely correct. The fact is that

THE HOLY SPIRIT WORKED THROUGH PROPERLY DISCIPLED PEOPLE.

This cannot be over-emphasized. Jesus spent His entire earthly ministry training, discipling, those who would begin the gospel explosion. And those men—and women, when you include the 120 who were, no doubt, discipled by the Apostles—began to make disciples of others according to the plan of the Great Commission. And those they discipled led others to Christ and discipled them; and on and on. The point is this:

WITHOUT DISCIPLEMAKING AS A FOUNDATION, THE HOLY SPIRIT WOULD HAVE NOTHING TO WORK WITH!

The Holy Spirit works through people—saved, discipled people—who are able to be used because they've been prepared according to God's plan. Had there been no discipling, had Jesus merely taught multitudes, had He not poured His life into His select few, there would have been no explosion, not even a fizzle! The power of the Holy Spirit energized the people who were obedient to the divine plan. And He will do the same today in the life of every believer who takes the Great Commission seriously and obeys it!

FAILURE TO MAKE DISCIPLES QUENCHES THE ACTIVITY OF THE HOLY SPIRIT.

Why? Because the Holy Spirit was sent specifically to empower disciplemakers (**Acts 1:8**) in order to bring about the fulfillment of the Great Commission! Christians who don't become disciplemakers grieve the Holy Spirit by being disobedient to Jesus' utmost command. The Holy Spirit moves through a channel...

John 7:38, 39

> "He who believes in Me, as the Scripture said, 'From his innermost being shall flow rivers of living water.' But this He spoke of the Spirit, whom those who believed in Him were to receive...."

...and that channel through which the Holy Spirit must flow is **YOU!** Don't stop God's love from flowing through you to the world by shutting the floodgate of disciplemaking with disobedience.

FACTOR TEN: LAUNCH

Jesus brought the time of instruction to a close and gave His disciples their marching orders.

Matthew 28:18-20

> "And Jesus came up and spoke to them, saying, 'All authority has been given to Me in heaven and on earth. Go therefore and make disciples of all the nations, baptizing them in the name of the Father and the Son and the Holy Spirit, teaching them to observe all that I commanded you; and lo, I am with you always, even to the end of the age."

(You do have these verses memorized by now, right?) As Jesus had planned all along, the disciples were to do with others what the Master had done with them— make disciples.

Disciplemaking isn't complete until the disciple becomes a discipler. The world is the target of discipleship. For any believer to ignore this fact and to settle for anything less than a personal ministry as a discipler is for that believer to live in overt spiritual rebellion.

MAKE DISCIPLES!

These ten factors of disciplemaking make up Jesus' disciplemaking methodology. There's only one way to make disciples, and that's His way.

But the Great Commission not only has this methodology, it also has a built-in

STRATEGY.

A strategy is an overall plan of action designed to reach a specific goal. Whereas the METHODOLOGY is the instrument of disciplemaking at the personal, individual level, the STRATEGY of the Great Commission is the orchestrated, over-arching battle plan for impacting the world with the gospel.

In preparing soldiers for war, a fighting methodology is taught which will enable troops to effectively and successfully engage the enemy in combat. They're taught to handle weapons and they learn the how-to's of hand-to-hand combat. Each soldier learns the methodology of fighting well. But when the time comes for battle, the soldiers don't (usually!) run onto the battlefield every-man-for-himself. That would prove disastrous. The methodology of combat trained into each soldier must be applied through a strategy in order to reach the larger goal. There must be a plan of attack!

In the same way, the methodology of disciplemaking is applied through a plan of action which will insure maximum results. Let's examine this strategy and see just how it works...

THE STRATEGY OF THE GREAT COMMISSION

Matthew 4:19, 20
> "And He said to them, 'Follow Me, and I will make you fishers of men.' And they immediately left the nets and followed Him."

At the outset of Jesus' ministry, He made this statement of His purpose for the lives of His followers-"I will make you fishers of men." By using the image of fishing, Jesus revealed the nature of the strategy of His Great Commission. (It's also interesting to note that Jesus emphasized reaching the world both at the beginning and end of His earthly ministry. It was His goal throughout.) They fished not with hooks, but with

NETS.

Remember, we discovered that each believer has a two-fold ministry to perform...

TO THE WORLD
and
TO THE CHURCH.

The ministry of the body is directed toward fellow believers. The ministry of discipleship is directed toward the world. When the body is gathered (**Hebrews 10:24, 25**), there is a building up of the church, spiritually. When the body is dispersed into the world—to jobs, homes, schools, etc.—it's like **CASTING A GREAT NET IN ORDER TO DRAW IN PEOPLE TO CHRIST AND INTO HIS BODY.**

But this can only occur when disciplemaking is the life-style of the believers involved. Each undiscipled person within a local church body represents a gaping tear, a hole, in the network of the Great Commission strategy—God's net for catching unbelievers for His glory.

DON'T BE A HOLE IN GOD'S NET OF DISCIPLEMAKING!

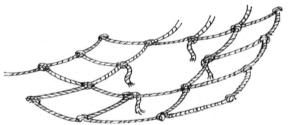

Great numbers of people are brought into the Kingdom only when disciples are properly related to Jesus' master plan. If you don't become obedient to Jesus' command to personally proclaim the gospel and make disciples of those you lead to Christ, then it will mean this: People will be slipping through your "hole in the net into an eternity of separation from God in a place called hell. **MAKE DISCIPLES!**

HOW IS THE NET MADE?

The net is made one "strand" at a time, by the application of the discipleship methodology to the lives of those brought to Christ.

DISCIPLEMAKERS MULTIPLY.

The goal of the methodology is to produce disciplemakers. The goal of the strategy is to consistently and systematically impact communities with the gospel until the entire world is reached.

The net of discipleship strategy grows by **SPIRITUAL REPRODUCTION**.

Spiritual reproduction is a process by which the Holy Spirit multiplies the number of believers using the vehicle of disciplemaking. Here's how it works, beginning with YOU...

Within just a few "generations" the network of disciplemakers begins to increase dramatically. At every juncture, new believers aren't allowed to become lost in any shuffle or to be overlooked. Each is thoroughly discipled and becomes a discipler, and the process continues on and on.

The object of the strategy is the numerical increase of the Church. However, the emphasis isn't on numbers, but on PEOPLE. Don't think for a moment that this is an easy thing to accomplish. Each disciple/disciplemaker is produced as the result of painstaking training, developing a deep interpersonal relationship, and the pouring out of one's life in self-sacrifice. There is a PRICE to be paid-the death of self.

DISCIPLEMAKING ISN'T MERELY MULTIPLICATION, BUT SELF-SACRIFICE.

How large can the net become? One example will be sufficient: If one disciplemaker, each year, won and discipled three others who, in the next year, each won and discipled three more, the number of disciplemakers at the end of two years would be 16.

YEAR ONE: 1 + 3 = 4

YEAR TWO: 4 x 3 = 12

+4 =   16 DISCIPLERS

If this same process is repeated for five years, the number of disciplemakers increases to over 1,000. At the end of ten years, the number is well over a million!

Now, you might think that this is a little idealistic. NOT AT ALL. Is it too much to expect that every believer could win and disciple three people in a year's time? It seems pretty realistic-it is possible! Why isn't it being done? Simply because the divine methodology and strategy has been almost entirely ignored.(By the way, in some parts of the world it is being done, with even more dramatic results than these.)

So, as we've seen, the net of discipleship is made and increased by **SPIRITUAL REPRODUCTION**.

HOW IS THE NET CAST?

The net is cast every time a body of believers departs after having gathered together. The body disperses, as disciplemakers, into the community, penetrating every niche of society. Each disciplemaker, being sensitive to the Spirit's leading and to the needs of others, applies the ten-factor methodology, beginning with evangelism. As a result, men and women find Christ.

HOW IS THE NET DRAWN IN?

The net is drawn in as disciplemakers personally train new believers and help them to become integrated in the local church body as functioning members. By the end of a discipling period, each new believer has not only taken up his symbiotic relationship with the church body, but also has become a part of the network of disciplemakers who are cast again into the world.

Remember, disciplemaking **IS** the Great Commission. There is one methodology and one strategy.

After His resurrection, Jesus re-emphasized His demand that the disciples become

FISHERS OF MEN

in a very powerful way: Study **John 21:1-19**.

Peter—a fisherman before being called by Jesus to be made a fisher of men—went fishing along with six other disciples. After fishing all night, they had not one minnow to show for their efforts. Unknown to them, Jesus was standing on the bank (He had already cooked breakfast). Jesus shouted to them across the water, commenting on their failure to catch any fish, and then told them to cast their net on the right hand side of the boat. They did. And to their surprise, they hauled in 153 big fish! Then they recognized Jesus and got to shore as fast as they could, with Peter diving in and swimming all the way (the typical Peter-approach!).

In this beautiful passage (verses 15-17) Jesus reminds Peter that people, not fish, are the calling of his life. And there's a significant lesson here for all disciplemakers, not just for Peter. Jesus made a point: When they followed His instructions, even in catching fish, they achieved maximum results. They didn't just catch some fish, they caught the maximum number of fish; their nets couldn't hold any more.

The Master's implication is obvious. In the three years the disciples spent with Him, Jesus had made them into fishers of MEN. Soon He would be casting them forth into the world, via the Great Commission, and He wanted them to remember that with men, as with fish, His precise instructions alone would bring about success. Jesus ended by reiterating to Peter the words He had spoken to him in the very beginning—"Follow Me." Then they turned to go to the mountain where they would receive Jesus' ringing command: "Go.. .make disciples," that is, "Go fishing for men by making disciples, and you'll draw in more than you can imagine!"

ONLY DISCIPLEMAKING CAN
REACH THE MAXIMUM NUMBER
OF PEOPLE FOR CHRIST.

Do evangelism in every way possible—personal evangelism, mass evangelism, every kind of evangelism. Dive off the Empire State building into a wet sponge if you want to—if it will result in people being saved! But remember, evangelism isn't the Great Commission. Those who do come to Christ as a result of evangelism must be made into disciplemakers by disciplemakers, so that the gospel has maximum penetration into the communities where they live.

There may be a hundred, even a thousand, different ways to do evangelism. **BUT THERE IS ONLY ONE WAY TO MAKE A DISCIPLE—THE WAY JESUS DID IT, AND COMMANDED IT.**

Believer, Satan will do everything in his power to keep you from becoming a disciplemaker. You must not let apathy and mediocrity rule your mind and heart. Being a disciplemaker means that you'll have to sacrifice many things—your time, your money, your emotions, your life—in order that the Holy Spirit may use you as a channel to reach many people for Christ. Don't rationalize away your responsibility. Don't think that the job is going to get done by attending church, studying the Bible, praying, teaching a Bible class, singing in a choir, preaching, or anything else. There's only one way to be obedient to the Great Commission—**MAKE DISCIPLES!**

THE LORD AND THE LOST AWAIT YOUR DECISION.

Let's close this section of our study with a review...

1. From memory, write out the Great Commission.

_____

_____

_____

_____

_____

_____

_____

2. Now, from memory, write out Acts 1:8.

_____

_____

_____

_____

_____

3. From what you've learned, what do these verses mean? Be brief.

_____

_____

_____

_____

_____

4. There are many ways to _____ but only

    one way to _____.

5. Who has the responsibility to carry out the Great Commission?

_____

6. What are the ten factors in disciplemaking?

_____

_____

_____

_____

_____

7. Why is it important to implement all ten factors when making disciples?

_____

_____

_____

_____

_____

8. The ten factors comprise the discipleship _____.

9. The goal of disciplemaking strategy is _____.

10. Why is a strategy important?

_____

_____

_____

11. The methodology of disciplemaking is drawn from what?

_____

_____

_____

_____

12. Why is the analogy of a "net" important to our understanding of disciplemaking?

_____

_____

_____

_____

_____

13. How does disciplemaking relate to the local church?

_____

_____

_____

14. What does discipleship do for the local church?

_____

_____

15. What has being discipled done for you?

_____

_____

_____

16. You realize that the next step in your discipling is to be launched as a disciplemaker. How do you feel about that?

_____

_____

_____

17. The Holy Spirit has given you the power to make disciples. Are you willing for Him to use you to reach others for Christ and to make disciples of them?

_____

_____

_____

At this point in your discipleship training it can be very meaningful to you and to your discipler to evaluate how things have progressed. Get together, one-on-one, with your discipler. Honestly and carefully evaluate your discipling relationship according to the ten factors of discipleship. State specifically how each factor has been applied, or what can be done to fulfill it. Especially be on the look-out for deficiencies, and make every effort to correct them. Together, fill out the following disciple/discipler EVALUATION:

FACTOR ONE: EVANGELISM

Disciple:

_____

_____

_____

Discipler:

_____

_____

_____

FACTOR TWO: PROXIMITY

Disciple:

_____

_____

_____

Discipler:

_____

_____

_____

FACTOR THREE: FRIENDSHIP

Disciple:

_____

_____

_____

Discipler:

_____

_____

_____

FACTOR FOUR: EXAMPLE

Disciple:

_____

_____

_____

Discipler:

_____

_____

_____

FACTOR FIVE: COMMITMENT

Disciple:

_____

_____

_____

Discipler:

_____

_____

_____

FACTOR SIX: RESPONSIBILITY

Disciple:

_____

_____

_____

Discipler:

_____

_____

_____

FACTOR SEVEN: KNOWLEDGE

Disciple:

_____

_____

_____

Discipler:

_____

_____

_____

FACTOR EIGHT: GOAL

Disciple:

_____

_____

_____

Discipler:

_____

_____

_____

FACTOR NINE: POWER

Disciple:

_____

_____

_____

Discipler:

_____

_____

_____

FACTOR TEN: LAUNCH

Disciple:

_____

_____

_____

Discipler:

_____

_____

_____

Next your discipler will introduce the Handbook section of this manual.

"GO...MAKE DISCIPLES!"

HANDBOOK
FOR
DISCIPLEMAKERS

CHAPTER 25
CALLED TO MAKE DISCIPLES

Jesus' ministry on earth climaxed with the giving of the Great Commission. The resurrection of Christ—that event unsurpassed, unequalled in the history of the world—was indeed of eternal proportions. But even with salvation secured through Jesus' death and resurrection, there remained one final and crucial task to be performed, without which the gospel itself might go virtually unnoticed by those for whom it was intended. The message must have a voice, yes, thousands, even millions of voices, by which the gospel can be proclaimed, so that mankind through the ages encounters Jesus

Christ, accepting or rejecting Him (**Romans 10:14, 15**). "Tetelestai!" Jesus cried from the cross. "It is finished!" Jesus had completed His substitutionary work for our salvation; He then assigned us, His followers, the final, critical task...

Matthew 28:19

> "Go. ..make disciples of all nations...."

Acts 1:8

> " ...you shall receive power when the Holy Spirit has come upon you; and you shall be my witnesses...."

The correct understanding of our Lord's words is absolutely essential for their proper fulfillment.

First, the Great Commission—Go...make disciples..."—is a command, not merely a suggestion or option. Not only is it a command, it's also directed to all believers. It isn't reserved for pastors or evangelists or professional ministers or "super-saints." It's directed at you, personally, no matter who you are. If you are a true believer in Christ, you have as your responsibility the fulfillment of this imperative. There are no exceptions.

Second, the imperative verb (in Greek) which makes **Matthew 29:19** a command is not "go," as many have wrongly assumed. The command isn't to "go" but to **"MAKE DISCIPLES."** The word translated "go" is a participle and means "as you go," conveying that wherever believers find themselves in the context of daily living, they are to make disciples. You need not become a vocational missionary and travel halfway around the world to be obedient to this command. It requires your obedience right where you are.

Third, Jesus meant for His followers to make disciples according to His established plan. This plan was thoroughly demonstrated in Jesus' own disciplemaking ministry. There's only one way to make disciples—the way Jesus did it. The Master's own discipling methodology and strategy are to be followed, and must be followed, in order for the Great Commission to be properly obeyed.

Fourth, it isn't enough just to be a disciple. You must become a disciplemaker. When Jesus gave the Commission, He transformed the meaning of "disciple" into "disciplemaker." One cannot be an obedient disciple without becoming, through disciplemaking, a disciplemaker. A disciple isn't merely a follower, but a proclaimer, for no one can please the Lord Jesus without being obedient to His most fervent command. It's His desire for us to be spiritually reproductive, proclaiming the gospel and making disciplemakers of those who receive Christ.

Fifth, those who receive Christ are to be properly integrated into a local church as they're being discipled. They're to be baptized in recognition of their adoption as children of God and joint heirs with Christ. Baptism is not only symbolic of their death and resurrection in Christ, but also of their acceptance by God into the body, their new family, the Church. Each disciple is to be taught about his relationship to the local church and his responsibility to be obedient to the command of Scripture concerning it (**Hebrews 10:24, 25**).

Finally, the power to fulfill the Great Commission is supplied by the Holy Spirit. The Holy Spirit is able to work through those who are committed to making disciples, empowering them as His witnesses. While there is no power to fulfill the Commission apart from the Holy Spirit, neither can the Holy Spirit fulfill it without willing, obedient, and properly discipled individuals, through whom He can work. Both must act in unison.

Disciplemaking is God's plan for impacting our planet with the gospel. As a disciplemaker, you are His personal representative to those within your own life-context. Your mission field is wherever you find yourself—at this or any moment in time. As you will discover, disciplemaking is not easy. In fact, it's hard work and there are many sacrifices involved. The fact that you have this handbook is, hopefully, evidence of your personal desire to make disciples. It's our prayer that God will multiply you spiritually through those you lead to Christ and disciple. May your personal ministry of discipleship be fruitful for God's glory!

As you begin to contemplate your personal spiritual reproduction through disciplemaking, it will be very beneficial for you to begin to visualize just exactly what your life-context includes. It is within the related spheres of your life-context that you'll minister, calling others to follow Christ and making disciples of those who receive Him. The following portion of this chapter is designed to help you get a mental picture of your life-context, and to begin to pray specifically for God to direct your personal ministry in each sphere. You can continue to use these for years to come as you continually become aware of the people the Lord brings across the path of your life.

Life-Context Spheres

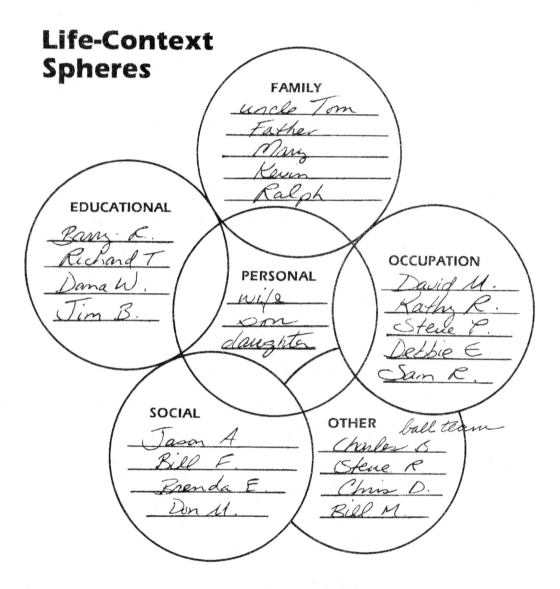

FAMILY
uncle Tom
Father
Mary
Kevin
Ralph

EDUCATIONAL
Barry C.
Richard T
Dana W.
Jim B.

PERSONAL
wife
son
daughter

OCCUPATION
David M.
Kathy R.
Steve P.
Debbie E
Sam R.

SOCIAL
Jason A
Bill F.
Brenda E.
Don M.

OTHER   ball team
Charles B
Steve R
Chris D.
Bill M

.....those who need Christ

FAMILY

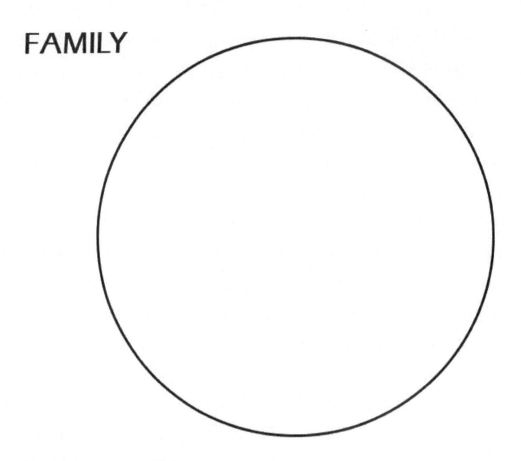

Life-Context Sphere

PERSONAL

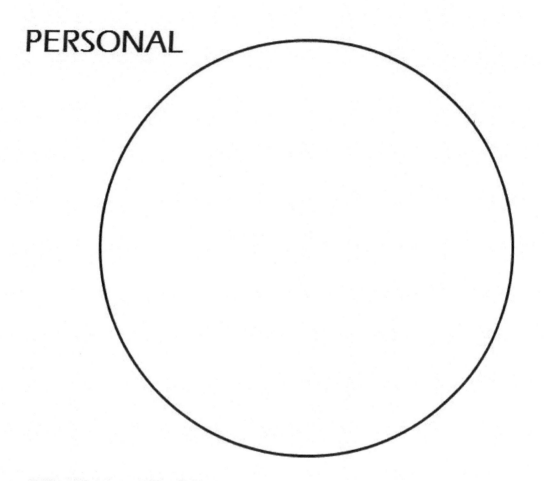

Life-Context Sphere

OCCUPATION

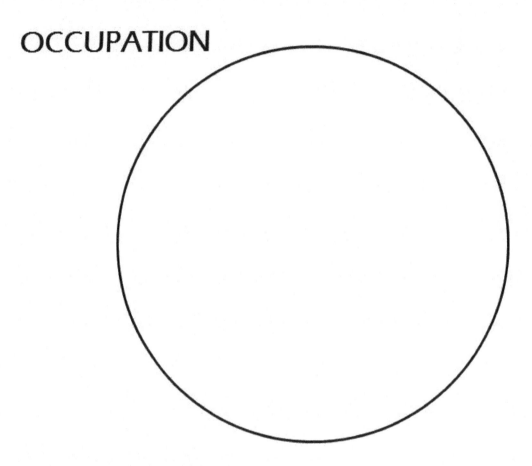

Life-Context Sphere

SOCIAL

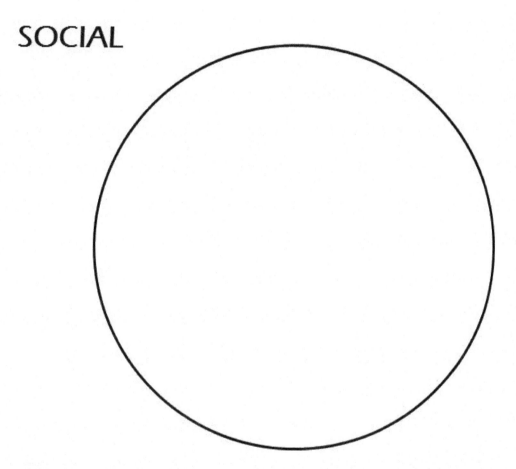

Life-Context Sphere

EDUCATIONAL

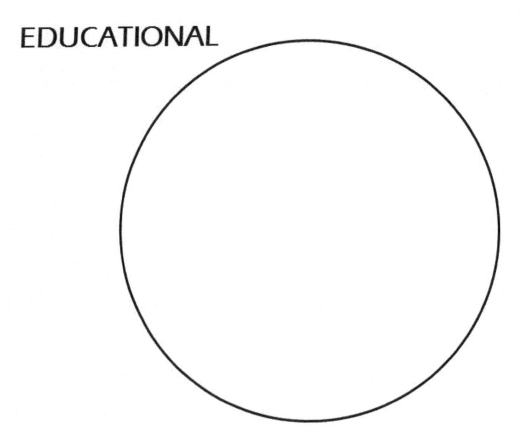

Life-Context Sphere

OTHER

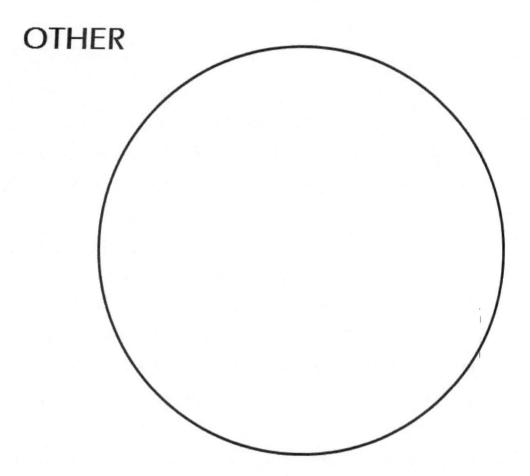

Life-Context Sphere

CHAPTER 26

THE DISCIPLER'S PERSONAL CHARACTER

As a disciplemaker, your own life will be your most important teaching aid. This is because you aren't just teaching knowledge (facts) to your disciples, but you are sharing your life with them. You're imparting your very being to them in order to make disciples of them (**I Thessalonians 2:8**). The quality of your life will provide a reflection of the person of Christ and will profoundly influence your ability to teach God's Word (**James 1:22**). Your personal character will significantly affect every person you seek to disciple. Certainly, you aren't perfect. But you must press toward that mark (**Matthew 5:48; Philippians 3:7-14**).

The Bible speaks about many qualities that should characterize every believer. One group of these qualities is called "the fruit of the Spirit" (**Galatians 5:22, 23**). Although these nine attributes—which are realized in your life as a result of the indwelling Holy Spirit—are specifically designated as being Spirit-related, this doesn't mean that the other character (personality) qualities mentioned in Scripture aren't Spirit-related. Actually, the word translated "such things" (**Galatians 5:23**) is a direct indication that this list of qualities is only representative of those "things" which develop in your life as a result of the Spirit's filling, which is brought about by your obedience to the lordship of Christ (**Ephesians 5:18**). Indeed, **Galatians 5:25** teaches us that every aspect of the believer's life is to be lived in obedience to and in the power of the Holy Spirit. To this list in Galatians can be added many other attributes of the spiritual life. As a disciplemaker, you will desire to walk by the Spirit. As you do you will develop these qualities...

LOVE

Love, according to Scripture, is the attitude which opens up one's life, unconditionally to a personal relationship with another. Love (Greek, agape) isn't given or expressed based on consciously or unconsciously determined prerequisites. Love expects nothing in return for its action, thought, emotion, or favor. Scripture says this beautifully:

1 John 4:19

> "We love, because He first loved us."

1 Corinthians 13:4-7

> "Love is patient, love is kind, and is not jealous; love does not brag and is not arrogant, does not act unbecomingly; it does not seek its own, is not provoked, does not take into account a wrong suffered, does not rejoice in unrighteousness, but rejoices with the truth; bears all things, believes all things, hopes all things, endures all things."

To ask the Lord to "love someone through me because I can't love that person myself' is to sadly miss the mark of the love we're to possess as believers. God wants you to love—with His quality of love, yes, but not passively or secondarily. He desires that you be transformed so that you are able to love actively and dynamically.

Study these passages: **Matthew 5:43-48; John 15:12, 13; Romans 13:8; Galatians 5:13, 14; Ephesians 5:2; Colossians 3:14; I Thessalonians 4:9; I John 3:14**.

JOY

Joy is closely related to grace (Greek, joy is "chara", grace is "charis"). The inner joy of the believer goes far beyond mere human happiness and contentment. Joy is that which permeates our beings as a result of the knowledge of who God is and the experience of the salvation which He has so graciously granted to us. Joy is the Spirit-imparted inner security that comes from a supernatural (faith) awareness that God is sovereign and in control of our lives and destinies. This joy is unshakable even in the midst of deep sorrow or persecution.

John 17:13

> "Jesus prayed, "But now I come to Thee; and these things I speak in the world, that they may have My joy made full in themselves."

James 1:2, 3

> "Consider it all joy, my brethren, when you encounter various trials; knowing that the testing of your faith produces endurance."

Romans 14:17

> "...for the kingdom of God is not eating and drinking, but righteousness and peace and joy in the Holy Spirit."

As you walk by the Spirit, this joy will become evident in your daily experience.

Study these passages: **John 15:11; Psalm 16:11, 43:4, 119:111; Jude 24; James 1:2.**

PEACE

Peace is one of the great themes in Scripture. Always, it is God who brings peace. Any peace offered by the world is only transitory or the result of delusion. Although the ultimate arrival of everlasting peace in the new heaven and new earth awaits future fulfillment, there is peace now for the people of God through a personal relationship with Him in the person of Jesus Christ. It's only through an abiding relationship with Jesus that we can experience true peace, His peace. We have no peace within ourselves, for even in our individual lives, as believers, we are at war (**Romans 7**). Again, this divine peace can be experienced only as you live a Spirit-filled life in obedience to Christ. This peace is not the facade of lack of conflict—there is a spiritual war constantly raging, initiated by Satan and his dark forces (**Ephesians 6:12**)—but it's the sense, the reality, of wholeness even in the path of pain and opposition. It's your confidence in God's absolute authority and victory.

John 14:27

> "Peace I leave with you; My peace I give to you; not as the world gives, do I give to you. Let not your heart be troubled, nor let it be fearful."

Romans 5:1

> "Therefore having been justified by faith, we have peace with God through our Lord Jesus Christ.'

Philippians 4:7

> "And the peace of God, which surpasses all comprehension, shall guard your hearts and your minds in Christ Jesus."

Study further in these passages: **Isaiah 32:17; Romans 8:6; Ephesians 2:14; Colossians 3:15; II Thessalonians 3:16; Hebrews 12:14; James 3:18; II Peter 3:14.**

PATIENCE

Patience isn't merely the art of waiting; that leads to procrastination. Patience is the ability to properly assess God's timing and to be obedient to His course of action. Patience (perseverance) is akin to endurance in that it causes one to remain faithful in the face of (seemingly) unresolved situations, knowing that God is still at work to accomplish His purposes. Patience doesn't mean that you are forbidden to act swiftly and decisively; it does mean that you will not seek to resolve matters according to your own whims and anxieties, but that you seek to learn God's lessons from the situations of daily living.

Romans 5:3

"And not only this, but we also exult in our tribulations; knowing that tribulation brings about perseverance [patience]."

James 1:3, 4

"Knowing this, that the trying of your faith worketh patience. But let patience have her perfect work, that ye may be perfect and entire, wanting nothing." (KJV)

Study also the following passages: **II Thessalonians 1:4; Titus 2:2; Hebrews 12:1; II Peter 1:6; Psalm 37:7; I Thessalonians 5:14; James 5:8; II Corinthians 1:6; II Timothy 3:10; Ephesians 4:2; Isaiah 40:31**.

KINDNESS

Kindness is that quality which give sensitivity to the personhood of others. In our fast-paced, technological age it's easy to overlook the individual worth of people as persons. Not to respect another's individuality is truly to be unkind. Each of us, through the intricate courses of our lives, has become exceedingly complex in the formation of our distinct personalities. To selfishly ignore the fragile complexity of others in the pursuit of our own egocentric comforts and pleasures is to preclude our being used by God to build up other persons in the faith. Kindness recognizes the delicate needs of others and orchestrates one's qualities and abilities in meeting those needs where possible.

Proverbs 19:22

"What is desirable in a man is his kindness...."

Kindness is one of God's attributes. Through a close personal relationship with Him, you will learn it.

Study these passages: **Romans 11:22; II Corinthians 6:5; Ephesians 2:7; Colossians 3:12; II Peter 1:7**.

GOODNESS

The word generally translated "goodness" can also be "uprightness." Goodness is personal transparency—the opposite of deception. To be upright is to invite others to examine one's life in the light of God's principles. Goodness is the foundation of a clean conscience before God and man.

II Thessalonians 1:11, 12

"To this end also we pray for you always that our God may count you worthy of your calling, and fulfill every desire for goodness and the work of faith with power; in order that the name of our Lord Jesus may be glorified in you, and you in Him, according to the grace of our God and the Lord Jesus Christ."

Study also: **Romans 15:14; Ephesians 5:9; Philemon 1:14**.

FAITHFULNESS

The word translated "faithfulness" in **Galatians 5:22** is simply the word "faith" (Greek, "pistis"). It's only by the context that one can determine how faith, or faithfulness is meant—whether referring to the faith that leads to salvation, or the faith necessary for the daily walk. Where "faith" is a reference to that faith in the believer's Spirit-led walk, it could be rendered "faithfulness." Either way, it's the attitude, the mind-set, of abiding in Christ (John 15). Faithfulness is the ability to trust God in every moment of life, day by day. Faithfulness leads to consistency in the Christian life. One's faithfulness to Christ produces a lifestyle which is exemplary and worthy of emulation.

Romans 1:17
"...the righteousness of God is revealed from faith to faith; as it is written, 'But the righteous man shall live by faith."

Galatians 2:20
"I have been crucified with Christ; and it is no longer I who live, but Christ lives in me; and the life that I now live in the flesh I live by faith in the Son of God, who loved me, and delivered Himself up for me."

Hebrews 13:7
"Remember those who led you, who spoke the word of God to you, and considering the outcome of their life, imitate their faith."

Whether in salvation (**Romans 6:23**) or in daily living, faith/faithfulness involves obedience.

Study these passages: **Matthew 23:23; II Thessalonians 3:5- 10; Romans 4:16-20; I Timothy 1:18, 19; II Corinthians 10:15**.

GENTLENESS

Gentleness has directly to do with our ability to relate properly to the problems of people. Gentleness (or meekness) causes one to withhold self-expression and self-exertion when the exercise of such would be at the expense of another's rights, feelings, or reputation. A domineering attitude is egocentric. Gentleness, while not without firmness and boldness, seeks to minister to others without self-centered attitudes of survival and conquest.

Galatians 6:1
"Brethren, even if a man is caught in any trespass, you who are spiritual, restore such a one in a spirit of gentleness; looking to yourself, lest you too be tempted."

II Timothy 2:24, 25
"And the Lord's bond-servant must not be quarrelsome, but be kind to all, able to teach, patient when wronged, with gentleness correcting those who are in opposition...."

Human nature impresses us to demand our rights in every situation. In your dealing with others, the Spirit-related quality of gentleness will allow you to reach out and meet the needs of people, trusting God, not yourself, for your preservation and protection.

Examine these Scripture passages: **I Corinthians 4:21; Ephesians 4:2; Colossians 3:12; I Timothy 6:11; I Peter 3:15**.

SELF-CONTROL

Self-control has to do frequently with sex because it is a biological appetite. The old nature (**Romans 7**) knows nothing of discipline in the biological appetites, especially in the realm of sexual function. Without the Spirit's control over these natural (soul/self-dominated) appetites, they will seek fulfillment without discretion or regard for the consequences. Self-control is the ability to direct one's physical desires toward the fulfillment of God's purposes, not for mere personal gratification.

I Corinthians 10:23, 24
> "All things are lawful, but not all things are profitable. All things are lawful, but not all things edify. Let no one seek his own good, but that of his neighbor."

In order for you to experience the abundant life, you must have this self-mastery. Without it there will be great anxiety, guilt, and, of course, God's severe discipline (**Hebrews 12**).

Study these passages: **I Corinthians 7:5, 8, 9; II Peter 1:5-8; Proverbs 2:10-22, 5:1-23**.

HOPE

Hope is the inner confidence in the omnipotence and sovereignty of God and His ability to carry out His plans and purposes. It's the assurance that God is at work to accomplish every facet of His will for this universe, specifically as Scripture has revealed it. It's that quality of the Spirit-controlled mind which causes one to see beyond the confines of immediate difficulties and pressures of life into the greater panorama of God's plan for the ages. it's to have a conscious perception (from God's Word) concerning the consummation of all things in the person of Christ.

Romans 5:1, 2
> "Therefore having been justified by faith, we have peace with God through our Lord Jesus Christ, through whom also we have obtained our introduction by faith into this grace in which we stand; and we exult in the hope of the glory of God."

Colossians 1:27
> "...God willed to make known what is the riches of the glory of this mystery among the Gentiles, which is Christ in you, the hope of glory."

I Timothy 4:10

> "For it is for this we labor and strive, because we have fixed our hope on the living God, who is the Savior of all men, especially of believers."

See these passages also: **Psalm 71:5; Romans 12:12; I Corinthians 13:13; Colossians 1:5; Titus 2:13; Hebrews 6:19; I Peter 1:3, 21; I John 3:2, 3**.

FORGIVENESS

Forgiveness is the spiritual ability to accept, in one's own mind and heart, the universal forgiveness of sin secured for all by Jesus' death on the cross—there is no true forgiveness in the heart of the carnal believer. Indeed, to personally deny our forgiveness to another is to make a mockery of what Christ has done on our behalf. Just as forgiveness (and acceptance) is basic to our relationship to God in Christ, so forgiveness is critical to the development of all relationships. To deny, by an unforgiving spirit, a person's access to one's life in the formation of a vital relationship is to deny Christ.

Matthew 6:14, 15

> "For if you forgive men for their transgressions, your heavenly Father will also forgive you. But if you do not forgive men, then your Father will not forgive your transgressions."

Ephesians 4:32

> "...be kind to one another, tender-hearted, forgiving each other, just as God in Christ also has forgiven you."

In your dealings with people, always remember that your fellowship with God is directly affected by your forgiveness-or lack of it-toward others.

Also look into these passages: **Matthew 6:12; Colossians 3:13; II Corinthians 2:5-11**.

SERVANT ATTITUDE

It's a patent natural trait of the human species (fallen) to seek to be served, for to be served is to exalt our egos. It's the characteristic of the Spirit-born, Spirit-led, to seek to serve others. This was Jesus' way. It must be ours. Truly, it's more blessed to give than to receive. A servant's attitude is one which is sensitive to the needs of others and not preoccupied with personal needs.

Galatians 5:13

> "...through love serve one another."

Study these passages: **I Peter 4:10, 11; Ephesians 4:12; Matthew 20:25-28**.

PURITY

Purity means sinlessness—not that we can attain sinlessness in this life, but purity must be a basic desire of every believer. Purity also means that one will not retain sin in one's practical experience, but will confess it and pursue freedom from sin (**I John 1:8-10**). One key to purity is the cleansing power of God's Word.

Psalm 119:9
> "How can a young man keep his way pure? By keeping it according to Thy word."

I Timothy 1:5
> "But the goal of our instruction is love from a pure heart and a good conscience and sincere faith."

I John 3:2, 3
> "Beloved, now we are children of God, and it has not appeared as yet what we shall be. We know that, if He should appear, we shall be like Him, because we shall see Him just as He is. And everyone who has this hope fixed on Him purifies himself, just as He is pure."

See these passages: **Psalm 73:1; Proverbs 20:11; Philippians 4:8; I Peter 1:22; Titus 1:15, 2:14; I Timothy 4:12**.

WISDOM

Wisdom—true spiritual wisdom as developed through one's walk in the Spirit—is the divinely given ability to make proper judgments concerning matters of daily living. Not to be wise, according to Scripture, is to be a fool. Wisdom not only chooses right over wrong, but discriminates keenly between good, better, and best. It's a spiritual sensitivity to the will of God based on realities, not merely on outward appearances which may deceive.

Proverbs 3:13, 14
> "How blessed is the man who finds wisdom, and the man who gains understanding. For its profit is better than the profit of silver, and its gain than fine gold."

James 1:5
> "But if any of you lacks wisdom, let him ask of God, who gives to all men generously and without reproach, and it will be given to him."

See these passages also: **Proverbs 1:20-33, 3:13-20, 8:1-9:18; Colossians 3:16; James 3:13-18**.

GENEROSITY

Generosity seeks to give to others before acquiring luxuries for one's self. A generous spirit prevents the believer from hoarding beyond the requirements of personal needs. This is a sore spot in the lives of many believers. Being generous does not mean giving to every outstretched hand and good cause; it does mean being open to God's leadership in the proper distribution of your time and possessions. We must follow God's leadership in this area with cheerfulness and humility.

Proverbs 11:25

"The generous man will be prosperous, and he who waters will himself be watered."

I Timothy 6:18

"Instruct them to do good, to be rich in good works, to be generous and ready to share."

II Corinthians 9:6, 7

"Now this I say, he who sows sparingly shall also reap sparingly; and he who sows bountifully shall also reap bountifully. Let each one do just as he has purposed in his heart; not grudgingly or under compulsion; for God loves a cheerful giver."

Study these Scripture passages: **Proverbs 22:9; Galatians 6:6-9; Luke 6:38**.

TRUSTWORTHINESS

The Bible has much to say about "whisperers" and "gossips." The one who is trustworthy keeps confidential information to himself. Trustworthiness is the ability to maintain silence concerning the faults, weaknesses, and sins of others, realizing that the broadcast of such information, in any context, is egotistical, and violates God's commands regarding such practices. Trustworthiness must be applied with enemies as well as with friends.

Proverbs 11:13

"He who goes about as a talebearer reveals secrets, but he who is trustworthy conceals a matter."

Trustworthiness also has to do with being Christ-like in all matters of speech, including telling the truth. Half-truths distort and deceive. One can do as much damage by telling only part of the truth as by lying.

Study these passages: **I Corinthians 4:2; Proverbs 12:17, 23:23; Psalm 51:6**.

INTEGRITY

"Integrity" as used in the Old Testament is related to the word "blameless" in the New Testament. Integrity is that quality developed in a Spirit-filled life which causes one to act, in all areas of life, according to God's ethic. A person with integrity doesn't live one way under scrutiny, supervision, or observation, and another way when all backs are turned. When you're watched, and when you're all alone without the possibility of being discovered, you must live according to the commands of God, who sees all.

Proverbs 10:9

"He who walks in integrity walks securely, but he who perverts his ways will be found out."

Proverbs 20:7

"A righteousness man who walks in his integrity-how blessed are his sons after him."

Ephesians 1:4

"...He chose us in Him before the foundation of the world, that we should be holy and blameless before Him."

Study these also: **Psalm 15:27; I Corinthians 1:8; Philippians 1:10, 2:15; Proverbs 2:7; Ephesians 5:27; Colossians 1:22**.

COURAGE

Courage is the mental attitude necessary for the completion of tasks which threaten us. Whether this threat is physical harm or mere personal embarrassment, courage leads us to act according to God's directive, knowing that the outcome is His will, whether deliverance or destruction (**Daniel 3:13-18**).

Psalm 27:14

"Wait for the Lord; be strong, and let your heart take courage; yes, wait for the Lord."

Micah 7:7, 8

"But as for me, I will watch expectantly for the Lord; I will wait for the God of my salvation. My God will hear me...Though I fall I will rise; though I dwell in darkness, the Lord is a light for me."

John 16: 33

"These things I have spoken to you, that in Me you may have peace. In the world you have tribulation, but take courage; I have overcome the world."

Study these Scripture passages: **Isaiah 35:4; II Corinthians 5:6-8; Acts 27:22-25; Philippians 1:14**.

HONESTY

The term "honesty" means not only being truthful, but it also conveys a willingness to be confronted with the truth and then to submit to it. Often it's a far easier thing to hide behind a lie rather than to face the truth. Without honesty, we weave a network of deceptions in order to live with ourselves and others, but a relationship with God isn't enjoyed in such a condition. Honesty recognizes and lives joyfully under the omniscience of God (**Hebrews 4:13**).

Proverbs 12:17, 19

> "He who speaks truth tells what is right, but a false witness, deceit...Truthful lips will be established forever, but a lying tongue is only for a moment."

You must never use the truth to damage another. Better silence than slander (**Proverbs 10:18**).

Study these also: **Ephesians 4:24, 25; 5:9; 6:14; Proverbs 3:3; 23:23**.

HUMILITY

Humility is viewing one's self from God's perspective and living accordingly. A person can only think higher of himself than he ought when God's perspective is blurred or obliterated. The truly humble see themselves as important to God's plan, yes; but they also realize that the extent of their personal worth is calculated only on the basis of who Christ is and their personal relationship to Him. Without Him they are nothing. With Him they are divinely significant.

Romans 12:16

> "Be of the same mind toward one another; do not be haughty in mind, but associate with the lowly. Do not be wise in your own estimation."

Isaiah 66:2

> "But to this one I [the Lord] will look, to him who is humble and contrite of spirit, and who trembles at My word."

This life offers ample opportunities for you to take the spotlight, and the flesh will pursue it. But remember, God can't do great works through a prideful heart (**Micah 6:8**).

Study these passages also: **Zephaniah 2:3; Philippians 2:3, 4; Proverbs 16:19; 29:23; Matthew 23:12; Colossians 3:12; Isaiah 57:15; James 4:6; Ephesians 4:2; I Peter 3:8; 5:5**.

COMPASSION

Compassion is that character trait which relates to the suffering—spiritual, mental, or physical—of others, resulting in genuine sorrow, and a desire to give personal aid. Compassion is more than sympathy. The word connotes empathy, or a projection of oneself into another's situation. It's one thing to watch in pity; it's quite another thing to act in compassion. Compassion means personal involvement even at the expense of one's reputation. Remember, the Lord ate with sinners, with those who needed a physician!

Matthew 9:10-13

> "And it happened that as He was reclining at table in the house, behold many tax-gatherers and sinners came and joined Jesus and His disciples at the table. And when the Pharisees saw this, they said to His disciples, 'Why does your Teacher

eat with the tax-gatherers and sinners?' But when He heard this, He said, 'It is not those who are healthy who need a physician, but those who are ill."

Colossians 3:12

"...as those who have been chosen of God, holy and beloved, put on a heart of compassion, kindness, humility, gentleness and patience...."

Study these passages: **Matthew 12:7, 20:34; Mark 1:41; Philippians 2:1.**

STEADFASTNESS

Steadfastness is often cited along with patience, but they are significantly different. Steadfastness can be applied to a number of areas. One must be steadfast in hope, through persecution and trials. One must also be steadfast in doctrine and faith. Steadfastness is the unrelenting tenacity which enables the believer to remain firmly anchored in God's principles in the face of opposition, whether human, natural, or demonic.

Isaiah 26:3

"The steadfast of mind Thou wilt keep in perfect peace, because he trusts in Thee."

I Corinthians 15:58

"Therefore, my beloved brethren, be steadfast, immovable, always abounding in the work of the Lord, knowing that your toil is not in vain in the Lord."

Look up these also: **I Thessalonians 1:3; Psalm 51:10, 57:7, 108:1; Hebrews 6:19; II Peter 3:17; Colossians 1:11, 23; II Thessalonians 3:5.**

HOLINESS

Holy means "set apart." Holiness, then, is "set-apartness." One may not often think of holiness as being very practical, but, in reality, it is a most practical quality. First, holiness is an attribute of God Himself. He is wholly set apart by His infinite uniqueness—there is no one in God's category but God Himself. Our holiness is from Him through Jesus Christ and sets us apart for His special use. By our position in Christ, we are holy. But holiness in daily living comes through obedience to Christ as one walks in the Spirit. This experiential holiness is realized by consciously setting one's self apart for God's use on a moment-by-moment basis, to do His will. It's living in God's will, by His power, therefore, in His holiness. Holiness has a great deal to do with doing, not only being (II Corinthians 1:12).

II Corinthians 7:1

"Therefore, having these promises, beloved, let us cleanse ourselves from all defilement of flesh and spirit, perfecting holiness in the fear of God."

Hebrews 12:9, 10

> "Furthermore, we had earthly fathers to discipline us, and we respected them; shall we not much rather be subject to the Father of spirits, and live? For they disciplined us for a short time as seemed best to them, but He disciplines us for our good, that we may share His holiness."

Study this marvelous quality in these passages: **I Thessalonians 3:13; I Corinthians 3:17; 7:34; Colossians 1:22; 3:12; I Peter 1 :15, 16; Romans 12:1; Ephesians 1:4; 5:27; II Timothy 1:9; II Peter 3:11**.

GODLINESS

Godliness is the attitude of fear and reverence which follows from a comprehension of the awesome magnificence of Holy God. Even the frail human thought of God's greatness and majesty brings the wise to their knees (**Proverbs 9:10; Psalm 8:3, 4**). Truly, one's perception of who God is most directly affects the character of one's life.

I Timothy 4:7, 8

> "...On the other hand, discipline yourself for the purpose of godliness; for bodily discipline is only little profit, but godliness is profitable for all things, since it holds promise for the present life and also for the life to come."

As you pursue godliness in your walk with Christ, your entire approach to life will be so transformed that you may very well be criticized or persecuted—mostly by "religious" people (**II Timothy 3:12**). But a godly life will lead many to salvation.

Study these passages also: **II Peter 1:3; I Timothy 2:2; 6:3-6, 11; II Peter 2:9; 3:11; Titus 1:1; Psalm 4:3; 37:28; 116:15**.

Obviously, the 24 qualities listed are only a sampling of those found in Scripture, but they do represent the major ones. Many Hebrew and Greek words give us a beautiful spectrum of spiritual attributes, the meanings of which shade into one another, creating a sense of their interwovenness in the believer's life. This orchestra of character qualities will become a reality in your life as you are obedient to the moving of the Holy Spirit, directly in connection with God's Word. It's by the Word that the Spirit of God deals with your old nature and causes the Spirit-born new self to become dominant, resulting in the development of these qualities in your conscious life (**Hebrews 4:12**).

We strongly suggest that you take each of these 24 spiritual qualities and make them the focus of your quiet-time for at least 24 days—and even repeat their study in your Bible study time. The following section of this chapter is for use in your quiet time for the purpose of becoming acquainted with these qualities. Use Scripture passages from this chapter and others as you discover them.

EXAMPLE:

DATE: 5-25

LOVE

PASSAGE: I Corinthians 13:4-7; I John 4:19;
Ephesians 5:2; Romans 13:8

THOUGHTS: It seems, especially from I Cor. 13,
that love is a lot more than just emotion—
it is an action as well.

PRAYER: Lord, fill me with your Spirit so that
I might be able to develop an attitude of
love.

LOVE
DATE:

PASSAGE:

THOUGHTS

PRAYER:

JOY
DATE:

PASSAGE:

THOUGHTS

PRAYER:

PEACE
DATE:

PASSAGE:

THOUGHTS

PRAYER:

PATIENCE

DATE:

PASSAGE:

THOUGHTS

PRAYER:

KINDNESS

DATE:

PASSAGE:

THOUGHTS

PRAYER:

GOODNESS

DATE:

PASSAGE:

THOUGHTS

PRAYER:

FAITHFULNESS

DATE:

PASSAGE:

THOUGHTS

PRAYER:

GENTLENESS

DATE:

PASSAGE:

THOUGHTS

PRAYER:

SELF-CONTROL

DATE:

PASSAGE:

THOUGHTS

PRAYER:

HOPE

DATE:

PASSAGE:

THOUGHTS

PRAYER:

FORGIVENESS

DATE:

PASSAGE:

THOUGHTS

PRAYER:

SERVANT ATTITUDE

DATE:

PASSAGE:

THOUGHTS

PRAYER:

PURITY

DATE:

PASSAGE:

THOUGHTS

PRAYER:

WISDOM

DATE:

PASSAGE:

THOUGHTS

PRAYER:

GENEROSITY

DATE:

PASSAGE:

THOUGHTS

PRAYER:

TRUSTWORTHINESS

DATE:

PASSAGE:

THOUGHTS

PRAYER:

INTEGRITY

DATE:

PASSAGE:

THOUGHTS

PRAYER:

COURAGE

DATE:

PASSAGE:

THOUGHTS

PRAYER:

HONESTY

DATE:

PASSAGE:

THOUGHTS

PRAYER:

HUMILITY

DATE:

PASSAGE:

THOUGHTS

PRAYER:

COMPASSION

DATE:

PASSAGE:

THOUGHTS

PRAYER:

STEADFASTNESS

DATE:

PASSAGE:

THOUGHTS

PRAYER:

HOLINESS

DATE:

PASSAGE:

THOUGHTS

PRAYER:

GODLINESS

DATE:

PASSAGE:

THOUGHTS

PRAYER:

CHAPTER 27

THE DISCIPLER'S PERSONAL DISCIPLINE

The life of a disciplemaker must be not only a life of **BEING** but also one of **ACTION**.

Matthew 7:24, 25

"...every one who bears these words of Mine, and acts upon them may be compared to a wise man, who built his house upon the rock; and the rain descended and the floods came, and the winds blew, and burst against that house; and yet it did not fall; for it had been founded upon the rock."

James 1:21-25

"Therefore putting aside all filthiness and all that remains of wickedness, in humility receive the word implanted, which is able to save your souls. But prove yourselves doers of the word, and not merely hearers who delude themselves. For it any one is a hearer of the word and not a doer, he is like a man who looks at his natural face in a mirror; for once he has looked at himself and gone away, he has immediately forgotten what kind of person he was. But one who looks intently at the perfect law, the law of liberty, and abides by it, not having become a forgetful hearer but an effectual doer, this man shall be blessed in what he does."

Why must action be the product of your relationship with Christ and your eternal position in Him? Because God has not saved us to sit, but to march! The Bible compares believers to soldiers and athletes...

II Timothy 2:3-5

"Suffer hardship with me, as a good soldier of Christ Jesus. No soldier in active service entangles himself in the affairs of everyday life, so that he may please the one who enlisted him as a soldier. And also if any one competes as an athlete, he does not win the prize unless he competes according to the rules."

II Timothy 4:7, 8

"I have fought the good fight, I have finished the course, I have kept the faith; in the future there is laid up for me the crown of righteousness, which the Lord, the righteous Judge, will award to me on that day; and not only to me, but also to all who have loved His appearing."

Hebrews 12:1-2

"Therefore, since we have so great a cloud of witnesses surrounding us, let us also lay aside every encumbrance, and the sin which so easily entangles us, and let us run with endurance the race that is set before us, fixing our eyes on Jesus the author and perfector of faith, who for the joy set before Him endured the cross, despising the shame, and has sat down at the right hand of the throne of God."

The common denominator of the soldier and the athlete is **DISCIPLINE**. Without discipline, nothing can be accomplished, not as an athlete, not as a soldier, not as a Christian. Studying the Bible requires discipline. Praying requires discipline. Witnessing requires discipline. Disciple-making requires discipline. Being an active church member requires discipline. Let's face it—doing anything effectively and with regularity requires discipline! The fact of the matter is that nothing significant is ever accomplished apart from the application of discipline. One must beware, however, of the great difference between discipline and that insidious robber of the joy of serving...legalism.

DISCIPLINE VS. LEGALISM

The most disciplined (perfect) life ever lived was that of our Lord Jesus Christ; yet He condemned the legalism of the religious elite. The Law (Old Testament) demanded obedience, but the religious leaders of Jesus' day approached obedience without regard for God and His leadership.

Law (command) does not exclusively lend itself to legalism; in fact, any form of order or call for obedience, whether under law or grace, is in danger of being invaded by attitudes of legalism. You, as a New Testament Christian, are as much in danger of legalistic entanglements as were the Pharisees of Jesus' day. This is shown to be true by Paul in Romans, where he strongly asserts that "...the Law is holy and the commandment is holy and righteous and good...for we know that the Law is spiritual...." Carefully study **Romans 5-8**, for a thorough lesson on this principle (the entire book of Galatians is also devoted to this problem).

Legalism is imposed upon the observance of the Law but is not a provision or inherent characteristic of the Law itself. The Law was a "tutor" to lead us to Christ (**Galatians 3:24, 25**). That we as Christians are "not under the Law, but under grace" (**Romans 6:14**) does not mean that we're removed from the possibility of slipping into legalism. Law does not equal legalism; in contrast, grace does not mean that we're allowed to "sin that grace might increase" (**Romans 6:1**). Obedience is required under both law and grace. In every age (dispensation)-yes, even today- obedience has been demanded. The issue is not whether or not the Christian has specific commands to obey (we do!); the key issue is how we're to respond to God's call for obedience. How can we be obedient believers and avoid the pitfall of legalism? First, we must understand the difference between legalism

282

and discipline. Legalism is the improper approach to obedience; discipline is the correct response.

BASIC DEFINITIONS:

Discipline: The spiritual attitude, derived from inner transformation, which allows the believer to be trained, instructed, and guided, leading to self-control, orderliness, and efficiency.

Legalism: The carnal attitude which insists upon strict adherence to laws, rules, regulations, forms, and tradition, as if to produce a change in the life or to bring "more" acceptance before God.

Each of the personal disciplines to be presented in this chapter has a Scriptural command (principle} directly related to it. In order to follow God's desires in these areas, we must be obedient, not legalistically, but through discipline. You see, legalism produces a response based on reward or punishment; but discipline produces a response based on love and gratitude. You can get a clear picture of the difference between the two from the following:

Legalism leads to hypocrisy.
Discipline leads to consistency.

Legalism expects a reward.
Discipline serves without thought of gain.

Legalism exalts the self.
Discipline means death to self.

Legalism leads to pride.
Discipline brings humility.

Legalism must conform to the law as an end in itself.
Discipline is obedient with intent to build character.

Legalism attempts a conformation from without.
Discipline is the product of an inward transformation.

Legalism requires the same from others.
Discipline desires to instruct others in love.

Legalism is based on works.
Discipline is centered in grace.

Legalism brings bondage.
Discipline is the true expression of Christian freedom.

Legalism makes time for duties.
Discipline gives time for service.

Legalism says "no" to protect "piety."
Discipline says "no" because of insight and understanding.

Legalism is religion.
Discipline is relationship.

Discipline is our response of love and gratitude to God for what He has done for us in Christ. It's the practical outworking of our desire to please Him in all aspects of life.

Legalism threatens when we approach the tasks of the Christian life with no conscious thought of our personal relationship with Jesus Christ.

Abiding in Him (**John 15**) is the key to discipline. Your conscious awareness of His presence will guard against treadmill-like living and will open the gate to the exciting path of walking in the Spirit.

Proverbs 23:12

"Apply your heart to discipline, and your ears to words of knowledge."

Colossians 2:5

"For even though I am absent in body, nevertheless I am with you in spirit, rejoicing to see your good discipline and the stability of your faith in Christ."

I Timothy 4:7

"...discipline yourself for the purpose of godliness."

II Timothy 1:7

"For God has not given us a spirit of timidity, but of power and love and discipline."

As believers we're to discipline our lives in order to fulfill the commands of the Lord. We're to be living sacrifices (**Romans 12:1, 2**). God's commands for believers aren't burdens, but are joyous opportunities for us to express commitment to His lordship and love for our wonderful Savior.

I John 5:1-3

"Whoever believes that Jesus is the Christ is born of God; and whoever loves the Father loves the child born of Him. By this we know that we love the children of God, when we love God and observe His commandments. For this is the love of God, that we keep His commandments; and His commandments are not burdensome."

The following personal disciplines are crucial for your life as a disciplemaker. These are the commandments of Christ concerning your daily life—these are the "dos" of the Christian walk.

YOU MUST STUDY GOD'S WORD

II Timothy 3:16,17

> "All Scripture is inspired by God and profitable for teaching, for reproof, for correction, for training in righteousness; that the man of God may be adequate, equipped for every good work."

Study also these important passages: **Matthew 4:4; II Timothy 2:15; I Peter 2:2; Hebrews 4:12**.

Satan abhors disciplemakers because they're doing what God requires for reaching the world with the gospel. One of the ways the evil one will attack you in order to keep you from making disciples is by getting you out of God's Word. Satan knows that the Word is the only offensive weapon that the believer possesses (**Ephesians 6:13-17**), and he'll do everything in his power, through his dark forces (**Ephesians 6:10-12**) to keep you from reading and studying the Bible. But don't be deceived. Stand firm in your commitment to the Word. Read it. Study it. Memorize it. Meditate on it. Your spiritual growth depends of your daily feeding from God's Book. Set out a specific daily Bible study plan and stick to it!

YOU MUST PRAY

Philippians 4:6, 7

> "Be anxious for nothing, but in everything by prayer and supplication with thanksgiving let your requests be made known to God. And the peace of God, which surpasses all comprehension, shall guard your hearts and your minds in Christ Jesus."

Study also: **Ephesians 6:18; I Thessalonians 5:17; Hebrews 4:16**.

Prayer is the privilege of communicating one-on-one with God. The power of prayer is God's power, active in and through your personal relationship with Jesus Christ. Jesus' model prayer (**Matthew 6:9-13**) gives you an idea of the kinds of things you should pray about. Prayer is communicating with God in His presence, and includes many facets such as petition, intercession, desiring, supplication, asking, inquiring, beseeching. The ability to pray is supplied by the indwelling Holy Spirit who enables us to know God's mind in matters for which we pray (**I Corinthians 2:10-16**). Even when we don't know how or what to pray, the Spirit intercedes for us directly with the Father, and, therefore, God's will is accomplished in spite of our weaknesses in prayer (**Romans 8:26-28**). Prayer is the vital, practical link between God's will and our own lives. Pray often. Go to the Lord in prayer daily.

YOU MUST RELATE PROPERLY TO YOUR FAMILY

Turn in your Bible to **Ephesians 5:22-6:4**. Read and study these verses carefully.

How very important it is to relate in a proper manner to each member of your family. Your relationships with your family members-whether to parents, children, or mate-must be directed by the Holy Spirit. Poor family relationships damage all other areas of life, even our ability to pray (I Peter 3:7-9). As a disciplemaker, your example in this area will greatly influence those you disciple. Your family must have first priority in your personal relationships. Neglect in this area will have serious results.

YOU MUST MAKE DISCIPLES

Matthew 28:19

> "...Go...make disciples...."

You must proclaim the gospel to the lost within your life-context, and make disciples of those who receive Christ. Disciples are made by your personal application of Jesus' ten disciplemaking factors, training them from the Word until they, too, are able to make disciples. This is the will of God for every Christian's life. Disciplemaking isn't an option.

YOU MUST PRACTICE FELLOWSHIP

Hebrews 10:24, 25

> "...and let us consider how to stimulate one another to love and good deeds, not forsaking our own assembling together, as is the habit of some, but encouraging one another; and all the more, as you see the day drawing near."

See also these passages of Scripture: **I Corinthians 12:18, 20, 25; Hebrews 3:13**.

Specifically, the act of fellowship is carried out in a local church body. You cannot be in God's will and ignore your personal responsibility to the local body of believers. Through the fellowship of the body we receive spiritual motivation from other believers through the Lord's special presence (**Matthew 18:20**), and we receive spiritual support for daily living (**II Corinthians 1:3, 4; I Thessalonians**

5:11). Through fellowship of the local church body we also experience mutual love (**John 13:34, 25; I John 4:11, 5:11**).

We're to be bound to other believers—not unbelievers (**II Corinthians 6:14-16**)—in the exercise of spiritual gifts and abilities so that the body might be built up (**I Corinthians 12:4-7; Ephesians 4:11-16**). Your ministry to the body is as vital to the body as the body's ministry is to you.

YOU MUST SACRIFICE

I Peter 2:5

> "...you also, as living stones, are being built up as a spiritual house for a holy priesthood, to offer up spiritual sacrifices acceptable to God through Jesus Christ."

See these verses also: **Romans 12:1; Philippians 2:17**.

The key to sacrifice is cost. Jesus gave the ultimate, eternal sacrifice—Himself—and it was the greatest price possible (**I Corinthians 6:20; 7:23**). As His followers we, too, have a great price to pay in living godly, holy lives. In order to follow Christ, one must count the cost (**Luke 14:25-30**). But, be sure, the rewards of being His faithful disciple are great, and anything you might give up, lose, or suffer for Jesus' sake will be far outweighed by the benefits of belonging to Him (**Philippians 3:7-10; I Corinthians 2:9**).

YOU MUST BE A GOOD STEWARD

Luke 16:10

> "He who is faithful in a very little thing is faithful also in much; and he who is unrighteous in a very little thing is unrighteous also in much."

This verse is from the parable of the unrighteous steward (**Luke 16:1-13**). A steward is one who supervises or administrates the estate of another. The point of this story—which is very revealing—is found in verse 8, and, put simply, is this: The unsaved have more acumen in monetary affairs than do believers. By way of application, we might say this: If believers handled their material dealings as prudently for the cause of Christ as non-believers do for worldly gain, the advancement of the gospel would greatly benefit. You must realize that everything you have in this life-time and possessions-belongs to God and you're only a steward of these things, being responsible for the proper and prudent use of all for God's glory.

YOU MUST SERVE OTHERS

James 2:15

> "If a brother or sister is without clothing and in need of daily food, and one of you says to them, 'Go in peace, be warmed and be filled,' and yet you do not give them what is necessary for their body; what use is that?"

Also carefully study **Matthew 25:34-40**.

How easily it is to overlook our responsibility to minister to others—physically as well as spiritually. Don't become blinded to the spiritual quality of rendering service for the physical welfare of people. Don't be satisfied only with that which appears "spiritual," but be disciplined to reach out to others with "non-spiritual" hurts.

YOU MUST DISPLAY
PROPER CONDUCT

Colossians 4:5

> ...conduct yourselves in a manner worthy of the gospel of Christ...."

See also: **Philippians 1:27; I Peter 1:17**.

Conduct applies to every facet of your life. It has to do with your actions, practical and moral. As a disciplemaker, your conduct is highly important. Your actions are an outward reflection of your inner transformation and a powerful influence on those you disciple. Others cannot look at your heart, as the Lord does, but will view your conduct as the manifestation of your relationship to Christ. We're able to have holy conduct, that is, a conduct which is set apart (distinct) from that of the world, witnessing to the life-changing power of Christ.

There are other aspects in the Christian life which are directly related to discipline, such as decision-making (**Matthew 5:37**), influence (**I Corinthians 9:19-23**), rest (the Sabbath principle; **Exodus 20:8-11**), and living in general (**Colossians 3:17**), including that which is done in education, business, homemaking, recreation, etc. God does require obedience. It's basic to our love for Him. Obedience is the mark of the Spirit-filled life, not some spiritual gift (the Corinthian believers lacked in no gift, yet they certainly weren't walking by the Spirit). Being filled with the Spirit (**Ephesians 5:18**) is a matter of obedience—one's volitional response of obedience to the Holy Spirit in every aspect of life. The fruitful Christian life, abiding in Christ, is a matter not just of relationship, but of obedience in our relationship to Him.

Take time to consider your personal disciplines. Make a conscious commitment to express your love and gratitude to Christ by obedience to His desires. Use each of the disciplines cited above as themes for a series of quiet times. The strength to carry out these disciplines-the Holy Spirit-is resident within you. Allow God to speak to you during these quiet times, leading you to an understanding of His will in each matter. As your desire to obey God grows, the Holy Spirit will empower you to master these disciplines.

GOD'S WORD

DATE:

PASSAGE:

THOUGHTS

PRAYER:

PRAYER

DATE:

PASSAGE:

THOUGHTS

PRAYER:

FAMILY

DATE:

PASSAGE:

THOUGHTS

PRAYER:

DISCIPLING

DATE:

PASSAGE:

THOUGHTS

PRAYER:

FELLOWSHIP

DATE:

PASSAGE:

THOUGHTS

PRAYER:

SACRIFICE

DATE:

PASSAGE:

THOUGHTS

PRAYER:

STEWARDSHIP

DATE:

PASSAGE:

THOUGHTS

PRAYER:

SERVING OTHERS

DATE:

PASSAGE:

THOUGHTS

PRAYER:

CONDUCT

DATE:

PASSAGE:

THOUGHTS

PRAYER:

CHAPTER 28

PROCLAIMING CHRIST

Your initial responsibility as a disciplemaker is to proclaim the Gospel of Jesus Christ to those who don't know Him. Proclamation is the first factor of making disciples. Obviously, if one is to be discipled, there must be a conversion first. To every believer has been given the task of telling the good news to the lost.

YOUR TASK

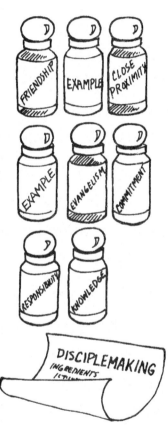

The word "task" is a good one in relation to witnessing because it implies doing something. "Task" also emphasizes the non-accidental nature of sharing Christ. In order to present the gospel, you must attend to it consciously. Witnessing is a conscious effort because there is no such thing as a silent witness! Certainly, a holy, godly life is important as proof of your own walk with Christ, but unbelievers are spiritually blind (**II Corinthians 4:4**) and, therefore, incapable of reading your actions in order to understand the message of salvation. You must speak in order for that message to be heard. God has placed you in a unique life-context for the purpose of proclaiming Christ to the people within your sphere. This is your task.

YOUR TRAINING

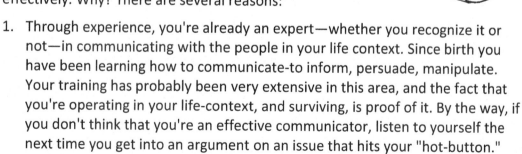

Contrary to much popular opinion, you don't need a great deal of training to be able to share Christ effectively. Why? There are several reasons:

1. Through experience, you're already an expert—whether you recognize it or not—in communicating with the people in your life context. Since birth you have been learning how to communicate-to inform, persuade, manipulate. Your training has probably been very extensive in this area, and the fact that you're operating in your life-context, and surviving, is proof of it. By the way, if you don't think that you're an effective communicator, listen to yourself the next time you get into an argument on an issue that hits your "hot-button."

2. If you're a believer, you already know what the gospel is-or you wouldn't be a Christian.

3. The people to whom you will present Christ-those in your life context-share at least a part of the same life-context you do; therefore, a common ground for communication already exists.

So why don't more believers share Christ? There are at least six things that will keep you from witnessing to others...

1. **PRIDE**—You don't want to harm your "image."

2. **FEAR**—You may be afraid of embarrassment or rejection. These are Satan's ploys. You talk about everything else under the sun. Why would you be afraid to mention Jesus?

3. **FALSE DOCTRINE**—Someone (not God's Word!) has said that witnessing is a special gift for some people, but you "don't have it."

4. **NOT FEELING LED**—Your feelings may depend on what you ate for lunch!

5. **APATHY**—There may be a spiritual problem in your life that gives you a "don't care" attitude about sharing your faith. Identify it and deal with it. Seek help from mature Christians who are witnesses.

6. **COMPENSATIONS**—All of your Bible studies, prayers, fellowships, church activities, etc., aren't going to make up for ignoring your responsibility to witness.

Satan will do everything in his power to keep your mouth shut when it comes to Jesus Christ. The deceiver will gladly let you talk about Sunday School, your preacher, the church choir, the youth group, the revival. But when it comes down to sharing about Jesus Himself, Satan will provide a million excuses and rationalizations for your not doing so. Face up to this possibility: Satan may have your tongue in his grip when the gospel threatens to roll off it! This need not be the case. All that's necessary to free your voice for the proclamation of the gospel is **OBEDIENCE**. When you obey, the Holy Spirit empowers you—you become a Spirit-filled witness who cannot be silenced.

I Corinthians 9:16
"For if I preach the gospel, I have nothing to boast of, for I am under compulsion; for woe is me if I do not preach the gospel."

Start sharing the gospel because Jesus commanded it, and you'll be filled with God's love for the lost; your fear will dissipate; your apathy will evaporate.

This doesn't mean that you need no training at all. Certainly, you must be discipled. You must be grounded in God's Word, in prayer, in fellowship. The fact that you (1) already know how to communicate effectively within your life-context, (2) already know what the gospel is, and (3) share a common ground for communication with everyone in your life-context, can be enhanced considerably by whatever you do to become a more proficient witness-whether specialized training or just gaining lots of personal experience. You can also learn how to increase your life-context, for example, by penetrating into new areas of society. It's true that the more often you share the gospel, the more fluent you become in communicating it.

But is it possible to become, through time, very mechanical in witnessing? Can you say the same basic words so many times that they become more or less automatic? Most of the time this possibility is overplayed. Of course, one can get to be almost "impersonally mechanical," but the problem isn't with the practice, but with the person. The answer to this is a very simple one: ABIDING IN CHRIST. Your witnessing will be as personal, sensitive, and Spirit-led as is your daily walk with the Lord. Your conscious relationship with Christ will directly affect your witnessing, and everything else that you do.

Don't, however, confuse the impersonal/mechanical with the trained/efficient. Just because you're able to present the gospel with clarity and, if need be, with brevity, doesn't mean that you're destined to become robot-like. Actually, a well-practiced presentation can allow you to be more sensitive to the other person because you aren't preoccupied with "getting it right" but with the person's spiritual need.

YOUR MESSAGE

It's at this point that many Christians fail in their witnessing. Why? Because they fail to be scripturally specific about the gospel they're sharing. The best way to get an idea of this failure in its different forms is to enumerate some of them:

1. talking about God in generalities

2. talking about church involvement

3. letting people know that you're a Christian

4. talking about how Christ has changed your life

5. talking (arguing?) about issues such as creation vs. evolution, morality, etc.

6. trying to influence another's behavior (someone stops cursing around you because they know you don't approve)

7. inviting people to church functions and programs

8. getting in a "good word" about being a Christian

9. using a lot of "Christian jargon" and clichés

10. displaying "Christian paraphernalia" (lapel pins, bumper stickers, etc.)

11. passing out tracts or pamphlets

12. conspicuously carrying a Bible

Certainly, there's nothing basically wrong with any of these things; in fact, there may be times when some of them are quite appropriate in instances when there's absolutely no other means of witnessing. Indeed, such things as your personal testimony can be very effective. But the point is that, alone, none of the things listed above is New Testament proclamation.

Witnessing in the New Testament sense is proclaiming (telling, informing, announcing) the gospel to unbelievers. The gospel is a very specific thing. It's God's message to people about the salvation available through Jesus Christ. The Bible tells us precisely what the gospel is...

John 3:16

"For God so loved the world, that He gave His only begotten Son, that whoever believes in Him should not perish, but have eternal life."

I Corinthians 15:1-4

"Now I make known to you, brethren, the gospel which I preached to you, which also you received, in which also you stand, by which also you are saved, if you hold fast the word which I preached to you, unless you believed in vain. For I delivered to you as of first importance what I also received, that Christ died for our sins according to the Scriptures, and that He was buried, and that He was raised on the third day according to the Scriptures."

II Corinthians 5:18-20

"Now all these things are from God, who reconciled us to Himself through Christ, and gave us the ministry of reconciliation, namely, that God was in Christ reconciling the world to Himself, not counting their trespasses against them, and He has committed to us the word of reconciliation. Therefore, we are ambassadors for Christ...."

These representative verses show us exactly what the gospel is. The following elements, given clearly in the above passages, comprise the gospel message (additional Scripture passages are cited with each point):

1. God loves each person and desires to have a personal relationship with him/her (**I John 4:19; II Peter 3:9; I Corinthians 8:3**).

2. People have been separated (spiritual death) from God because of sin, and there is nothing any person alone can do to bridge this separation and gain access to God. This separation is eternal (**Romans 3:23, 6:23; Revelation 20:11-15**).

3. Jesus Christ—God in human form, the Son of God—came to earth and paid the penalty for the sins of every person by dying on the cross in our place. Jesus then rose from the dead thereby conquering death and giving eternal life to those who follow Him. Jesus is the only way to God (**John 14:6; Romans 5:8, 8:2; II Corinthians 5:21; Hebrews 9:26**).

4. Those who personally receive Christ through faith are granted eternal and abundant life, having been born again into a personal relationship with God through Jesus Christ (**John 1:12, 3:1-8; Ephesians 2:8, 9**).

5. One follows Christ by placing one's faith in Him, for He alone has the ability to provide eternal, abundant life. This faith involves willfully turning from self (repentance) and turning one's life over to Jesus as Lord and Savior. When one receives Christ, the Spirit of Christ, the Holy Spirit, instantaneously comes to live within that life, resulting in a new creation who possesses the power to live for Him (**Revelation 3:20; Romans 10:9, 10; I John 5:11-13; Matthew 16:24, 25; II Corinthians 5:17**).

You must be prepared to share this message succinctly or at length. It can be presented in a few short minutes or explained over many hours, depending on the person with whom the message is being shared and the circumstances involved (time, environment, etc.). Regardless of the time factor or the circumstances, however, you must share the whole message—**THE GOSPEL**. Again, the elements of the gospel are these:

1. God loves people, but...

2. people are eternally separated from God because of sin;

3. Jesus Christ removed the separation by His death and resurrection, so that...

4. those who follow Christ receive His free gift of eternal life.

5. To follow Christ, one must turn from self and personally receive Him through faith.

From Scripture, we see that the gospel is proclaimed in the second person (see Acts). This personalizes the message, and can be done by using phrases such as...

1. God loves you, but...

2. You are eternally separated from God because of sin.

3. Jesus Christ died in your place, and rose from the dead so that you need not be separated from God any longer.

4. By following Christ you will receive His free gift of eternal and abundant life.

5. You can follow Christ by turning from self and putting your faith in Him as your Lord and Savior.

Why is it so important to tell the whole gospel? Because it is POWERFUL. The previously-mentioned "failings" are just that, if they stand alone. Unless the gospel itself is specifically verbalized, there is no power in what is shared...

Romans 1:16

> "For I am not ashamed of the gospel, for it is the power of God for salvation to every one who believes, to the Jew first and also to the Greek."

People might scorn it, laugh at it, or ignore it, but the gospel is God's Word to them. The only thing God has to say to an unbeliever is "Repent, turn to Jesus Christ, or you will spend eternity under condemnation, separated from your Creator."

Disciplemaker, it's not your job to make the gospel "acceptable." It is your task only to declare the message of salvation in Christ and leave the results to God. Some will reject the message, yes. In fact, many will shun it (**Matthew 7:13, 14**). But there are many people yet hungering for the gospel, and if you're a faithful witness, you'll find them and experience the joy of leading them to Christ! Then you'll have the added joy of discipling them in the Faith!

YOUR TECHNIQUE

There are as many techniques for witnessing as there are believers. But whatever the approach, the message of the gospel is still paramount. If you'll remember the following things and put them into practice, your individual technique(s) in presenting the gospel will be what the Lord desires:

1. Stay prepared. This means keeping your walk with Christ vital and personal.

2. Continue to pray daily for those in your life-context who need Christ. Make a list if necessary.

3. Be sensitive to openings for presenting Christ.

4. Be yourself, empowered by the Holy Spirit.

5. Be genuine. Don't put on a verbal facade.

6. Always speak from a heart of love.

7. Be courteous and friendly.

8. Know the points of the gospel message and the accompanying verses.

9. As far as possible, put off answering any questions until you're finished sharing the gospel. If you run out of time or are interrupted, it's better to have shared the gospel than to have given only your answers and opinions.

10. Always have a Bible handy so that Scriptures can be looked up.

11. Share the whole message.

12. Close each presentation of the gospel with the challenge to receive Christ. Give each person an opportunity to respond to Him.

13. If necessary, help the person express the desire of his/her heart in prayer. Remember, the words of the prayer to receive Christ are not all-important, but the attitude of the heart is.

14. Help the person to formulate his/her prayer to the Lord according to the gospel, so that God is addressed personally.

15. Never force a decision. Respect each person's response. Remember, "No" is a legitimate answer.

16. Follow up, when possible, on those who do not receive Christ at the first presentation.

17. When a person receives Christ, make arrangements to begin to disciple him/her immediately.

One brief word about opportunities...

Many believers never present Christ to anyone (or very few) because they're always waiting for the opportunity to arise. Often believers rationalize away a lost opportunity by saying, "Well, I just didn't feel led to share," or "The timing wasn't right." Be very cautious here. Such a subjective approach to witnessing can easily lead to no witnessing at all. You should realize that you're not just looking for an opportunity to share Christ, but you are someone's opportunity to meet the King of kings and Lord of lords. You must give others the opportunity to come to Jesus Christ.

Your personal technique in witnessing should utilize:

1. your developed ability to communicate within your life- context;

2. your personal knowledge of the gospel; and

3. the common ground shared with an unbeliever from your overlapping life-contexts.

We have already discussed the second of these, so let's briefly examine the first and third.

Each one of us is involved daily in interpersonal communication. The verbal dimension of interpersonal communication is one enjoyed by most human beings, and it's the fact of expression which causes believers the greatest anxiety—not so much in general conversation, but specifically in witnessing. What we must realize is that God doesn't require a wholesale shift in our vocabulary in presenting Christ. We don't even have to put on a white robe! You can present the gospel accurately and effectively using the same language that you use every day. This language is, most often, also the language of your peers. You know how to talk to them about business, school, ball games, the weather, the opposite sex, family, auto repairs, income taxes, and the economy—and somehow you're understood!

A student will present Christ from a student's perspective. An executive will present Christ from an executive's perspective. A mother will present Christ from a mother's perspective. A carpenter will present Christ from a carpenter's perspective. And all of these, when not witnessing to their vocational peers, will simply share Christ from the perspective of a person. This also applies culturally and socially. All of us must take our witness into our life-context and communicate the gospel in an understandable way using the communicative abilities we've already gained through living. The apostle Paul did this effectively. You can, too.

In most witnessing situations, not only is there the ability to communicate within a life-context, but also there is the shareability of the life-context. Almost everyone you meet in daily living shares some common ground with you. This ground might be as significant as a classroom or an office, or as slight as the weather or an interest in a local sports team. Common ground is where, conversationally, you can meet every person in your sphere of living.

I Corinthians 9:1 9-22

> "For though I am free from all men, I have made myself a slave to all, that I might win the more. And to the Jews I became as a Jew, that I might win Jews; to those who are under the law, as under the Law, though not being myself under the Law, that I might win those who are under the Law; to those who are without law, as without law, though not being without the law of God but under the law of Christ, that I might win those who are without law. To the weak, I became weak, that I might win the weak; I have become all things to all men, that I may by all means save some."

Paul didn't' mean that he put up a facade or gimmick to gain access to people. Paul was expressing the fact that everything he was, or had been, gave him a share of common ground with all men which he used as a foothold for the gospel. You'll never have to pretend to be something you're not in order to share the good news. Never! But by being sensitive to others, by being aware of each situation, by being alert to the lives of people, you'll find a starting point for sharing Christ. And once that common ground, however slight, is used to open a conversation or discussion, a transition to the gospel is only a simple phrase away...

"Could I share..."

CHAPTER 29

FACTORS IN DISCIPLEMAKING

You know from your own discipleship training that there are ten factors involved in making disciples (Section 3 of this manual). The purpose of this chapter is to give you some practical suggestions concerning each of these ten factors. Listed under each heading will be several ways in which a factor can be applied in disciplemaking. You'll want to be creative with the people you disciple, in order to insure that all ten factors are integrated into your personal disciplemaking. When all factors aren't applied, deficiencies in training disciples can result. Maximum discipleship occurs when Jesus' methodology for disciplemaking—the ten factors—is employed. When this happens, disciples become disciplemakers.

1. THE EVANGELISM (WITNESS) FACTOR

As stated in the previous chapter, witnessing means proclaiming the gospel to the unsaved. The reason witnessing is the first factor in disciplemaking is, of course, that you can only disciple a believer.

One crucial matter bears repeating: When a person receives Christ as Lord and Savior, discipling must begin immediately. Why? Because when a person receives Christ, he/she is willing to be discipled THEN. The more time that elapses between the moment of conversion and the beginning of formal discipling, the more remote the probability of successful discipling becomes. This is so because the new believer is a spiritual infant with a great hunger for the nourishment of the Word. He's in critical need of spiritual parenting. If these fresh and vital desires aren't satisfied, they'll decrease and, in time, become very difficult to revive.

Think back to that day when you first received Christ. Do you recall the excitement, the peace, the joy? Do you remember how totally willing you were to follow Christ anywhere? Then, were you immediately discipled by a trained disciplemaker who was able to spend personal time with you, teaching you essential principles from God's Word and providing encouragement, support and love? If you were discipled in this way, you're very fortunate, because most believers today haven't had the opportunity. If your experience is typical of the majority of believers today, you were, after you received Christ, left to yourself and, for the most part, had to go it alone. This should never happen. Sure, you may have become involved in church activities and programs and maybe you became a faithful church member, but no one took enough interest in you, personally, to train you in the daily walk with Christ. No one poured his/her life into you so that you could begin to mature spiritually-until you yourself became a disciplemaker.

Because discipling never took place, you probably experienced a period of time—whether months or many years—when you didn't grow in Christ. You weren't in the Word; you didn't have a consistent life of prayer and fellowship; you never witnessed to others; you didn't experience victory in daily living. Then, one day, the Lord sent someone your way who challenged you to be discipled. This person offered to teach you, to pour his/her life into yours. You agreed. Remember how difficult it was at first. Recall how hard it was to revive the love for God's Word and to muster the discipline to become a true disciple.

Reflect on these things and also on the wasted months or years that could have been productive for Christ had you been properly discipled beginning the very day of your conversion. Disciplemaking is crucial, not only for the spread of the gospel through spiritual reproduction, but also because it is fundamental to proper spiritual growth and maturity. The fact that you have reached the Handbook section of this manual indicates that you have now been discipled and have become, or are ready to become, a disciplemaker.

Please be very sensitive to the importance of sharing your faith with others in your life-context, and **DON'T NEGLECT YOUR PERSONAL RESPONSIBILITY TO MAKE DISCIPLES OF THOSE YOU LEAD TO PERSONAL FAITH IN JESUS CHRIST.**

2. THE PROXIMITY FACTOR

Spend time with those you disciple; not just teaching time, but time enough to allow them to view your actions and reactions in real daily living. There are many ways to accomplish this. Here are some suggestions: (Note: It's always more convenient and effective, and very wise, to disciple only those of the same sex, unless in a couple-to-couple or group situation.)

1. Share in recreational activities such as sports, hobbies, etc.

2. Get together for meals.

3. Attend church, school, civic, and/or social functions together.

4. If you work with or go to school with a disciple, plan to spend some time there together, even if only passing in the hall, or at the coffee pot, Coke machine, or lunch room.

5. When you're together, talk about family, job, school, finances, problems—giving a Christian perspective.

6. Go witnessing together.

7. Go shopping together.

8. Plan special outings such as camping, boating, fishing—whatever might allow more than a few hours together.

9. Pray together.

10. Study the Word together.

11. Minister to others together—to those in nursing homes, the sick, the needy, imprisoned, shut-ins, etc.

12. Share crises—be there, be available in times of illness, death, tragedy of any sort.

Jesus allowed His personal disciples to see how He operated in real life. As you do the same, you'll be giving more than just words-you'll be giving your life.

3. THE FRIENDSHIP FACTOR

In developing this factor of disciplemaking, be aware of several areas of life from which true friendships can arise:

1. common interests

2. common problems

3. common goals

4. common vocation

5. common tasks

From these mutually shareable areas such aspects of friendship as caring, concern, help, trust, burden-sharing (fellowship), and joy can develop. As a disciplemaker, be on the alert for these common areas.

4. THE EXAMPLE FACTOR

Don't get caught teaching something without also providing an example from your personal life. Each teaching session you spend with your disciples must be reinforced with the real thing. For example: When teaching about God's Word, you need to let your disciples see how you study it; when teaching on prayer, show how you pray; when teaching on the importance of church involvement, allow those you're discipling to observe your own commitment to your local church; when teaching about fruit in the believer's life, let your disciples see fruit in your own life; when teaching on Christ-like attitudes, display yours; etc.

Be a worthy example!

5. THE COMMITMENT FACTOR

Commitment seems to be a sore spot with many these days. Don't wear out the word for the sake of "sanctimonious semantics." Commitment means action, pure and simple. It isn't something about which one merely says, "I have that!" Commitment means doing. This can and must be taught to those you disciple. How is it learned? By providing the opportunity for disciples to do what they say. Try these:

1. Give them the opportunity to be on time-and lovingly, but firmly, reprove them when they aren't.

2. Help them set and keep priorities-like discipleship meetings.

3. Check up on how they follow through on Bible study, prayer, church involvement, etc.

4. Give opportunities to sacrifice-giving up other activities in order to be discipled.

5. Continue to encourage them through your own personal commitment to Christ.

6. THE RESPONSIBILITY FACTOR

The most obvious area in which responsibility can begin to be assigned and learned is the teaching time. Ask each disciple to complete the fill-in segments of each chapter as proof that they have adequately dealt with each lesson. Check answers and make necessary changes. Other responsibilities can be assigned, such as:

1. praying for others,

2. studying specific Bible passages,

3. providing refreshments,

4. applying what is learned, and reporting back to you (and the group) through testimony, and

5. group projects in service to others.

7. THE KNOWLEDGE FACTOR

This highly important factor involves teaching disciples basic principles and doctrines from God's Word, bearing in mind that what is taught to those disciples they will soon be teaching to disciples of their own. Because of this, teaching should be both understandable and systematic. By using materials prepared with disciplemaking specifically in mind, teaching can be effectively accomplished. The goal of teaching materials is to clearly present Biblical truths in a direct manner which allows maximum comprehension. The discipleship training manual you're now using is designed to present lessons from Scripture in this way. We have attempted to provide a solid knowledge foundation upon which the disciple can spend a lifetime building as he/she studies personally from God's Word, and learns from other teachers.

You don't need to be an expert teacher to train a disciple although your teaching skills will improve with practice. As you teach these lessons to disciples, consider the following suggestions:

1. Use the Bible freely, looking up passages in the Word as often as possible.

2. Always stress the centrality and importance of the Bible itself as the only authority for Christian living.

3. Keep the teaching time open to discussion, but without detracting from the lesson.

4. Don't try to teach too fast, or to teach too many lessons in one sitting. Take your time.

5. Make use of the drawings and diagrams for emphasis.

6. Select a teaching place that's conducive to study—whether home, restaurant, outdoors, school, business, etc.

7. Spend time in prayer as you prepare to teach.

8. Continue to apply what you teach in your personal life.

9. Make sure each person understands what's being taught before proceeding.

10. Each disciple should have his/her own copy of CHRISTIAN DISCIPLESHIP.

11. Make sure that the review sections and fill-in-the-blanks are completed by each disciple for their own use in teaching later on.

Remember, you aren't trying to teach your disciple(s) everything—only basic, foundational truths from God's Word. They'll spend a lifetime learning from the Bible. What you're doing is laying the groundwork upon which a structure of sound doctrine and practice can be built.

8. THE GOAL FACTOR

This factor is highly important and easily accomplished. Each disciple must never forget, as you must not, that the goal of discipleship is not merely spiritual growth and stability, but the fulfillment of the Great Commission by becoming a disciplemaker. You must continually remind those you disciple that they, too, will win and disciple others. Talk about it and live it!

9. THE POWER FACTOR

The power to make disciples is from the Holy Spirit. As you develop your disciples, you must help them gain the practical knowledge of walking in the Spirit through obedience to Christ as Lord. Remind them that the Holy Spirit resides in them and will empower them as they become obedient in personally carrying out the Great Commission as disciplemakers. They must realize that being filled with the Holy Spirit isn't just for the purpose of personal growth, but for reaching others with the gospel.

10. THE LAUNCH FACTOR

How will you know when a person has been properly discipled and is ready to begin making disciples? When all ten discipleship factors have been adequately applied and have become evident as you evaluate a disciple's life, then that disciple is ready to be launched as a disciplemaker. Commission that disciple with **Matthew 28:18-20**.

Challenge each disciple to begin to make disciples as they have been discipled. Always be available to help when necessary.

When disciples are launched as disciplemakers, then you are ready to begin again with others...

UNTIL THE LORD COMES!

CHAPTER 30
PERSONAL EVALUATION

The following evaluation sheets are designed to help you evaluate your performance and effectiveness as a disciplemaker in relation to each individual you disciple. These evaluations should help to insure that you're consciously aware of how you apply the ten discipleship factors to each disciple.

Throughout each discipling period—the time it takes until a disciple is launched as a disciplemaker—keep a record on these pages of your disciplemaking experiences. An example page has been completed to show you how.

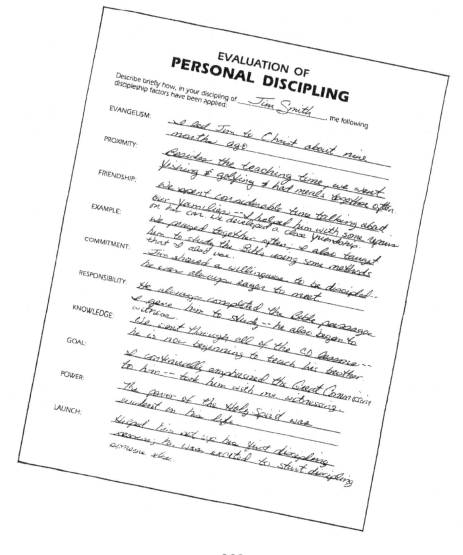

EVALUATION OF
PERSONAL DISCIPLING

Describe briefly how, in your discipling of _____,
the following discipleship factors have been applied:

EVANGELISM: _____

_____

PROXIMITY: _____

_____

FRIENDSHIP: _____

_____

EXAMPLE: _____

_____

COMMITMENT: _____

_____

RESPONSIBILITY: _____

_____

KNOWLEDGE: _____

_____

GOAL: _____

_____

POWER: _____

_____

LAUNCH: _____

_____

EVALUATION OF
PERSONAL DISCIPLING

Describe briefly how, in your discipling of _____,
the following discipleship factors have been applied:

EVANGELISM: _____

_____

PROXIMITY: _____

_____

FRIENDSHIP: _____

_____

EXAMPLE: _____

_____

COMMITMENT: _____

_____

RESPONSIBILITY: _____

_____

KNOWLEDGE: _____

_____

GOAL: _____

_____

POWER: _____

_____

LAUNCH: _____

_____

EVALUATION OF
PERSONAL DISCIPLING

Describe briefly how, in your discipling of _____,
the following discipleship factors have been applied:

EVANGELISM: _____

_____

PROXIMITY: _____

_____

FRIENDSHIP: _____

_____

EXAMPLE: _____

_____

COMMITMENT: _____

_____

RESPONSIBILITY: _____

_____

KNOWLEDGE: _____

_____

GOAL: _____

_____

POWER: _____

_____

LAUNCH: _____

_____

EVALUATION OF
PERSONAL DISCIPLING

Describe briefly how, in your discipling of _____,
the following discipleship factors have been applied:

EVANGELISM: _____

_____

PROXIMITY: _____

_____

FRIENDSHIP: _____

_____

EXAMPLE: _____

_____

COMMITMENT: _____

_____

RESPONSIBILITY: _____

_____

KNOWLEDGE: _____

_____

GOAL: _____

_____

POWER: _____

_____

LAUNCH: _____

_____

EVALUATION OF
PERSONAL DISCIPLING

Describe briefly how, in your discipling of _____,
the following discipleship factors have been applied:

EVANGELISM: _____

_____

PROXIMITY: _____

_____

FRIENDSHIP: _____

_____

EXAMPLE: _____

_____

COMMITMENT: _____

_____

RESPONSIBILITY: _____

_____

KNOWLEDGE: _____

_____

GOAL: _____

_____

POWER: _____

_____

LAUNCH: _____

_____

If you liked this study, you'll also like these outstanding selections:

The Defendable Faith: Lessons in Christian Apologetics, Steven Collins (Trinity Southwest University Press, 2010), paperback, 300 pages, ISBN 978-0615689753.

Discovering the City of Sodom: The Fascinating, True Account of the Discovery of the Old Testament's Most Infamous City, Steven Collins, Latayne Scott (Howard Books//Simon & Schuster, 2013), hardcover, 334 pages, ISBN 978-1451684308; eBook ISBN 978-1451684377.

Handbook for Holy Land Travelers, John Witte Moore, Steven Collins (Trinity Southwest University Press, 2011), paperback, 220 pages, ISBN 978-1466430884.

Let My People Go: Using Historical Synchronisms to Identify the Pharaoh of the Exodus, Steven Collins (Trinity Southwest University Press, 2005), paperback, 142 pages, ISBN 978-0615687940.

Revelation: What Did John Really See?, Phillip J. Silvia (Trinity Southwest University Press, 2005), paperback, 142 pages, ISBN 978-0615687940.

ABOUT THE AUTHOR

Dr. Steven Collins is Executive Dean of Trinity Southwest University, where he lectures in the College of Biblical and Theological Studies, and serves as Dean of the College of Archaeology and Biblical History. He is Director and Chief Archaeologist for the Tall el-Hammam/Sodom Excavation Project in Jordan, and is one of the world's foremost biblical archaeologists. Although Dr. Collins' "day job" is as an academician, biblical scholar and archaeologist, he is profoundly committed to the Gospel of Jesus Christ and to the fulfillment of the Great Commission—making disciples! His many books include: *Let My People Go: Using Historical Synchronisms to Identify the Pharaoh of the Exodus* (TSU Press, 2005); *The Defendable Faith: Lessons in Christian Apologetics* (TSU Press, 2012); and *Discovering the City of Sodom* (Howard Books/Simon & Schuster, 2013).

605 - 313 -5867

6306152

Made in USA - North Chelmsford, MA

12.18.2020 1344